CHRISTIANS AND PAGANS
IN ROMAN BRITAIN

CHRISTIANS
AND PAGANS
IN ROMAN BRITAIN

Dorothy Watts

London and New York

First published 1991
by Routledge
11 New Fetter Lane, London EC4P 4EE

Simultaneously published in the USA and Canada
by Routledge
a division of Routledge, Chapman and Hall, Inc.
29 West 35th Street, New York, NY 10001

Disc conversion in 11/12 pt Garamond 3 by
Columns Typesetters of Reading
Printed in England by
T.J. Press, Padstow, Cornwall

British Library Cataloguing in Publication Data
Watts, Dorothy
Christians and pagans in Roman Britain.
1. Great Britain. Christianity, ancient period
I. Title
209.361

Library of Congress Cataloging in Publication Data
Watts, Dorothy.
Christians and pagans in Roman Britain/Dorothy Watts.
p.   cm.
Includes bibliographical references and index.
1. Great Britain—Church history—To 449.
2. Christianity and other religions—Roman.
3. Christianity and other religions—Celtic.
4. Great Britain—Religion—To 449. 5. Great Britain—Antiquities, Roman.
6. Great Britain—Antiquities, Celtic. 7. Christian antiquities—Great Britain.
8. Excavations (Archaeology)—Great Britain.
9. Rome—Religion. 10. Celts—Great Britain—Religion. I. Title.
BR748.W38   1991
274.1′01—dc20   90–49531
ISBN 0–415–05071–5

To the one who provided the challenge to start
and the incentive to finish

CONTENTS

LIST OF FIGURES

PREFACE

There has been a growing interest in the religions of Roman Britain in recent years, stimulated, no doubt, by the discovery of several important hoards with a religious component. This has resulted in a number of publications on the topic, most of which emphasise the Celtic or Roman cults. Christianity is usually treated as a minority eastern religion; the major archaeological sites and finds are mentioned, and the authors generally come to some conclusion about the possible continuity of Christianity into the post-Roman and Saxon periods. There are very few attempts to distinguish any pagan elements in Romano-British Christianity, and none made to evaluate such elements. It seemed that here was a fertile field for research.

Such was the background for this study. In the search for the pagan material, however, it was found that the evidence for Christianity itself was often far from clear, despite recent publications specifically of this aspect of Romano-British religion. This in turn prompted a wider-ranging investigation which meant looking beyond the published works to archaeological projects completed but not yet in press, and to others still in progress. Undoubtedly, further evidence for Christianity awaits recognition in storerooms of museums or amongst unpublished material held by various individuals or institutions, but problems of accessibility make an even wider search impracticable for the time being.

The investigation has tended to confirm the generally accepted view of Christianity as a minority religion in Britain at the time of the withdrawal of the Romans; but it has also, I hope, resulted in a more accurate assessment of the extent of Christianity, and of its place in the religious tradition of Roman Britain. Moreover, the criteria developed for the identification of Christian sites will assist further expansion of this knowledge.

For a person normally living outside Britain, detailed research on any aspect of the Roman period is daunting. My task was made much easier and more pleasurable by the generosity of many scholars and archaeologists who provided information on their specialist fields, or made material available to me in advance of publication. In this regard, the present work has been greatly improved by discussions or correspondence I have had with Ms Brenda Dickinson, Ms Catherine Johns, Rev. Professor William Frend, Professors Henry Chadwick and Charles Thomas, Drs Edward Yarnold, SJ, John Drinkwater, Mark Hassall and Martin Henig, Messrs William Putnam, Christopher Sparey Green and Nigel Wilson; in addition to their help with details of their particular projects, the following have given permission to use unpublished material: Messrs Philip Crummy, Carl Crossan and the Colchester Archaeological Trust; Messrs David Miles and John Moore and the Oxford Archaeological Unit; Ms Susan Davies, Mr David Farwell and the Trust for Wessex Archaeology; Mr Brian Dix and Northamptonshire County Council Archaeology Unit; Mr Michael Jones and the City of Lincoln Archaeological Unit; Mr David Wilson, for excavations carried out by the University of Nottingham, with assistance from the Department of the Environment; Mr Robin Turner, for excavations conducted with the assistance of English Heritage; Dr Ann Woodward, Emeritus Professor Philip Rahtz, and Messrs George Boon and Christopher Guy. I am especially grateful to Bro. Eoin de Bhaldraithe, who not only advised me on matters of church history and ritual, but also wrote a note on the use of various instruments in the early Mass which is incorporated in this work as an Appendix. I offer my sincere thanks to all these busy people who still found time to share their knowledge and the fruits of their labour. For the views expressed in this work, however, I alone am responsible.

For permission to use copyright material, acknowledgement and thanks are extended to B. T. Batsford Ltd (fig. 27), the Trustees, British Museum (cover illustration), Oxford University Press (fig. 10a), the Royal Archaeological Institute (chap. III.1), the Society of Antiquaries of London (chaps V.1, V.2; figs 23–5), the Society for the Promotion of Roman Studies (figs 7a, 10b) and Dr Stanley West (fig. 7b).

There are, in addition, a number of people to whom I have a

considerable debt for the final product. My family – husband, daughter and son – have been chief supporter, critic and computer consultant respectively; their enthusiasm for the project has been matched only by their patience and forbearance in the face of wholesale neglect. It is also my pleasure to thank Mr Don Barrett for his great help and constructive criticism, and for counsel so often sought and so freely given; Professor Keith Branigan, for his guidance and invaluable assistance while I carried out research under his aegis in the United Kingdom and Ireland; Professor Robert Milns, for his critical reading of the various drafts, and for his encouragement and administrative assistance; and Professor Trevor Bryce, who opened doors and made possible the first faltering steps.

Dorothy Watts
University of Queensland
Brisbane, Australia
July 1990

I

THE RELIGIOUS BACKGROUND

In AD 391, the Roman Emperor Theodosius closed all temples in the Empire and banned all pagan cults. Thus Christianity was endorsed as the official religion of an empire which, despite barbarian incursions, internal strife and economic hardship, even then stretched from the Euphrates to Britain.

Undoubtedly the decree of Theodosius reached the shores of Britain and was acted upon in due course by the provincial administration. This remote part of the known world had, after all, been part of the Roman empire for more than three centuries. Yet its religions included not only those found at Rome and Constantinople but also the native Celtic cults. The destruction of paganism might have seemed a difficult task. Close observation would, in fact, reveal many pagan influences in the British version of Christianity, suggesting that the religion, while it may have been found in Britain for up to two centuries, was not so firmly established there as elsewhere in the Empire. This conclusion and its implications will be considered later (ch. VII).

A search for the pagan elements in Romano-British Christianity led to the present work. Before these elements could be established, however, it became clear that it would be necessary to reappraise the evidence for Christianity in Britain and, where appropriate, to devise methods for identification. Once that was done, it would be possible to determine the links with pagan religions and practices and to assess the impact of these pagan elements on Christianity in the late Roman period, prior to the withdrawal of the Roman forces about AD 410. In the process, a reassessment could also be made of the nature of Romano-British Christianity and its place in the history of the religions of Roman Britain.

At the outset, a study of the other major religions found in Britain both prior to and during the Occupation would be useful; but as that task has already been carried out in depth by various scholars,[1] only a brief general survey will be undertaken here, beginning with the immediate pre-Roman (Late Iron Age) period.

The Celts were a warlike, rural people, and their religion reflected this. Their many gods, named or nameless, were associated with war and also with nature and fertility: the earth itself, the sun, trees or groves, streams, marshes, animals and birds. While in Britain the Celts were less disposed than their continental counterparts to represent humans and animals in their religious art (Green 1986: 9),[2] anthropomorphic representations such as those found at the Iron Age site of Garton Slack in Yorkshire (Brewster 1976) indicate that the religion was not purely animistic. It has been suggested (Green 1986: 107, 206–7) that Celtic art, far from being crude or simple,[3] was meant to be abstract in conception and execution. The religious imagery was not intended to be representational and would be obvious only to initiates; it was the result of stimuli other than the mimesis which governed classical art. Notable examples of presumed votive or religious objects from Iron Age Britain include the Aylesford Bucket with human head and horse motifs, and the Witham Shield, decorated with a stylised boar (Kruta and Forman 1985: 64–5, 94–5; Green 1986: 10, fig. 2).

There was, too, a vast difference between the religious rites of the Celtic and Roman worlds. Classical writers found nothing to admire in the barbaric rituals of the Celts: Strabo (4.4.5) describes the practice of displaying as trophies the heads of victims in war (and indeed, the head, whether human or animal, had great significance in Celtic religion); Caesar (*De bello Gallico* 6.16) tells of sacrifice, including that of humans, presided over by the Druids; and Pliny (*Naturalis historia* 30.13) claims even cannibalism occurred. The Druids, Celtic priests, dominated the religious life of the people, and it was this influence, translated into a resistance movement, that was to be stamped out by the Romans (Tacitus, *Annales* 14.30).

In pre-Roman Britain, many places which were part of the natural environment were sacred to the Celts, but cult buildings were also erected. Iron Age shrines were found in hillforts or sites with defined boundaries, others in prominent locations within unenclosed, nucleated settlements (Drury 1980: 45–62). In some instances, these round or rectilinear structures were the precursors of Romano-Celtic temples. A number, such as those at Frilford, Harlow, Hayling Island and Maiden Castle, were followed by Roman buildings on the same site; in other cases, a building of Roman date was erected on or beside what may have been a sacred spot: an example is at Gosbecks, Colchester, where the later Romano-British building was placed off-centre in its *temenos*, presumably to leave room for a Celtic sacred tree or grove (Hull 1958: 229–30). But Iron Age shrine sites are not always readily identifiable, and it is only lately that they have been recognised; recent scholarship has gone some considerable way in establishing criteria for identification (Wait 1986: 156; see below, ch. II).

In the main, the pre-Roman Celts do appear to have associated burial with religion, although their actual beliefs are not readily ascertainable, particularly in regard to a belief in an afterlife. The written evidence is Roman: Pomponius Mela (*De chronographia* 3.2.19) writes of Celts in whom a belief in an afterlife was fostered in order to make them fearless in war; and Caesar (*De bello Gallico* 6.14) implies that a belief in the transmigration of souls was inculcated by the Druids for the same purpose.[4] Only a small percentage of all pre-Roman burials have been discovered, however; many bodies must have been cremated (Whimster 1981: 195) or deliberately exposed to predators, as suggested for Danebury (Cunliffe 1983: 165). But neither cremation nor excarnation would have necessarily reflected any change in religious belief if the Celts saw death as a release of the soul from the body, thus facilitating its removal to an afterworld or (if transmigration was the belief) to another body (Brunaux 1988: 85–6). This would also explain the deliberate destruction of weapons placed in graves, noted below.

Funerary practices varied considerably. The early La Tène burials of Celtic chieftains, described in most works on the Celts, were not typical for the inhabitants of Iron Age Britain, and it is difficult to generalise about the burial rites of ordinary folk. Nevertheless, it has been determined that, by the time of the Roman occupation, there were a number of regional inhumation practices in addition to cremation, while in other areas the dead were disposed of without any apparent ritual or care (Whimster 1981: 195). An identifiable Celtic burial of the period immediately before the Occupation might be one found in a rough grave, in crouched or foetal position, aligned north–south, with one or two pots for food and drink, and maybe a weapon (sometimes deliberately destroyed), some jewellery or even parts of an animal,[5] intended presumably to accompany the deceased to the hereafter. It might be located in a recognisable burial ground or, more frequently, merely deposited along with other burials in a convenient ditch or pit associated with a settlement.

The coming of Rome had a considerable impact on the outward appearance of the Celtic cults, but probably less on religious thought and ritual, particularly in the countryside. Romanisation was at its most effective in the towns. Since, therefore, the vast majority of Romano-Britons lived in the rural areas, the influence of Roman practices would often have been superficial at best. Even so, Romano-Celtic temples evolved, neither as primitive as their Celtic predecessors nor mere copies of Roman cultic buildings. The characteristic *cella*-and-ambulatory plan was a departure from both traditions and evidently served the purpose well, as it was still in use into the fourth century. Yet simple circular, rectangular or polygonal structures continued to be erected, especially in the less romanised areas. At the same time, classical Roman temples were built. Examples have been identified at Bath, Colchester and Verulamium; a number of other towns have possible evidence. It is known that the structure at Bath was dedicated to Sulis–Minerva, but classical temples would also have been constructed for the Imperial cult. The Temple of Claudius at Colchester was probably the provincial centre for emperor worship.

Roman influence meant that Romano-Celtic iconography now took on a more classical appearance; and rough local stone, pipeclay and terracotta figures came to outnumber the skilfully wrought imported marbles and bronzes which were still found in the more urbanised parts of the province. Nevertheless, the lack of realism in their execution proclaimed the native influence in some artefacts. On occasion, the impact of Rome seemed to have been negligible or non-existent. This is exemplified by a recently published chalk figurine, 'Deal Man' from Kent, which bore no sign of classical influence; it is similar to other Celtic finds from Britain and Gaul, yet pottery evidence suggests a late first- or second-century date. The object was found in a pit which may have had a votive purpose (Parfitt and Green 1987).

The elimination of druidism and its associated threat to political stability meant that Roman and Celtic religions could co-exist, and their gods were, in time, accepted in both cultures. Roman soldiers made dedications to Celtic gods[6] and rural dwellers erected temples to Roman gods.[7] Virtually the whole Roman pantheon came to be found in Britain. Native deities acquired a Roman veneer, and often a fusion of Celtic and Roman took place: Mars–Lenus, Apollo–Cunomaglus, Sulis–Minerva and numerous other examples testify to the syncretism which was a feature of Romano-British religion. Offerings might now include small models of parts of the body, if the god was considered a healing one, such as Nodens, at Lydney (Wheeler and Wheeler 1932). More commonly, gifts to the gods, both Celtic and Roman, included sacrificial animals, metal plaques and figurines, coins, pins and other personal items; the votive weapons of pre-Roman times disappeared, though miniature weapons, also votives in the earlier period, were still offered. But even in the late fourth century, and after the advent of Christianity, offerings were being made to purely Celtic deities.[8] It is difficult to argue with Branigan (1980: 264) that 'in their hearts' the Britons probably still clung to their ancient gods.

Burial practices changed with the coming of Rome in that generally more care now seemed to be taken with the disposal of the body, but here too, the changes seem superficial. Following the Roman example, cemeteries were established beside the roads leading to the towns. Cremation was widely practised until the third century, when it was replaced by inhumation, yet cremation persisted alongside inhumation in some cemeteries. Although crouched or prone burials were found, bodies were usually laid out supine and extended. They were sometimes placed in wooden coffins or on biers. Alignment might still be north–south but, by the beginning of the fourth century, there was a move to west–east burial. In other cases positioning of graves seems to have been dictated merely by the presence of earlier features such as ditches. Usually little care was taken to avoid intersecting or disturbing other burials. On occasion the body was decapitated, the head either placed on the pelvis, between the knees or ankles, or missing altogether. Grave deposits included jewellery, combs and hobnailed shoes, sometimes worn, sometimes not; vessels (pottery and, more rarely, glass), perhaps containing food remains such as animal or bird bones; and coins, sometimes in the mouth. Other Roman practices such the insertion of lamps in graves were known, but were not common.

Pagan hoards and ritual objects have been found from the

Romano-Celtic period. Religious ritual may have changed but little with the Occupation, although the extent of any change is impossible to assess. The sceptre heads from Wortlington, Willingham Fen and Amersham, for instance, suggest Roman iconography but not necessarily Roman ritual, since similar objects are known from the Celtic period (Henig 1984b: 136–41). Fishwick (1988) has proposed that some of these sceptre heads, probably of Roman emperors, represent the 'incorporation of an imperial element into the rites associated with a Celtic deity'; they were normally found in shrines as offerings to a deity, and were brought out for religious processions. Regrettably, it has often been only the syncretic element in the artwork of the pagan hoards which has attracted comment and conjecture; the purpose of the objects has rarely been discussed. The recently discovered spectacular hoard of late fourth-century silver utensils and gold jewellery from Thetford (Johns and Potter 1983) demonstrates further the syncretism of Romano-British religion: the objects have links with both an ancient Latin and a Celtic cult – and, it has been argued (Watts 1988b), a strong connection with Christianity. This hoard and the possible use of its spoons and strainers will be discussed at length below (ch. V.1).

Where 'oriental' cults were imported into this Romano-Celtic world, their impact would undoubtedly have been evident. Isis and Serapis, Cybele and Atys, and Mithras and his companions Cautes and Cautopates had probably been brought to Britain by soldiers or merchants; but their presence in Roman Britain has tended to be overrated. There is little evidence for them other than in military areas, such as Hadrian's Wall, Gloucester and York, or in London; and while there may have been up to a dozen temples to Mithras in Britain in the period from the mid-second to the early fourth century, the buildings (with the exception of London) were very small and cult membership limited (Henig 1984b: 108; Branigan 1980: 266). By and large they would have had a minimal impact on Romano-British religion.

Among the religions introduced into Britain was Christianity. It has become almost the received opinion that Christianity was an 'oriental' cult introduced to Britain along with worship of the various eastern deities. Most writers on Romano-British religion make this association,[9] but such an interpretation must be seriously questioned. An examination of the evidence suggests that the separation of Christianity from Judaism and the growth of

Rome, rather than Jerusalem, as the focus for the new religion were the factors which led ultimately to the introduction of Christianity to Britain as a *Roman* religion – as Roman, perhaps, as the worship of Apollo. This conclusion warrants elaboration as the distinction is important in a later discussion of continuity of Christianity into the sub-Roman period (below, ch. VII).

Historically, Christianity was an offshoot of Judaism. But in the very early Christian records, the writer[10] of Acts (15.19–20) is aware that the gentile members of the Church were already to have a different law from the one traditionally followed by the Jews. Paul, in his letter to the Galatians (2.1–10), makes a similar differentiation and goes still further by distancing himself from the Jewish Christian community at Jerusalem led by Peter, James and John. It may be that, even in this early period, Christians, being conscious of the distinction, chose to hold their meetings in the porch of the synagogue (Acts 5.12–13)[11] or in private houses (Acts 5.42), rather than in the synagogue itself.

The Church was already active in Italy (Hebrews 13.24) prior to Paul's arrival there in about AD 60. The apostle seems to have planned to take his mission westward to Spain (Romans 15.24, 28), still further removed from direct Jewish influence and from tensions which may already have surfaced. It has been suggested (Chadwick 1967: 21) that the reference by Suetonius (*Claudius* 25) to the disturbances caused by the Jews 'at the instigation of Chrestus'[12] could indicate that, as early as 50, violence between Jews and Christians had occurred at Rome.

The Jews took the initiative following the fall of Jerusalem to Titus in 70 and, rallying to their traditional leaders, used the liturgy of the synagogue to denounce the 'Nazarenes' as heretics. Anyone who acknowledged Jesus as the Messiah was to be expelled from the synagogue (John 9.22, 12.42). Meanwhile, in this sub-apostolic period, the Church continued to grow in areas such as Bithynia-Pontus (Pliny, *Epistulae* 10.96); but, where organised Judaism was very strong, Christianity could not compete (Frend 1984: 128).

At Rome, towards the end of the first century, leadership of the Church was taken by Clement, probably the third bishop after Peter. It was Clement (1.44.1–5) who first enunciated the principle of apostolic succession. This placed Rome in a prominent position because it was the site of the martyrdoms of Peter and Paul. But, of course, Jerusalem enjoyed greater prestige. The situation was to change with the accession of Hadrian (emperor AD 117–38). In 135 the emperor excluded all Jews from Jerusalem and Judaea; this meant a shift of focus for Christianity from Jerusalem to Antioch, Alexandria, and particularly to Rome, and a final separation of gentile Christianity from its origins. From a rescript of Hadrian, recorded mid-century by Justin Martyr (1 *Apology* 69), it seems that Romans already distinguished between Christians and Jews,[13] and Justin himself considered converts to Judaism the enemies of Christianity (*Dialogue* 122). Bitterness between them increased when the Jews played a part in the martyrdom of Polycarp at Smyrna in 155 (Eusebius, *Historia ecclesiastica* 4.15.26, 29, 41), and with the stinging attack on the Jews by Melito, Bishop of Sardis (d. *c.*190), for the crucifixion of Christ (*Peri pascha* 72–99). His theology seems to have influenced Irenaeus and Tertullian.

The separation of Jew and Christian was evident in the writings of new Christian leaders who owed little or nothing in their theology to Judaism, but were thoroughly hellenised in their outlook. Justin Martyr attempted to show that the whole of the Old Testament pointed to Christianity, as did all good and valuable thought of past times. He was particularly influenced by Plato's philosophy. Justin, in turn, influenced one of the most eminent of the early Church leaders, Irenaeus, bishop of Lyons (d. *c.*200). Irenaeus lent his authority to the principle of apostolic succession (*Adversus omnes haereses* 3.3.4), expounded almost a century before by Clement of Rome. This did much to enhance the claim of Rome to leadership of the Christian church.[14]

The Church, with its focus on the capital of the Empire, thus entered the Severan Age and the third century as a religion of the Roman Empire and indeed 'one of the major religions of the Greco-Roman world' (Frend 1984: 257). The first Latin-speaking Pope (Victor I, AD 189–99) had been enthroned, and the first major theologian to write in Latin, Tertullian (*c.*160–225), was extending the influence of Christianity in the western part of the Empire; a younger contemporary, Origen (*c.*185–254), was to write of Judaism in disparaging terms as a lesser sister of Christianity (*In cantica canticorum* 2.3); and Cyprian (d. 258), bishop of the powerful church at Carthage, despite a quarrel with Stephen of Rome over the issue of rebaptism, was to acknowledge the primacy of the see of Rome and its role as the source of unity (*Epistulae* 68, Oxford edn). This was the first known acknowledge-ment by a bishop of the pre-eminence of Rome.

The authority of Rome increased during the third century, as Christian communities came to be found in the west in North Africa, Spain, southern Gaul, the Rhineland and Britain. The Church was not eliminated in the persecutions of the age; after the conversion of Constantine following the Battle of Milvian Bridge in 312, Christianity emerged the religion of the emperor, if not yet of the empire. It was left to Theodosius to ban paganism, and to make a once-proscribed sect the official religion of the Roman world.

Against this background Christianity reached Britain, perhaps some time towards the close of the second century. It appears to have been fairly widespread, although probably not numerically strong. Tertullian (*Adversus Iudaeos* 7) could write of its presence in even the remoter parts of Britain, beyond Roman settlement; some years later Origen described Christianity there as a unifying force (*Homily 4 on Ezekiel*). While the value of these sources as evidence has been questioned in recent times by Thomas (1981: 43), even he accepts a Christian presence in Britain by the last quarter of the second century.

There is, however, little reason to doubt the evidence of Tertullian, although there may some element of exaggeration. It is known that Christianity was well established in Gaul by the time of reign of Marcus Aurelius (161–80). The martyrdom in Lyons of forty-eight Christians from all walks of life (Eusebius, *Historia ecclesiastica* 5.1) is significant, first, because it demonstrates the attraction of the religion to all strata of society and, secondly, because it implies a closely knit community of converts there. The number of converts in Lyons at the time of the persecution in 177 cannot be estimated, but the fact that such a large group refused to recant suggests a congregation of some considerable size.

This may be confirmed by the fact that the town had a bishop. Irenaeus, the successor to the martyred Pothinus, not only reinforced the principle of apostolic succession, as mentioned above, but, by carrying the Gospel to the Celts in their own language, did much to spread the influence of the Church in the west. That this influence was able to spread and grow in Britain after 177 cannot be doubted, despite the sporadic but violent persecutions under Septimius Severus in 203 and 206–10, Maximinus in 235–8, Decius in 249–51, Valerius in 257–60 and in the 'great persecution' of Diocletian in 303–5.

Britain produced its own early martyrs. The names of only three are known – Alban, Aaron and Julius – and there has been considerable debate over dates. Scholars are generally agreed that the martyrdoms would have been unlikely to have taken place during the persecutions of Diocletian, since the Caesar in Britain, later Constantius I, took little action against Christians (Lactantius, *De mortibus persecutorum* 15.7; Eusebius, *Historia ecclesiastica* 8.13.13). Morris (1968), in an influential study, proposes a date of 209 for Alban's death. This has been challenged by Thomas (1981: 50), but his arguments are not conclusive.[15] He sees 251–9 as the 'least improbable' period for the martyrdom. Stephens (1987) argues that Morris's appeal to the authority of the Turin manuscript is not valid, since an earlier version of the *Passio Albani* did not use the term 'Caesar' as the title of Alban's judge[16] – the basis for Morris's date of 209 for the martyrdom. Stephens dates the execution of Alban only to the third century.

As for the deaths of Aaron and Julius, citizens of Caerleon, Stephens (1985) proposes that their trials took place at Caerwent, although he accepts their execution and burial at Caerleon. He does not suggest a date, other than the third century. He believes there is no reason to assume the two were put to death on the same occasion or even in the same reign. To some extent this is true, but the traditional linking of the two, transmitted down to Gildas (*De Excidio et Conquestu Britanniae* 10.2), itself implies that the executions had been carried out on the one occasion. Moreover, there would seem to be only a remote possibility that a town could produce martyrs in two different persecutions, especially when that town, although a major Roman military centre, can only have had a limited civilian population; the tribal capital, Caerwent, was but 12 kilometres away. It is reasonable to accept the martyrdoms of Aaron and Julius as occurring on the one occasion, in the third century, but probably before *c.*290, when the legions were withdrawn from Caerleon.

From the literary sources nothing more is known of a definite Christian presence until after the Peace of the Church, which came into effect with the issuing of the so-called Edict of Milan in 313. In 314, the Council of Arles, summoned by Constantine to discuss the Donatist schism, was attended by three British bishops. From this it is presumed that the Church was organised on a regional basis at least by the early years of the fourth century. It may have been a religion of little material wealth, however, even by mid-century; the evidence from Sulpicius Severus (*Chronicon* 2.42) suggests this. Further literary references to Romano-British Christianity are virtually non-existent for the period up to the withdrawal of the Roman forces. In order, therefore, to determine the extent of Christianity in the period from the conversion of Constantine to *c.*410, we must turn from the literary evidence to that of archaeology.

Collingwood, writing in 1930 (145, 176) of the archaeology of Roman Britain, emphasised the very limited evidence for Christianity. Even in 1968, Morris, in his paper on the date of Saint Alban, concluded that, at the time when Constantine became sole emperor, there were but few Christians in the Latin west, and that it was only after the reforms of Martin, Ambrose and Damasis and between the years 370 and 400 that Christianity came to dominate the Roman world. It would seem, however, that Christians had been in Britain for at least a generation before 312, and probably up to a century before. A reappraisal of the earlier evidence and of new archaeological material will, it is hoped, shed more light on the history of Romano-British religion, and of Christianity in particular.

II

SIGNIFICANT PRIOR RESEARCH

The title of this work, *Christians and Pagans in Roman Britain*, indicates initially a study or reappraisal of the evidence for Christianity, followed by an assessment of the links with pagan religions and practices. In surveying prior research, it will be found convenient to consider separately the two aspects of the topic. With regard to Christianity, while there has not been a great deal written specifically on the subject, there is a considerable corpus of material on the religions of Roman Britain generally, and on individual sites and practices. Few authors, however, have touched on the relationship between pagan and Christian even in passing, although two (Toynbee 1968 and Huskinson 1974)[1] have dealt with pagan motifs in Christian art, with particular reference to Roman Britain.

Advances in archaeological techniques and the spate of discoveries since and because of World War II make it unnecessary to refer to accounts of Christianity in Roman Britain written prior to 1945. Indeed, the subject received little attention from the first publication by Williams in 1912 until Toynbee collated all the available evidence in 1953. Since then, new discoveries have been published frequently, and knowledge of the extent to which the religion penetrated the provinces expanded, until it has been possible for a major topic on the work to be produced (Thomas 1981).

In the pioneer study, Toynbee considers both literary and archaeological evidence. She first examines the primary sources and concludes that, even allowing for rhetoric, Tertullian and Origen show that the Church in Britain was a 'living force' by about the beginning of the third century. From the writings of Bede, Gildas,

Constantius and Venantius Fortunatus, she determines that the traditions of the early British martyrs Alban, Aaron and Julius are probably based on historical fact.

In looking for evidence of churches, Toynbee's examination of the ecclesiastical list of the Council of Arles of 314 leads her to conclude that the three British bishops there represented London, York and Colchester,[2] although no evidence of their presumed cathedrals has yet been found. Other sources do, however, mention churches: two at Canterbury – one probably on the site of the present cathedral, the other, dedicated to St Martin, outside the city walls – and a martyr church at St Albans. Buildings which had been excavated are then discussed. Toynbee is careful in her identification of the basilical building at Silchester, warning that although it has been 'almost unanimously accepted as Christian', and is probably so, it cannot be proved on the basis of the ground plan alone; re-excavation is urged – a task later carried out by Richmond (Frere 1975). The apsidal building on the site of the Roman baths at Caerwent Toynbee proposes is a sub-Roman or post-Roman church. The suite of rooms at Lullingstone is identified as the house chapel, while a similar identification for the two rooms, one apsidal, at Frampton, is rejected. Toynbee concludes her examination of evidence for churches with a discussion on possible religious continuity. She notes the incidence of Roman villas under a number of village churches across England, and wonders if there might be a link between Roman house chapels and later churches, or if the siting of some Saxon religious buildings had been due merely to the fortuitous presence of suitable building materials.[3] In pursuing this theme, she suggests that the church of St Bride in Fleet Street, London, could be the site of a Roman extra-mural cemetery church, since the cemetery there was known to have been in use at least in the Saxon period.

Toynbee also looks at objects which may have a Christian identity, and reviews the evidence. After considering the main theories on its origins, she concludes the *rotas-sator* word square at Cirencester is probably Christian. Of the several lead tanks found throughout civilian Britain, those with Christian symbols are believed to have been made for adherents of the faith, and probably fulfilled a religious function; even those without such symbols may also have had the same purpose. What purpose is not clear, but

Toynbee seems to favour baptism by affusion. Of other inscriptions she is less than certain. The arguments for a Christian identity for tombstones with the words *plus minus* instead of the exact age of the deceased[4] are 'not quite conclusive'. Similarly, she does not subscribe to the theory that the villa at Chedworth necessarily came into the hands of Christians: all that can be deduced is that someone who was familiar with the Christian (*chi-rho*) monogram lived at, or visited, Chedworth. She then describes smaller objects found throughout Roman Britain and, although not claiming to have collected all the evidence, points out that there is, in total, a wide range of evidence and a broad distribution of sites in an area covering southern, south-eastern and south-western England.

The conclusions drawn by Toynbee are, even more than three decades later, still relevant to a study of Romano-British religion. The most important of these include: the evidence is almost wholly civilian in context, although she accepts as negative evidence the destruction of Mithraea at military sites; the wide range and distribution of evidence reveals a mixed Christian following – town and country, rich and poor; the quality and type of evidence (here the reference is particularly to the Lullingstone frescoes and the Cirencester word square) suggest that Christianity was not insular in character, but was part of the mainstream of the religion in the Late Empire; and (perhaps her most controversial finding) Christianity did not end with the Roman epoch, but it remained 'submerged' until the arrival of Augustine, to flower once more in mediaeval England. It was not, she maintains, 'completely wiped out from sight and memory': the Celtic Church which survived in the remoter parts of Britannia, the north and west, was 'thoroughly Roman in creed and origin'.

Frend has a much more conservative view of the spread of Christianity, and he tends to consider the problem from an historical rather than an archaeological viewpoint. In his first analysis of Romano-British religion, published in 1955, he proposes that Christianity, although part of the Western tradition of church government and doctrine, was neither as widely accepted nor as popular with the masses as it was in other parts of the Empire, and that it remained to the end of the fourth century a minority religion. It was affected, no doubt, by the strength of the pagan revival which he sees as mirroring a trend towards the Bacchic salvation-type cults in the Mediterranean provinces in the previous century. By the time of Augustine's arrival at Canterbury in 597, Christianity was all but forgotten. In a later paper specifically on Romano-British Christianity (Frend 1968),[5] he expands on the theme of fourth-century minority religion, citing archaeological and literary evidence for the relative unimportance and poverty of the new religion even in urban centres. However, he does concede, presumably in view of further archaeological discoveries, that the Church had made some gains towards the end of the century to the extent that, by the time of the Pelagian heresy, there must have been a well-established, educated and articulate Christian community in Britain. In fact, he appears to extend the date for the 'demise' of Christianity[6] to about 450, by which time, he believes, Britain had become 'as Christian a country as northern Gaul had . . . a generation before'.

In the same study, Frend deals with specific evidence for Christianity, accepting the Cirencester word square and a presence at Lullingstone, Hinton St Mary, and Frampton, and probably also at Horkstow and Woodchester, in view of the Orpheus mosaics found there. He sees the Church as making ground in the major towns of Britain and in the wealthy rural areas, although paralleled by continuing, if generally declining, paganism; he proposes that evidence for Christianity should be found in military areas, especially after 375 and the accession of Valentinian II.

A third study by Frend (1979) relates particularly to the fate of the Church in the fifth century. Here, while he still holds to the view that the religion in Britain virtually perished along with the Latin language after 450, he allows that a complete hiatus between Romano-British and Anglo-Saxon Christianity is most unlikely. As in his earlier publications, he examines both literary and non-literary evidence and, in keeping with his scholarly interests, is at his most authoritative when dealing with Church history.[7] He sees Christianity early in the fifth century as having the same pattern as before, that is, organised on an urban and episcopal basis but having no developed parochial system; and, while there is no evidence that it had become the religion of the masses, the Church did seem to have emerged as a 'vigorous movement' in some towns. As Gaulish and Roman influences waned in Britain in the fifth century, so too did Christianity. Its decline was due not to the incursions of pagan Saxons, but to the failure of the religion to achieve popular appeal.

In his examination of the archaeological evidence, Frend covers areas explored in his previous papers and also looks at other material, although he does not include all available at the time. He brings together some evidence on cemeteries, suggesting as probable Christian inscriptions two bone plaques from York: one from a burial in Castle Yard, inscribed *DOMINE VICTOR VINCAS FELIX*, the other from Sycamore Terrace and previously listed by Toynbee (1953), bearing the words *S{OR}OR AVE VIVAS IN DEO*. He ascribes a Christian identity to the Poundbury cemetery, on several separate pieces of evidence.[8] In his appraisal of churches and baptisteries, Frend does not doubt that the Silchester basilical building is a church, but refers to the presumed baptistery there merely as a *piscina*, perhaps for ablutions before entering the church. He has, however, no argument with the identification of the hexagonal structure at Richborough as a baptistery. In his discussion of the lead tanks he is cautious, proposing a Christian purpose for them, probably in the baptismal rite, but does not enter into the debate over what actual function they performed. On treasures and hoards, he limits himself to a brief discussion of Mildenhall and Water Newton: he does not accept Painter's theory (1977a: 22–3) on the deposition of the Mildenhall Treasure, describing it as 'unproved'; in the Water Newton hoard he sees the presence of votive 'leaves' as illustrating the slow progress from paganism to Christianity in fourth-century Britain.

The most recent work by Frend (1982) specifically on Romano-British Christianity reviews later evidence. He accepts the buildings at Silchester, Richborough, and St Pancras at Canterbury as the 'only . . . indubitable Romano-British churches' and an 'almost certain' Christian identity for burials at Poundbury Camp, Dorchester and Lankhills, Winchester; he seems inclined to accept the *rotas-sator* word square at Manchester (Hassall and Tomlin 1979: 353) as Christian, despite its early date. He compares Christianity in Britain with that in other parts of the Empire in the fourth century, and questions why, when the same conditions prevailed in sub-Roman Italy and Gaul, Latin Christianity did not triumph in Britain as it did on the Continent. He proposes internal weaknesses in the province as the main reason: the lack of an effective parish system; the absence, apart from the shrine of Alban at Verulamium, of evidence for the cult of martyrs and of any missionary effort such as that by Martin of Tours; and the continuation and revival of paganism. In his overall assessment, he sees a gradual penetration of Christianity among the upper classes and that it was strongest in some of the towns and villas; he holds that the period 430–50 saw the 'practical destruction of episcopally based Christianity in Britain', a stance somewhat modified from his earlier writings.

Frend's approach to the study of Christianity is primarily historical. His use of the texts of the early Church is of great help in putting Christianity in Britain into its setting in the Late Empire. His contribution to research on Romano-British religion is considerable; and his conclusion that 'the *ecclesia Britannorum* failed to provide the foundations for the *ecclesia Anglicana*', based as it is to a large extent on his examination of the literary sources, has provided the challenge to Thomas (1981) to show, more on linguistic and archaeological evidence, that there was a line of continuity from the Romano-British to the Anglo-Saxon Church.

Though some of Thomas's conclusions are contentious, the importance of his book cannot be overestimated; undoubtedly it will remain the standard reference for the study of Christianity in Roman Britain for many years to come. In view of its importance, it is felt that a fairly detailed analysis of this work would be appropriate here.

Thomas gathers together most of the literary and archaeological evidence on Christianity available to 1979. He builds on the work of Toynbee and Frend[9] and also makes use of publications such as those by Wall (1965; 1966; 1968) on the evidence for Christianity in the north and south-west of Britain – gazetteers rather than critical analyses. Thomas carries his narrative to 500, which date, he believes, roughly corresponds with the end of Romano-British Christianity. He argues strongly for continuity between the Roman and Anglo-Saxon Church:[10] he proposes that the spread of Christianity to the north and west of Britain took place earlier in the fifth century than has generally been accepted, and that, far from being expunged in the fifth and sixth centuries, it continued and gradually spread east and south into English-occupied territory. While the details of this late period of Romano-British Christianity are not pertinent to the present study, his conclusions are, as it will be argued below (chs IV and VII) that the theme of continuity is one which is constant throughout the whole history of Romano-British religion.

Thomas puts Christianity in its conventional setting as one of the oriental mystery cults introduced mainly in the Late Empire; he concludes that the number of Christians was 'substantial' in late Roman Britain, though still constituting a minority religion. In his second chapter, he examines the literary evidence, which, as he says, is 'neither isolated nor particularly specific', and arrives at some controversial conclusions: as noted in Chapter I, he takes a date of mid-third century for the martyrdom of Alban,[11] and he relegates Pelagius to a far from central figure in early fifth-century Christianity;[12] in an important chapter (his ch. 3) Thomas explores the use, spread, and retention of Latin, and takes the view that Latin usage (and thus the Latin-speaking Church) was more widespread than is usually allowed; and he believes that the Church, whose distribution and organisation in the fourth century has been underestimated, played an important part in the retention of Latin in the fifth and sixth centuries (cf. Frend 1984: 793).

Having considered the literary evidence, Thomas then looks rather briefly at Christian symbolism, after which he examines the material evidence for Christianity. This is classified on a 3–0 scale: 3, 'nearly certain', includes churches, church–baptistery combinations, items with Christian ornament such as hoards, lead tanks, mosaics, building stones, tiles and bricks, fragments of pottery and glass, and cemeteries with an apparently Christian component; 2, 'reasonably probable', includes complete vessels with Christian symbols, lead tanks without such decoration, plaster or gypsum burials, and tombstones where the wording is ambiguous; 1, 'possibly Christian', relates to portable and valuable items such as finger rings, individual items of silver, decorative pieces such as strap tags and glass, and to 'negative' evidence such as the destruction of pagan shrines, presumably by Christians; a scale of 0, that material which he considers 'chronologically irrelevant or dubious', such as the word squares from Cirencester and Manchester, the pewter ingots with *chi-rho* from London, and the Traprain and Mildenhall Treasures.

Although there are a few minor omissions,[13] there is little quarrel with Thomas's actual classifications, given the material available for study at the time he was writing. His ranking of plaster or gypsum burials as reasonably probable evidence for Christianity might now be revised, however, in the light of further archaeological discoveries.[14] A few other classifications may be queried here. A weighting of 2 for the presence of bishops and martyrs seems insufficient, in view of the literary evidence Thomas himself cites for London, York and probably Lincoln for bishops, and the ample evidence for the martyrdom of Alban at Verulamium. The low evidential weighting for portable and valuable objects such as finger rings is probably warranted, but it cannot be just coincidental that many of these items have been found in areas where a Christian presence has been postulated on other grounds.[15] One further weighting should be questioned – the pewter bowl with *chi-rho* found at Caerwent. This would have been originally a complete vessel, apparently purposely buried (Boon 1962: 338–9); it should therefore surely rank with hoards such as the Appleshaw pewter.[16] The rejection of the Mildenhall Treasure as evidence, an omission based on Painter's thesis (1977a: 22–3; Thomas 1981: 103), is to be regretted, since Painter's reconstruction of events leading to the deposition of the hoard is far from conclusive.

In a chapter devoted to the identification of churches in Roman Britain, Thomas looks for analogies in Gaul, from which he is led to classify churches under three heads: intra-mural or congregational, extra-mural or cemetery, and estate churches. These categories are adequate, though some refining might be necessary as more sites are identified as Christian.[17] As before, his classifications are generally appropriate, though the criteria for identification are not always clear, and his omissions thus appear arbitrary. The apparent inclusion of Littlecote as an estate church is perhaps premature, since the debate over the mosaic and the purpose of the building continues.[18]

A study of baptism and baptisteries follows in which the possible methods of administering the sacrament are examined; Thomas concludes that affusion would have been the most likely method in Roman Britain. In a discussion on the lead tanks unique to Britain and their possible use in the baptismal rite, he argues that the churches would have had fixed or portable fonts and that the lead tanks were, therefore, alternatives to fixed fonts.[19]

Thomas then turns to burials and cemeteries in what he admits is a defective and unsatisfactory chapter (his ch. 9). He stresses the problems of identification, and deplores the 'surprisingly low emphasis' accorded studies of Romano-British cemeteries, with the exception of a few such as Trentholme Drive, Lankhills and Poundbury. Poundbury and feature 6 of Lankhills he ranks on a 3 scale, and suggests that Ancaster may also be Christian in character. While he describes some of the features of the cemeteries, he does not indicate what criteria he is applying in his identification of them as Christian. An important point made is that the lack of continuity in the use of burial grounds from the

19

Roman to the post-Roman period makes it difficult to identify pre-400 burials.

The last section of Thomas's book relates to fifth-century Britain and is not particularly relevant to this study. Apart from his belief in the continuity of Christianity into the post-Roman period, however, two of his final points are pertinent here: he believes that, while Christianity remained a minority religion, by about 500 in certain areas its followers were more numerous than those of any other distinct religion; and he advocates a new interpretation of old material on Christianity in Roman Britain in conjunction with the study of new archaeological discoveries.

Three new studies of Romano-British religions have appeared since Thomas's publication, one of which (Webster 1986) does not touch on Christianity. It is doubtful if, with regard to Christianity, either of the other authors (Henig 1984b: Green 1983) has systematically re-interpreted the old material, or, for that matter, incorporated any new archaeological discoveries into his or her respective works.

Henig's volume on religion in Roman Britain has only a small section devoted to Christianity, no part of which contains new evidence found since Thomas's book was published, although it does describe two Christian engraved gems not mentioned by Thomas but previously listed in Henig's own major study of Roman engraved gemstones (Henig 1978: nos 361–2). Henig has taken a fresh look at one inscription supposedly relating to Christians, the Jupiter column at Cirencester (*RIB* 152) which refers to desecration by 'insolent hands', and concludes that it does not look Constantinian and is probably earlier. He follows Walters (1981; 1984) in giving an Orphic identity to the Littlecote triconch mosaic and chamber, and supports the contention of King (1983) that the basilical building at Silchester was not a Christian church, but a *schola*. Even so, he believes that, while the process of christianisation was slow, a 'large proportion' of the British population was Christian by the early part of the fifth century.[20] Overall, Henig's work is a timely and useful addition to the study of Romano-British religion. So far as Christianity is concerned, however, he has not brought together additional material published since 1979.

The other recent work, by M. Green (1983), does not purport to be a study of Romano-British religions but of the gods of Roman Britain,[21] and the brief uncritical section on Christianity does not incorporate all available evidence. The work is based to a large extent on her earlier book (1976) collating and analysing evidence for religion from the civilian zones of Roman Britain. In that study, her account of Christianity expands little on the work of Toynbee and Frend. She concludes that 'in real terms Christianity does not seem to have gained any but a precarious foothold in Britain' (M. Green 1976: 64). However, she is able, as the result of further discoveries, to amend this view seven years later: 'The evidence . . . is . . . scattered but enough survives . . . to demonstrate archaeologically that the cult gained a substantial foothold in Britain during the fourth century' (Green 1983: 70). The strength of this book lies in the pagan section and the excellent illustrations therein.

One further work might be examined, a study by Morris (1983) on the Church in British archaeology, which has one chapter on Romano-British Christianity, and another in which he discusses the question of continuity into the Anglo-Saxon period. He summarises earlier studies, and draws his own conclusions on probable churches, stating, 'No building which can be un-equivocally identified as a Romano-British church has yet been found'. Those he accepts as Christian are the buildings at Silchester, Icklingham and Richborough, with, as possible examples, Verulamium 6 (using the identification of Lewis, 1966), and two buildings at Caerwent. He gives briefly and without comment the evidence for the first three but, for the last group, gives no supporting evidence. It does not appear that, when writing, he had access to Thomas's work of 1981, with the additional sites proposed by that author. It noted that Morris is inclined to accept Littlecote as a possible Christian site analogous to an Anatolian church as cited by Smith (1978).[22] On cemeteries he suggests only Poundbury and the Sycamore Terrace burial at York as Christian. In his map he shows other possible churches and cemeteries, but does not indicate why some of these have been included. With regard to continuity, Morris is of the opinion that Christianity survived in many areas until the second quarter of the fifth century, that British churches existed when Augustine landed in Kent in 597, and that it is 'conceivable' that some of these had their origins in Romano-British Christianity.

The works discussed above constitute the rather slight body of major publications on Christianity in Roman Britain. There have been, however, a considerable number of studies on specific sites.

It would not be practicable to list all such works, but the main ones may be identified.

On churches, temples and shrines, the seminal study is that by Lewis (1966). He classifies all religious buildings according to shape, provides plans, tables of dimensions and dates, and makes comparisons with continental examples. His work on pagan buildings will be considered later in this chapter. His treatment of Christian sites is limited by the paucity of material available at the time of writing and is, therefore, probably the least useful section for this present study. Nevertheless, it is worth recording that the Romano-British Christian sites he lists include Silchester 9 (his notation for the basilical building; Lewis's notational identification will be adopted throughout this work), Lullingstone, Canterbury Cathedral, St Albans Abbey, York, London, Lincoln or Colchester (these last four on the evidence of the Council of Arles of 314), the fifth-century rectangular building at Whithorn, and the apsidal building on the site of the Roman public baths at Caerwent.[23] Lewis's work has been brought up to date by Rodwell (1980c), who has published a gazetteer of known sites using the former's classifications.[24] Here the list of potential Christian sites does not include any not mentioned by Thomas (1981), but in other publications he has suggested further possibilities (Rodwell 1980a: 220, 238; Rodwell and Rodwell 1977: 37). These will be considered below (ch. IV).

For individual buildings which are almost certainly Christian, the material comprises few fully published reports. The Silchester 9 building, first reported by Fox and St John Hope (1893) was in recent times re-examined by Richmond, whose death prevented the publication of his findings. That task has been undertaken by Frere, who, while not disputing a Christian identity for the building, is not convinced that the small rectangular platform and associated pit just to the east of the building is a baptistery (Frere 1975: 295–6). The early excavations of the fort at Richborough were carried out by Bushe-Fox (1926–49) and the remains of a baptistery found but not recognised as such; years later, Brown (1971) demonstrated convincingly that what has survived here was a baptistery and the outline of a church, parallels for which could be found on the Continent.[25] Perhaps the most extensive of all those sites considered Christian is the one at Icklingham (West 1976). Here excavations have uncovered not only what is thought to be an apsidal church and cemetery, but also a baptistery and a lead tank. The immediate locality has yielded at least one more tank; both have *chi-rho* decoration. Of the sites not yet fully published, a very significant one is that at Uley, in Gloucestershire (Ellison 1980). Ellison's findings so far have been accepted by scholars such as Henig (1984b: 225) and P.A. Rahtz (pers. comm.), and have been important in the present study in developing the theory of continuity of religious tradition at a sacred site (below, chs IV, VII). The site seems to be an excellent example of religious continuity from the Late Iron Age down to the seventh and eighth centuries AD. In Essex, work at Witham has produced a small rectangular building and a presumed baptistery on an earlier pagan sacred site. This excavation has appeared only in an interim report (Turner 1982), and its final publication will be of considerable interest. Others reported only in brief to date are the apsidal building (Colchester 9) associated with a cemetery at Butt Road, Colchester (Crummy 1980), St Pancras at Canterbury (Jenkins 1976), given a ranking of 3 by Thomas, and St Paul-in-the-Bail, Lincoln (Jones 1984). This latter is assuredly Christian, the only doubt being whether it is Roman or sub-Roman. It is discussed in some depth in chapter IV.

In addition to those sites generally considered Christian, there are several which are probably so (see below, ch. IV), and which are reported in some detail. These include the rectangular building associated with the temple at Brean Down (ApSimon *et al.* 1961; ApSimon 1965), a site whose adjoining cemetery was much eroded long before excavation. ApSimon himself does not ascribe a Christian identity to the building, however; this has been suggested by the excavator of nearby Lamyatt Beacon (Leech 1973–82; 1980: 349–50; 1986). The cemetery at this latter site was undisturbed, but the temple and adjoining rectangular structure had suffered much at the hands of treasure hunters. Leech sees ritual links between the two temples and suggests similar links between the two rectangular buildings. At Nettleton, in the same general geographical area, Wedlake (1982) uncovered an important octagonal shrine to Apollo which was converted to a cruciform, possibly a church, in the fourth century, and also a rectangular building which seems to have had a close connection with an adjoining cemetery. The original building at the site of Stone-by-Faversham, Kent, excavated by Fletcher and Meates (1969; 1977), was of Roman date, and was quite possibly a Christian mausoleum church. Finally, in the Verulam Hills Field, the careful excavation by Anthony (1968) of the apsidal building Verulamium 7 and associated cemetery allows a likely Christian identity, with a continental parallel.

House or estate churches constitute a special group; the most important studies are those by Meates (1979; 1987) on Lullingstone, Farrar (1957) on Frampton, and Painter (1968) on Hinton St Mary. Neither of the last two is a full archaeological report. The sites have generally been accepted as Christian, but more recently doubts have been expressed about the Frampton mosaic (Huskinson 1974: 77; Henig 1986: 164).

Cemeteries have not engendered the same interest that temples and churches have in the past, and few have been excavated and reported thoroughly. Here the literature on probable Christian sites will be summarised; those that do not appear to have any possible Christian component will be dealt with in a survey of research on pagan cemeteries and burial practices later in this chapter. A study of likely Christian sites shows that cemeteries often form only a secondary part of an archaeological report, for example, Anthony (1968) on Verulamium 7, Leech (1981) on Bradley Hill, ApSimon *et al.* (1961: 120–5) on Brean Down, and Wedlake (1982: 109) on Nettleton. A better coverage is given by West (1976) on Icklingham (although there is no detailed plan of the cemetery or individual burials), and by Leech (1986) on the burials at Lamyatt Beacon. The known Romano-British cemeteries at York have been collated by RCHM (1962: 67–110) while Ramm (1971: 193–4) lists the 'gypsum' burials there, but neither gives detailed analysis or plans since the evidence has long been destroyed and the nineteenth-century excavations poorly recorded. Much more satisfactory is Clarke's report on Lankhills, Winchester, which includes detailed plans and a close examination of feature 6, a possible Christian burial group in an otherwise pagan cemetery, but still no full skeletal analysis (Clarke 1979: 97–9, 193, 429–30 and figs).

What is yet to be published is likely to be of even greater importance to the study of Christian cemeteries: Wilson's excavations at Ancaster have so far been summarised only briefly and without plans (Wilson 1968; Anon. 1974: 16–17); Rahtz's work (1977)[26] on the Cannington cemetery is referred to in a paper devoted mainly to an attempt to classify sub-Roman cemeteries and to exploring grave orientation as a feature of late-Roman and sub-Roman burials; and C.J.S. Green's progress at the Poundbury cemetery is given brief coverage from 1967 to 1981, with a more detailed summary in 1982. Two further sites, the reports for which are in preparation, are the cemeteries at Butt Road, Colchester, (mentioned briefly by Crossan, in Crummy 1980) and Ashton (Dix 1984; Frere 1983: 305–6; 1984a: 300–1). Since the excavation on these sites is complete, the full reports are awaited with great interest, as it is believed that the careful excavation and analysis of the cemeteries will result in their being identified as Christian (see below, ch. III).

Studies of burial customs for the Roman period are not extensive; those on the early burial customs of Christians are even less so; and, so far as is known to the writer, studies specifically on Romano-British Christian burials are non-existent. Toynbee (1971) has published a thorough examination of death and burial in the Roman world which, as Thomas (1981: 229) remarks, has few references to Roman Britain, owing to the scarcity of evidence. Toynbee's work complements Richmond's research on the links between archaeology and the afterlife, published in 1947 (at which date there was even less evidence for Christian cemeteries in Britain), and that by Cumont (1922) on afterlife in Roman paganism. Although the early chapters of Rowell's study (1977) of the liturgy of Christian burial do not refer to early British burials, they have very useful detail and are well documented. Other works warrant close attention because of their relevance to Romano-British religions. In a paper on pagan religion and burial practices, Macdonald (1977: 38) concludes that during the Roman occupation of Britain the 'negative attitude' revealed in the Roman view of the afterlife was eroded, while the oriental cults 'strengthened the native tradition'. This view of 'oriental' (that is, Christian) influence on third- and fourth-century burial practices in Britain has been challenged by Jones (1981: 15–18), who endorses the opinion long ago expressed by Nock (1932: 357) that the change from cremation to inhumation was not due to the influence of any oriental philosophy. For Christian burials, the most significant analysis to date has been that by Leech (1980). In a paper on religion and burials in Somerset and Dorset, he not only provides a very useful list of the Romano-Celtic burials in the region but also makes a real attempt to single out the characteristics of Christian burial.

On studies of particular burial practices, the distinction between pagan and Christian cannot always easily be made.[27] Alcock (1980) has looked at classical burial practices in Roman Britain, which include some found in Christian burials. Black (1986b) examines Celtic and Romano-British burial customs in the south-eastern part of England, but does not always separate the Celtic and Roman customs.[28] He has a little to say on Christian burials, as part of discussions on plaster burials and the orientation of graves. The paper is useful for his collation of material from nineteenth-century excavations, and his fresh look at the cemetery at Ospringe, Kent. A major study of Iron Age burial customs by Whimster (1981)[29] has some which were found in Christian burials of the fourth century. His book also contains a gazetteer, as does that by Toller (1977) on lead coffins and ossuaria; this latter does not attempt to classify pagan and Christian. C.J.S. Green's research on plaster and gypsum burials is of great importance, as is his cautionary note that 'not all plaster burials occur in a Christian context, and they are not the sole feature distinguishing these cemeteries from others' (Green 1977b: 52). Rahtz (1978) and Kendall (1982) have written on grave orientation, Rahtz giving greater weight to the burial and the solar arc than is accepted by Kendall.

Unlike cemeteries and burial practices, Christian symbolism has received attention from Victorian times, stimulated, paradoxically, by the pioneer work in the catacombs of Rome by De Rossi (1864–77); the earlier part of his work is conveniently summarised by Northcote and Brownlow (1869). One of the least-dated nineteenth-century studies of symbolism is that by Hulme (1899). More recent publications, of differing quality, include the well-documented, but limited, work of Daniélou (1964) and the more comprehensive, but little-documented, study by Child and Colles (1971). By far the most important research on the cross and the Christian monogram is that by Sulzberger (1925), an authoritative if at times rather controversial work.[30] A number of other works on symbolism do not touch on origins, however, and have little value for the present study. For the Graeco-Roman origins of many Jewish and Christian symbols, the multi-volumed study by Goodenough (1953–68) is useful, while Cabrol and Leclerq's vast *Dictionnaire* (1920–53) contains references to the whole Roman Empire including Britain, is well documented and generously illustrated. The scale of this work, however, allows errors to creep in.

An examination of symbolism leads to a consideration of the major hoards with a Christian or likely Christian component. It is instructive to look at publications on hoards from both the Roman period and later. The studies on Romano-British treasures include those by Haverfield (1914) on the finds near Corbridge, presumably from a hoard; Dalton (1922) on the Dorchester, Dorset, silver and Johns and Potter (1985: 345–50) on the spoons from Dorchester-on-Thames; Curle (1921) on the Traprain Treasure, a hoard of *Hacksilber* which should, it is believed, be reappraised in view of more recent discoveries; Mattingly *et al.* (1937) on the Balline (Coleraine) hoard of similar *Hacksilber*; Painter (1977a; 1977b) on the Mildenhall and Water Newton Treasures, hoards which are among the most important of all late Roman Christian silver found, but the studies of which are, unfortunately, rather slight; Painter (1965; 1972) and Johns and Potter (1985) on the Canterbury silver, found at different times but believed to be from the one hoard; and Johns and Potter (1983) on the Thetford Treasure, a find of such importance that it has merited a full reappraisal elsewhere in this study (below, ch. V.1; see also Watts 1988b). One post-Roman hoard is particularly relevant to this study: that found at St Ninian's Isle on the site of a pre-Norse church. It was first published by O'Dell *et al.* (1959), who identified only a portion of it as Christian. Since then McRoberts (1965) has argued very persuasively for a Christian, indeed an ecclesiastical, identity for the whole treasure.[31] An examination of the contents is useful, especially when assessing the Thetford Treasure.

It is useful also to compare the Romano-British hoards with those from other parts of the Roman Empire. These include the silver treasures from Hama (Diehl 1926) and Canoscio (Giovagnoli 1935), both of which have been generally accepted as eucharistic plate,[32] the Esquiline Treasure (Shelton 1981) and that from Kaiseraugst (Cahn and Kaufmann-Heinemann 1984), the last-mentioned of as much value for the parallels drawn (and illustrated) as for the sometimes contentious conclusions reached.[33]

But Christian symbolism occurs not only on silver plate. Adherents of the faith also seem to have decorated their floors with such devices. There has been much debate over the identification of fourth-century mosaics in Britain; several publications have appeared interpreting or re-interpreting designs which may be Christian, crypto-Christian or purely pagan. Apart from those previously mentioned on Frampton and Littlecote, the most relevant to this work are the studies by Toynbee (1963; 1964a),

Painter (1976) and Eriksen (1982) on Hinton St Mary; Smith (1983) on the Orpheus mosaics; Henig (1984a; 1986: 162–4) on Frampton; and Black (1986a) who re-examines some of the motifs in the Hinton St Mary and Frampton mosaics.[34]

After consideration of the prior research on Christianity, it is necessary to analyse the material on the pagan cults, in order to determine what pagan elements, if any, can be found in Romano-British Christianity. To this end, such examination is restricted mainly to the aspects covered in the analysis of Christian sources. Studies on the Celts are not uncommon. The most significant of these include general studies by Powell (1959) and Chadwick (1970), and more specific studies by Piggott (1968) on the Druids, Green (1986) on the gods of the Celts, and Brunaux (1988) on the religion of the Celtic Gauls; all of these contain some reference to Britain. Much of the material covered by those writers is also found in a work by Ross (1967), in what has become to some extent the standard reference on the Celts in Britain. This author's conclusions warrant closer scrutiny.

In her study, Ross looks at shrines, sacred springs, trees and groves and discusses shrines as structures, pointing to several sites known in Britain; she notes some evidence for graves as foci for ritual, but stops short of concluding that Celtic graves and burial grounds themselves became shrines. Her treatment of burial practices is restricted to the more spectacular 'chieftains' burials' and its value as a study of Celtic practices generally is, therefore, fairly limited. Of more use is her lengthy discussion on the cult of the head, a theme developed from an earlier publication (Ross 1959). This is of importance in any discussion of decapitated burials (below, chs III, VI). On continuity in Romano-British religion she is guarded: 'Continuity of [religious tradition] is suggested wherever it can be reasonably envisaged' (Ross 1967: 5); but she believes that Celtic shrines may be found beneath Roman ones. The place of the Celtic cults in Roman Britain is assessed and she concludes that the coming of Rome did not mean their demise.

This view is shared by M. Green (1976), who argues that the *interpretatio Romana* (Tacitus, *Germania* 43) could as well have been termed the *interpretatio Celtica*, and that the origins of the Romano-Celtic cults lay in the pre-Roman past. On ritual structures, she follows the classifications of Lewis (1966) and refers only to exceptional or new finds. As likely locations for temples and

28

shrines she suggests Iron Age forts, near theatres, on tribal boundaries, and sometimes in association with graves.[35] Treatment of burials is limited to evidence of extraordinary ritual: she discusses decapitated burials, concluding (after a regional study only) that the bodies were mainly of middle-aged women, possibly queens or community leaders, or perhaps witches or medicine women.[36] On the theme of continuity, she finds analogies from Gaul, and suggests that, in view of their shape and architecture, shrines such as that at Heathrow are precursors of the true Romano-Celtic temple. With regard to iconography, Roman influence was apparent in the increased numbers of representations of deities, in comparison with the dearth of such objects in the Iron Age, but the superimposition of Roman art forms was merely a means of expressing basically Celtic beliefs. She concludes, 'It was the underlying, native religion which was most important, and this is echoed by, for example, the types of shrine, ceremonial object and ritual practices.'

In another recent work on the religions of Roman Britain, Henig (1984b) takes an opposite stance, that the Roman element was the dominant one. In arriving at his conclusions, he places much emphasis on art and inscriptions which, of course, had little or no place in a pre-Roman Celtic world in Britain. On the *interpretatio Romana*, he believes it was a 'dynamic concept, which did not destroy the ancestral [Celtic] gods but it most certainly changed them' (Henig 1984b: 22). However, his views seem rather equivocal, since elsewhere he says, 'A common fallacy is that the romanisation of the gods was simply a matter of dressing Celtic deities in *togae*. Beneath a very thin veneer they remained uncorrupted by Rome' (Henig 1984b: 41–3). He then goes on to say that the Britons, on the other hand, were not just superficially romanised; they aspired to become 'citizens of the Empire'[37] and this attitude was reflected in their religious beliefs.

Henig examines Romano-Celtic temples and, in a departure from Lewis (1966), classifies them according to their purpose rather than their shape: large urban, small rural, temples of pilgrimage, and centres of private or restricted cults. He accepts continuity of religious tradition between the Romano-Celtic and earlier Celtic cults. Henig's views on the association of burials with temples are also worth noting: such an association, he believes, seldom existed in antiquity since it was thought that corpses might pollute the site. On burials themselves, he considers it 'hazardous' to claim a completely native or Roman identity for any grave, and that social *mores* may have been as important as religious beliefs; his treatment of ritual burials does not expand on the work of earlier writers.

One of the most recent major publications on the religions of Roman Britain is that by Webster (1986), who takes the same view as M. Green, that the coming of Rome did not mean the absorption of the Celtic cults by the Roman ones. Evidence to the contrary is deceptive, as much comes from the frontier zones. In a fresh approach, he looks at the effects on the native cults of the Roman occupation, although he does not generally go far into the Roman period. On pre-Roman religious structures, he recognises the difficulty of identification, and observes that normally the only evidence is the close proximity to a later (Romano-Celtic) temple or shrine.[38] He believes that, with the advent of Rome, Britons soon learnt that shrines and temples could be located anywhere, in addition to the sites within hillforts they had always favoured. His discussion on burials concentrates on the major finds: Danebury, Maiden Castle, the La Tène and Aylesford–Swarling burials, and those at Welwyn and Lexden. He mentions briefly the characteristics of these and possible Roman influences, but draws no conclusions on burial practices from the Iron Age generally, nor does he take an overall look at burials in Britain after the arrival of the Romans, in any effort to detect Roman influence. Despite the new approach to the topic, his work does not provide new insights into Romano-Celtic religion in those aspects germane to this present study.

Of greater value is a work on ritual and religion by Wait (1986), who devotes much of his research to the pre-Roman Iron Age, but includes, in addition, some useful material on Romano-Celtic temples in a general analysis of Celtic shrines. He examines the literary and archaeological evidence for Celtic rituals, as well as providing a gazetteer of sites. For this study, his work on burials and shrines is of particular relevance.

On burials, Wait takes a different approach from that adopted in earlier research by Whimster (1981; discussed below); he categorises burials by the number and completeness of the skeletons in the deposit, rather than, as does Whimster, by the type of grave. Wait apparently believes that, since most of the known Iron Age burials have been found in pits or ditches, this is the most convenient way to classify them. It has the disadvantage that, though 449 deposits are studied, they are over such a long period (from the seventh century BC to the early part of the first century AD) that the sample for a particular period is often very small. The figures he arrives at can hardly be said to be representative, or even necessarily a rough guide to trends in burial practice,[39] and he himself makes the point that probably about 95 per cent of all Iron Age burials have disappeared without trace. Thus his conclusions here are at best tentative. Undoubtedly Wait was loath to duplicate the work of Whimster; nonetheless, it would seem that his contribution to the study of pre-Roman burial practices is not as significant as his work on religious structures of the period.

In his research on shrines (his ch. 6), Wait makes a great deal of progress in establishing the characteristics of Celtic religious structures, using criteria such as religious continuity into the Roman period, the presence of votive objects and the position of the shrine or shrines in relation to other buildings in a settlement. He then looks at the structures themselves, the preferred sites and the artefacts found in association with shrines. This same pattern of research is extended into his examination of Romano-Celtic temples, where he attempts to differentiate between '[those] Celtic traits that continue into the Roman period and the customs of Roman pagan cults which were adopted into Romano-British practices'.

Wait's conclusions on religious structures are well argued and, because of the growing archaeological evidence since the topic was first studied in depth, they are difficult to refute. He accepts continuity of religious tradition at various site from the Celtic to the Romano-Celtic period. He finds that Celtic religion was not, as had been earlier thought, atectonic; nor indeed, since Celtic iconography appears so well defined early in the Roman period, were the cults aniconic (cf. Lewis 1966: 4). Overall, Wait has made a considerable contribution to research on Romano-British religious practices.

Mention has already been made of the important study of the temples of Roman Britain by Lewis (1966), and of the general thrust of his research. Despite more recent publications, his remains the standard work on the topic. Some further points he makes in relation to his analysis of pagan structures may be added here. With regard to the location of Romano-Celtic temples, Lewis considers that in the towns the siting was 'predetermined by secular considerations' and, while some may have been given a prominent position, others were relegated to a position away from the town centre. He suggests a variety of reasons for the sites of temples in rural areas, not necessarily always in prominent locations. His statement that 'Roman cemeteries near temples were not unknown' could be construed as inferring an association of temple and burial. (This point is taken up again in Chapter IV.) For continuity of religious tradition he looks to Gaul for analogies, to find that at least eight temples there are known to have been replaced by Christian churches, but adds that, for Britain, 'there is virtually no evidence . . . for continuity as holy places into Saxon times' – a view which, as a result of more recent research, could now be modified.[40]

Since Lewis published in 1966, a number of Romano-Celtic temples have been reported. For the present study, only those having a relevance to the theme of continuity of religious tradition will be considered. These sites are Uley (Ellison 1980), Hayling Island (Downey *et al.* 1980), Witham (Turner 1982) and Harlow (France and Gobel 1985). What they have in common is a Romano-Celtic building on the site of a pre-Roman religious structure or sacred site; Uley and Witham also have probable links with Christianity, Harlow perhaps so (below, chs IV, VI and VII).

New studies of pagan cemeteries are not so numerous, but there has certainly been an increase in both the numbers published and the quality of the reports in the last two decades. Over the past sixty years or so, several sizeable cemeteries[41] of the fourth century[42] have been the subject of reports of varying thoroughness. Of the early publications, none has detailed plans, few have skeletal analyses, and much more interest has been taken in the accompanying grave goods than in the physical remains themselves. The later reports are much more comprehensive, but many still fall short of the ideal: the report on Lankhills, Winchester (Clarke 1979), for instance, while providing excellent plans, analysis of grave goods and details of individual burials, does not have a full paleopathology report, as previously observed; the Bath Gate, Cirencester, report (McWhirr *et al.* 1982) includes such an analysis, but there are some inconsistencies in the publication[43] and it is not easily followed. The recently published report on the Kelvedon cemetery (Rodwell 1987: 26–52) is disappointing, not from lack of detail on the excavation, but because most of the skeletons had dissolved in the poor soil conditions; the grave deposits can be studied, the cemetery population cannot. One further published cemetery, at Queensford Farm, Dorchester-on-Thames, (formerly designated Queensford Mill) might also be considered here. Much of the material from the 1972 excavation by Durham and Rowley and the analysis by Harman *et al.* of 1978 has been incorporated into a report by Chambers (1987); this last study gives details of a total of 275 burials from an original cemetery population of over two thousand, now lost. The details and plans of the actual burials are, regrettably, accessible only on microfiche.

Those reports of other presumed pagan cemeteries most useful here are: Fox and Lethbridge (1926) and Lethbridge (1936) on Guilden Morden; Whiting *et al.* (1931), Ospringe; Bradford and Goodchild (1939), Frilford; Atkinson (1952–3), Radley (supplemented by a short account by Frere 1984a: 302); Wenham (1968), Trentholme Drive, York; Jones (1975), Lynch Farm near Peterborough; Collis (1977a), Owslebury; Matthews (1981), Dunstable; and Davies *et al.* (1986), Alington Avenue, Fordington, Dorchester; the Winterbourne Down cemetery was reported in *Wiltshire Archaeology and Natural History Magazine* (Anon. 1961–3). Short accounts of excavations yet to be reported in full include those by C.J.S. Green (1982; 1977a) on Poundbury, Crossan (in Crummy 1980) on Butt Road, Colchester, and Frere (1983: 305–6; 1984a: 300–1) on the Ashton burials.

Burials in the Iron Age are the subject of a major work by Whimster (1981), referred to briefly above. He classifies burials according to method: pit, grave, ditch, rampart or bank, barrow, cave burial or cremation, and looks at the characteristics of each method, for example orientation, grave goods, position of body, evidence of ritual and age at death. This is a thorough study and is useful for determining what are 'typical' features of burial in a particular area, or at a particular time; but since much of the evidence is poorly recorded, dating is not always secure.[44] He comes to several significant conclusions, some of which were mentioned earlier in Chapter I: from 1000 to 400 BC, there was no common method of burial, and the great scarcity of material for this period was attributable to the practice of cremation, an 'archaeologically invisible rite'; at the time of the Aylesford Culture (400 BC to the first century AD, with a peak of *c.*100 BC), there were four regional inhumation traditions evident and a fifth sword-burial custom with a more widespread distribution – all five with common ritual features; cremation was re-introduced into funerary practice in the middle of the last pre-Christian century by the Belgic immigrants; and while there was an extensive cemetery tradition with bodies given decent burial, in other parts of Britain there appeared to be a 'lack of concern for conventional funerary rules'.

A similar study, though on a smaller scale, is that by Wilson (1981), who analyses Iron Age burials in southern Britain. He classifies his evidence on the basis of the degree of fragmentation of the skeletons, but this has the effect of cutting across geographical and chronological lines, so his conclusions are of less value for this present work. He does, however, make a useful study of position, treatment and orientation of complete skeletons, their location and the differential treatment of males and females, and adults and children, In addition, he provides a list of the sites he refers to in his text, with a summary of the burials found there, which is helpful in extrapolating evidence for particular burial customs.

Burial practices are often dealt with in anthropological studies, but not in relation to archaeology. A most important study, therefore, is a paper by Ucko (1969–70), whose research into the archaeological interpretation of funerary remains is most valuable, not only for his global view of the topic, but also for his caveats on the danger of generalisation in the interpretation of archaeological evidence. He stresses that ethnography must be taken into account when assessing the significance of various burial practices.

Several studies have been produced on particular burial customs: Grinsell's two papers on practices found in Romano-British burials and elsewhere – Charon's fee (1957) and the deliberate breaking of funerary objects (1961); Black (1983) on the incidence of ritual dog burials from Roman sites; and one of the most important studies, that by Harman *et al.* (1981) on decapitated and prone burials, which collates almost all examples of these practices known in Britain up to Saxon times.

An identification of pagan practices is essential so that they may be recognised as irregular in a Christian context. There can be little doubt that there were both Celtic and Roman influences in Romano-British Christianity, but research on this aspect has been negligible. Two significant studies are on the topic of pagan motifs in Christian art, and in particular the mosaics of fourth-century Britain.

Toynbee (1968) summarises the emergence of Christian art, and examines ecclesiastical opposition to it even up to the fourth century. Even so, the Church had, by the third century, come to interpret the ban on graven images as a ban only on the worship of such objects; the use of pagan motifs which could be given a Christian interpretation was widespread in the Empire and not peculiar to Britain. Toynbee then studies the Hinton St Mary mosaic, which she considers 'deliberately Christian', and thus reasons that the other motifs in the mosaic are Christian, or at least 'Christian-sponsored', and that the two rooms form a house church. The mosaic at Frampton is also believed to be Christian, in view of the *chi-rho* on the chord of the apse and since the other motifs here can also be fitted into Christian iconography. At Lullingstone, there is a strong probability that the fourth-century suite to the north constitutes a house church; as for the Bellerophon-and-Chimaera and Europa-and-Bull mosaics in the adjoining rooms, she suggests that, although they were probably laid before the owner's conversion to Christianity, he would have had no trouble in re-interpreting them as Christian allegories. In a final comment on the mosaics, she proposes that 'all or some' of the Orpheus mosaics in Roman Britain could be crypto-Christian.

This is followed by a commentary on the Vyne Ring, decorated with a bust of Venus and so inscribed, but bearing a secondary inscription *SENICIANE VIVAS IIN DE(O)*, which Toynbee sees as the christianising of the ring, perhaps stolen from its original owner.[45]

Toynbee's paper purports to be a study of pagan motifs and practices in Christian art and ritual, but she herself admits that she knows of only one possible instance of a pagan practice incorporated into a Christian burial – from Sycamore Terrace, York, where a female was interred with grave goods of glass and jewellery and an open-worked bone plaque reading *S{OR}OR AVE VIVAS IN DEO*. Since 1968, the evidence for pagan influences in Christian ritual has been enhanced by the discovery of votive 'leaves' in the Water Newton early-Christian Treasure (Painter 1977b).

The second study on the topic of pagan motifs in Christian art is that of Huskinson (1974), who looks at several motifs, only two of which are relevant to Roman Britain, Orpheus and Bellerophon. Some of her conclusions are diametrically opposed to those of Toynbee. Huskinson notes that, in the Orpheus frescoes in the catacombs, there was a tendency from about the third century on to portray tame rather than wild beasts; this was significant since the Church was unlikely to have sanctioned meaningless iconography. But the examples to which she refers are from continental sites; the British examples she dismisses as having no specific Christian associations, and relegates them to an appendix.

Huskinson is equivocal about the Bellerophon motif: she agrees with the views of Brandenburg (1968) that it is the Christian motifs at Hinton St Mary and Frampton which are out of place in an otherwise pagan setting, yet elsewhere she accepts that, at Hinton, Bellerophon is juxtaposed with Christ, and that the two rooms there were probably, as Toynbee suggests (above), used for worship by Christians; she also refers to the Bellerophon mosaics from Hinton and Frampton as coming from 'secular sites'. Her rejection of the Frampton mosaic as Christian has been referred to earlier, and is based on the thesis of Brandenburg (1969) that the pagan motifs as well as the *chi-rho* here are merely apotropaic. At Lullingstone she proposes, following Toynbee, that this mosaic, along with Europa and the Bull, was probably laid by a pagan owner, and retained after his conversion. Suggested reasons she gives for the retention of these mosaics are the thrift of the owner, or that he found them not incompatible with his beliefs, or that he discovered in them Christian allegories.

Huskinson considers that the portrayal of Orpheus, used in a Christian context before the Peace of the Church, may be intended to be a representation of Christ himself, whereas Bellerephon was not so intended. It is a pity that she did not look at the Orpheus mosaics of Britain individually as she has the Bellerophon examples, since it seems unlikely that none of the nine examples[46] she gives from Britain is Christian, given the popularity of the motif in Christian art elsewhere in the Empire.

From this survey of prior research, it is clear that, despite significant contributions made by a number of scholars (and in particular by Frend, Henig, Johns and Potter, Lewis, Thomas, Toynbee, Ross, Whimster, and Wait) considerable gaps remain in our knowledge of Christianity, of the pagan religions in Roman Britain, and of the links between the two. There is, as Thomas (1981: 352) points out, a need to reappraise evidence already uncovered and, a corollary of this, a need to question previous assumptions and conclusions. New finds must be published as speedily and as fully as is possible, since the delay in publication of a vital site inhibits the advance of knowledge. Deficiencies in that knowledge have to be recognised, and an effort made to rectify them. This is especially so in the identification of Christian cemeteries and, to a lesser extent, churches. Only when as complete a picture of Christianity as is possible has been drawn can it then be related to the pagan cults, and the place of Christianity in the history of the religions of Roman Britain assessed.

III

IDENTIFICATION OF
CHRISTIAN CEMETERIES

I: INFANT BURIALS AS A CRITERION[1]

Charles Thomas (1981: 230), in his survey of Christianity in
Roman Britain, observes:

> It still remains true, however, that the task of identifying any
> *Christian* cemetery . . . is a formidable one . . . Christian
> identifications attached in such areas as the Rhineland to the
> remains of late Roman buildings and to closely-defined
> cemetery areas actually rest more on the continuity of
> Christian tradition than upon any direct archaeological
> display.

It is generally acknowledged that tangible evidence of such
continuity of Christian tradition is lacking in Britain, at least so
far as burials are concerned, and up to now there have been no
certain Christian cemeteries identified from the Roman era. That
does not mean that they have not been found, or that they cannot
be identified, given close analysis of well-recorded sites. Despite
the problems associated with such a task, it would seem that, if a
set of ranked criteria is applied to any carefully documented fourth-
century cemetery, the site may be identified with a reasonable
degree of certainty as either Christian or pagan.

The problems in finding any cemeteries from Roman Britain are
almost as great as those associated with identifying them. The
damp and frequently acidic soils have taken their toll of bone as
well as of tissue, fabric and wood; the constant occupation by
urbanised humans of a small island for two thousand years and, in
particular, the vigour of Victorian railway and building construction have left pitifully few areas untouched; the introduction of

sub-soiling in rural areas has disturbed or destroyed sites previously untouched by the share; the time and financial constraints on contractors or merely their indifference towards the 'few old bones' in the way of trench-digger or bulldozer have caused many a works supervisor in service industries to 'keep on digging'. Any archaeologist could add to this list. It has been remarked, 'The more Christian a cemetery, the less chance of according it any detailed internal chronology' (Thomas 1981: 234). To this may be added the observation, the more Christian a cemetery, the less chance of its surviving at all, since the absence of quantities of grave goods, or of any artefacts, would in times past have made such a cemetery of little interest to archaeologists and antiquarians, or to students of early church history. Examples abound, even in post-war excavations, of the actual burials being accorded the most cursory examination, the interest in a cemetery being focused on the multifarious pots, plates, pins, coins and brooches which accompanied the departed to their graves. That is not to say, of course, that such items are not of the greatest value to the archaeologist in dating a cemetery, and their absence does make the task of dating and identifying the site even more difficult. The greatest resource of a cemetery is, however, its skeletal remains, and far too frequently these have received little attention. For this study it is indeed fortunate that we have for analysis the data from several recently excavated and extremely well-recorded sites where the value as evidence of the 'old bones', both human and non-human, has been thoroughly appreciated.[2]

The burial of 'popular conception', as depicted by Thomas – extended, perhaps enshrouded, laid with head to the west in a coffin of wood, lead or stone, devoid of the pagan trappings of Charon's fee, food, drink or other grave goods – has the features generally acceptable for a Christian identification. But, as he rightly points out, such criteria can be eliminated one by one when applied to Roman Britain, with the result that there is little progress towards identification. They do not take into account fads or fashions in burial, or the possible poverty of a community (Thomas 1981: 231). Even so, there is more than a grain of truth in the description. It is true these popularly accepted criteria are far too simplistic; the various features of a burial are not necessarily of the same importance in identification, or even of any importance, and some may be passed over. Additional evidence, both internal and external, seemingly important or only slightly so, must be adduced and evaluated. When put alongside other features, fads should be distinguished from that syncretism which was such a feature of religion in Roman Britain. Certain criteria are thus of greater importance than others. The presence of infant burials is one such criterion. While others have previously been proposed, as noted by Thomas, this particular feature of Christian burial grounds has not been explored, and such is its importance that it is dealt with separately in Part 1 of this chapter. In the following sections, other criteria are developed and all are then applied to a group of fourth-century cemeteries.

The occurrence of infant or neo-natal burials in the cemeteries of Roman Britain is a phenomenon not generally encountered before the fourth century. That it coincides with the rise of Christianity following the conversion of Constantine does not appear to be mere chance, and it is proposed here that a careful study of the disposal of the bodies of the very young will produce a reliable criterion for the identification of Christian cemeteries in Roman Britain.

Roman law was strict in its prohibition of intra-mural burials. Cicero (*De legibus* 2.23.58) says it had been a provision of the Twelve Tables, and this law[3] was reaffirmed by later emperors;[4] Ulpian (*Digesta* 47.12.3.5) tells how Hadrian imposed a fine for its breach. Cemeteries in Roman Britain, as in other parts of the Empire, were normally situated outside the defined limits of a town, often alongside a major road. Exceptions to this would have been sites such as the small rural complex at Owslebury (Collis 1977a), where over a period of almost seven centuries burials took place in various locations around the settlement, or in a village without clearly defined boundaries, such as at Ashton, where burials were found on individual properties (Dix 1984: 26).

On the other hand, the deposition of the bodies of very young children within the city bounds seems to have been the norm. Both Juvenal (*Saturae* 15.139) and Pliny (*Naturalis historia* 7.16.72) refer to the practice, the latter stating specifically that it was not customary to accord the cremation rite to infants who died before teething (that is, 6 months old). He adds that it was the custom to bury these infants under the eaves of buildings (*in subgrundariis*).[5] Some four centuries later, Fulgentius (*Sermones antiqui* 7), while interpreting *subgrundaria*, says that those who were buried thus were less than 40 days old.[6] It seems, therefore, that although there appears over the centuries to have been some divergence in the interpretation of what constituted an *infans*, the actual practice of intra-mural burial for the very young was long-established. As a reason for the custom, Fulgentius says that the soft bones of a baby did not require cremation and, if inhumation were the practice, that the body would not be big enough for a monument to be raised; he quotes Rutilius Gemius, who proposed that the bodies of infants should be sought under the eaves, rather than in graves,[7] to illustrate the scarcity of formal burials for infants. Implicit in this seems to be the belief that, in the Roman period, there was not such value placed on the life of the very young as to warrant a formal grave. It has been pointed out that, in many ancient and prehistoric societies, and even among present-day primitive peoples, the disposal of the bodies of infants was often characterised by 'an absence of, or at most perfunctory, burial ritual', and that this was probably due to the high incidence of infant mortality (Ucko 1969–70: 271).

Yet, in Britain in the late Iron Age, despite the fragility of the remains and the nature of the soil in which they often were interred, careful archaeological research indicates that the bodies of infants could be accorded some status, particularly in what might be termed 'ritual burials', and that this practice continued into the Roman period. An early example is that from Uley, where two, possibly three, infant burials marked the reconstruction of a pre-historic shrine from the first century of the Christian era (Ellison 1980: 308); another was found outside the entrance to the Iron Age shrine at Maiden Castle (Cunliffe 1978: 321). At Verulamium, of ten infant burials found either inside or just outside buildings, one, confined in a small cist of roofing tiles, had been inserted into an angle of a room; Wheeler and Wheeler (1936: 138–9) propose that it may have been a foundation burial at the time the building was rebuilt at the end of the third century. At Gatcombe, two infant burials were found against the wall footings of building 5, suggesting foundation interments in this fourth-century settlement (Branigan 1977a: 140, fig. 6). A number of burial shafts of the late third or early fourth century at Cambridge contained the body of an infant buried in a wickerwork basket, accompanied by the remains of a dog. In seven of the nine shafts, there were two such burials, one above the other. These shafts, apparently for ritual burial, seem to have been related to a nearby Iron Age sacred spot

(Anon. 1978). Two further religious sites where ritual burial of infants may be inferred are Springhead Temple 4 of Antonine date (Lewis 1966: 76), with four interments (two of them decapitated) in the corners of the building, perhaps as foundation burials (Penn 1967), and Witham, with the burial of two infants, one in a ditch surrounding a ritual building, possibly from the mid-fourth century, the other associated with a deposit of eggshells (Turner 1982: 12, 17).[8]

But another type of infant burial known in Britain probably indicates that infanticide was carried out from pre-Roman times. Collis (1977a: 29, 34) has proposed that the high incidence of infant burials at Owslebury in the century before the Christian era (about 60 per cent of total burials) points to this practice, maybe as the result of an economic slump in the fortunes of the homestead; at Springhead, in a building just north of where the late-second-century Temple 3 would later stand, a kitchen floor yielded fourteen similar burials (Penn 1967); and at Hambledon, the bodies of ninety-seven infants were found in the vicinity of a Romano-British house (Cocks 1921: 150); they probably date to the late third century. None of these examples seems to be in any way related to religious sites, and an interpretation of the burials as evidence of infanticide is reasonable, given that there are many other examples of babies being buried individually on domestic sites.

From his study of burials within settlements in southern Britain in the pre-Roman Iron Age, Wilson (1981: 153–61) records many infant and neo-natal interments in pits, ditches and rubbish dumps, but rarely in graves. Ucko (1969–70: 264) has explained, 'An attitude to burial simply as a means of disposal, even when a specially designated burial area exists, is not uncommon ethnographically.' With the coming of Rome, however, there was a move to the interment of the bodies of the very young within or just outside buildings (the *subgrundaria* of Pliny), at least in the more romanised areas. The excavator of Poundbury cemetery notes that, in the early period, infant burials were found only on the actual site of the houses in the nearby settlement (Green 1982: 62). This suggests the practice of interment within dwellings was adopted very soon after the Roman occupation in the Dorchester region. A few other examples will suffice to illustrate this widespread practice: from the south-west, Crandon Bridge, Churchie Bushes, Bradley Hill, Ilchester Mead, Ilchester and

Catsgore (Leech 1980: 338); another from Colliton Park in Dorchester, where the skeletal remains of four infants were found in building I (Drew and Selby 1937: 11). There are also those from Verulamium mentioned above; and from Ashton, twenty-nine neo-natal or foetal burials possibly from the second to the fourth century found in houses in the small Roman town (B. Dix, pers. comm.).

Negative evidence for intra-mural burial of babies comes from a number of third- and fourth-century Romano-British cemeteries, and some of the larger of these could be profitably examined,[9] although the quality of the reporting is uneven.

From Ospringe, Kent, the account of which (Whiting *et al.* 1931) has recently been re-examined in some detail (Black 1986b), in a cemetery in use from the first to the fourth century, no burials of infants have been recorded in approximately 387 cremations and inhumations excavated. From the report, it is clear that the accompanying grave goods were of much more interest to the excavators than any skeletal remains; and this added to the heavily decomposed state of many of the skeletons makes it most unlikely that any very small burials would have survived or even been noted had they survived unaccompanied by grave deposits. In this cemetery, twenty-five graves of the sixty-one of known alignment were west–east (that is, with heads to the west).[10] There has been no published plan of the cemetery, but it has been suggested that its development was from cremation to north–south burials, and that the west–east interments were the latest (Black 1986b: 216–17, 232). A similar development might have been the case at the cemetery at Lynch Farm near Peterborough (Jones 1975), which was in use in the third and fourth centuries, and contained at least one cremation and about fifty inhumations. Here the only infant burial is one with an adult female, the pair considered by the pathologist to be a premature baby dying with its mother (nos 24 and 40: Fulton 1975, 129–30). This double inhumation was among the west–east burials in the cemetery. One further site where there were cremations and burials which were north–south probably followed later by others of west–east orientation is the second cemetery at Radley, reported as yet only briefly (Frere 1984a: 302), and situated some 200 metres to the south of the cemetery excavated in 1945 (Atkinson 1952–3). This later site comprised at least nine cremations, thirty-eight north–south inhumations and, in a cluster at the southern end, nine west–east burials. The last-mentioned group included decapitated and hobnail burials, but there were no infants or neo-natals here, in what the excavator believes could be a family grouping (D. Miles, pers. comm.), or elsewhere in the cemetery.

This absence of infant burials is also evident in two cemeteries which have in common not only that they began with cremation and appeared to become exclusively inhumation burial grounds, but also that there is no systematic alignment of graves, with later burials indiscriminately cutting earlier ones. The site at Trentholme Drive in York (Wenham 1968) seems to have had inhumations exclusively from around the year 280. Of about 260 burials it is noted that there were very few of young children, and no certain evidence of very young infant or neo-natal burials. In his comments on the skeletal remains, Warwick (1968: 147) expresses surprise that so few infants' remains were found, as infant mortality must have been very high. The siting of the graves here was to all points of the compass. At Guilden Morden, in excavations carried out in 1924 (Fox and Lethbridge 1926) and 1935 (Lethbridge 1936), about fifty cremations and one hundred inhumations were found, lying in all directions excepting west–east, with no respect for earlier burials (Lethbridge 1936: 110). There is no record of any infant or neo-natal burial in either report on this site.

A cemetery which was orientated west–east might now be examined briefly. Excavations at Frilford from the nineteenth century through to 1937 (Buxton 1921; Bradford and Goodchild 1939) have produced almost a hundred inhumations placed west–north–west to east–south–east in nearly parallel rows in the cemetery of a village settlement of the late Roman period. One burial had a coin in the mouth, at least three were disturbed by later interments, yet another was crammed into a grave that was too small, and to this end the legs had been broken. There was no record of any infant or neo-natal burial.

In addition to those mentioned above, there are three other sites which, although not yet fully published, are central to this study and should, therefore, be examined in as much detail as possible. These are the burial grounds at Ashton, Butt Road in Colchester, and Poundbury Camp, Dorchester.[11] At Ashton, two distinct burial customs prevailed: backyard burials or burials on individual properties, singly, in pairs or groups of pairs of no fixed orientation, and a formal, west–east cemetery to the south of the small town. In the former, there were no infant or neo-natal burials among the sixty or so found, but, as has been mentioned above, such burials did occur inside buildings within the town. The west–east cemetery will be discussed below. At Butt Road, Colchester, in the north–south cemetery of the third to early fourth century underlying the later west–east inhumations, there were no infant burials, although these, as at Ashton, also occurred contemporaneously within buildings in the town. This cemetery comprised mainly inhumations, and a handful of cremations. Similarly, cemetery 2 at Poundbury consisted mainly of inhumations with only a few cremations. This was a north–south cemetery dating to the third and fourth centuries; there was considerable disturbance of burials. Some infants' graves were found with those of adults, but Green (1982: 62) reports that there were also seven found below the floor of domestic building R16.[12]

It would seem, therefore, that, although inhumation replaced cremation in popularity in the third and fourth centuries (Jones 1981), the practice of burying babies other than in formal cemeteries persisted. But there is further evidence that by the fourth century they were also being interred, as at Poundbury 2, alongside and even with adults.

At Dunstable (Matthews 1981), where there were almost as many inhumations in convenient ditches and wells as in the 'managed' part of the cemetery, probably of the fourth century,[13] the 112 burials included four neo-natals and eleven infants under 1 year. Several of these were found above earlier burials; others, in shallow holes or in the fill of ditches and cesspits; one was buried with an adult, possibly its mother, and another was found beheaded, with the skull resting on the legs. The indications are that most of these burials were of late-fourth-century date, that often little care was taken with the deposition of the tiny bodies (although one was interred with a bracelet found resting on the skull), and that their interment with the adult part of the community and a number of complete animal bodies was a matter of convenience, rather than reflecting any particular religious beliefs. Orientation in the cemetery appeared to coincide with the alignment of existing ditches, and cannot be taken to be predominantly east–west or west–east overall.

The site at Bath Gate, Cirencester, also contained infants and neo-natals in what is seen not as an organised cemetery but as a recognised burial area of the late third to early fifth century

(McWhirr 1973: 199). Of 453 burials of no consistent alignment and with considerable intersection and disturbance, about sixteen were neo-natal, and two more under the age of 1 year. According to the report, 'several' infants were found at the feet of adults, and these adults were all male, with the exception of one, a woman with a physical deformity, who, at an age between 48 and 54, was unlikely to have been the mother of the newly born child with whom she was interred. About eight neo-natal burials were discrete, at least two in a ditch, and there were also two double burials, perhaps of twins. Another interesting aspect of these burials is the concentration of a number of them (nine) in one part of the cemetery. But it was suggested this could as readily indicate an increased recognition of the difficulty of recovering fragile remains as a genuine concentration of this type of burial in a particular part of the cemetery (McWhirr *et al.* 1982: 110).

The fourth-century cemetery at Lankhills, Winchester, (Clarke 1979) was a far better 'managed' cemetery than the last two mentioned. Here the burials were almost all west–east, though some had irregular burial positions, and there were a number of decapitations; in a total of about 450, there were seventeen which could be classified as neo-natal and another nine aged 9 months or less. Of the neo-natals, eleven were cut by later burials, and six remained wholly discrete. Clarke has charted the development of the cemetery on coin evidence from west to east from 310 to 410, but the distribution of neo-natal burials does not show any corresponding growth in incidence from the earlier to the later part of the cemetery.

The site of Queensford Farm, Dorchester-on-Thames, (Chambers 1987) should also be considered here: a total of 162 west–east and two east–west burials (including two prone and one crouched burial) have been excavated from what has been estimated was a cemetery population of 2,000, dating from the late fourth to the mid-sixth century. At this site, only one neo-natal, either *in utero* or dying after a premature birth (excavation conditions did not allow a more exact identification), was found with an adult female; this is likely to have been a mother–child interment.

This now leads to a consideration of cemeteries which have been proposed by various writers as likely to be Christian. The first is the site at Icklingham (West 1976), where two lead tanks with *chi-rho* symbols were found. In the cemetery of phase III of the site, about forty west–east burials were found in two groups to the west and the south or south-east of an apsidal building and an associated small D-shaped structure. Three burials were of 'small infants', at least one of which was newly born (Wells 1976: 103). Although the cemetery plan has not been published in great detail, it appears that all burials were discrete and did not disturb others. West (1976: 120) believes the site was probably Christian: 'The generalised east–west orientation of the graves [that is, with head to the west], the lack of grave goods, and the association with the lead tank strongly suggests a Christian cemetery'.

The second site is that at Colchester, where the phase II cemetery at Butt Road adjoining an apsidal building has also been proposed as a Christian burial ground (Crossan, in Crummy 1980: 264–6; Black 1986b: 232). Here two neo-natals and four infants under six months were buried in discrete graves, in a west–east cemetery of 664 burials, mainly unaccompanied; it is likely that others have been lost, particularly in the southern part of the site which had been subjected to nineteenth-century terracing, since the bodies of infants were often interred in shallower graves. Care had been taken not to cut or intersect other west–east burials, although there had been little regard for the north–south burials over which the later cemetery lay (C. Crossan, pers. comm.).

There appears to have been at least three phases of burial at Poundbury, and the excavator has proposed a Christian identification for the third phase (Green 1982). Cemetery 1 dated to the first century. Cemetery 2 commenced in the third century, and seems to have continued in use after the third cemetery came into being, employing a different rite. Cemetery 3, of which over a thousand burials have been excavated, was a west–east cemetery, generally unfurnished, with several features suggesting a Christian identity. The graves of neo-natal and very young infants tended to occur in clusters; some accompanied the small groups of adults interred within mausolea. A number were in wooden coffins, some in stone cists, and others were uncoffined. In all cases these infants were treated with the same ceremony as the adults, and care was taken with all burials not to disturb previous interments. There was at least one case when the burials of the very young were not discrete: in grave 116, two infants were placed one each side of a woman's body as secondary interments (D. Farwell, pers. comm.). Examples of mother–child burials may also have occurred. It was noted that, in addition to those burials found, there were also infant-sized pits which, while containing grave furniture, no longer preserved the remains of the tiny occupants (D. Farwell, pers. comm.).

At Ashton, too, small empty graves were found in the orderly west–east cemetery. About 170 inhumations, carefully laid out supine and extended in rows and unaccompanied by grave goods, were found in 180 graves. Of these burials, four were classed as neo-natal, at least seven as under 40 days old, and another three, 'infants'. There were none of the characteristics generally accepted as pagan, such as decapitated or hobnail burials, and the only coins found were two of Constantinian date found associated with, but not in the grave of, a very young child (B. Dix, pers. comm.).

Two further cemeteries which were very possibly Christian were those at Cannington and Ancaster.[14] For Cannington, a stumbling block to such identification has been the early belief that this west–east cemetery dated from the second to the seventh century (Rahtz 1977: 58). This assumption was based on uncorrected radio-carbon dates. However, the corrected dates indicate that the site centres on the fourth century, with activity up to the seventh. The inhumation cemetery of about 570 burials can now readily fit the pattern of other fourth-century cemeteries, and several features point to a Christian identity, not the least being the presence of what seems to be a 'focal' grave, and an absence of hobnail or decapitated burials. Some sixty to seventy neo-natals or infants were found. Unfortunately, owing to the speed of the excavation and the fragility of the remains, it is not possible to say if these were all discrete burials. Nevertheless, the fact that, even if there was some cutting of adjacent graves, care had been taken not to disturb the contents (P.A. Rahtz, pers. comm.), suggests that the infants here would have been treated with the same respect as adults.

With regard to Ancaster, a fourth-century cemetery of mainly west–east graves,[15] it was noted that there were burials of very young babies in the cemetery, and that these probably included neo-natals, and almost certainly babies under 6 months old (D. Wilson, pers. comm.). The cemetery was carefully laid out, with care taken to avoid previous burials.

A survey such as this shows that, just as there were trends or fashions in burial rites, for example from cremation to inhumation, from north–south to west–east orientation, so, too, it became the trend to bury the newborn and the very young in cemeteries along with adults, although the earlier practice of interring them within or just outside domestic buildings persisted, often in the same town. The reason for this development, it would seem, was the growth of Christianity and of the influence of Christ's teachings. The Gospels reflect his care for the young. Probably the best-known illustration of this is from Luke 18.15–17: 'Suffer the little children . . .' A further example is the incident recorded in Matthew 18.2–5, the importance of which is reflected in the fact that it is repeated in both Mark (9.36–7) and Luke (9.47–8). Paul follows a similar theme in exhorting Christians to be childlike (Ephesians 5.1).

Such teaching was taken up by the early Church. In the third century, Tertullian, in his defence of Christians (*Apologeticus* 9.4–11), thunders at pagans who are guilty of infanticide – of killing babies about to be born, or of exposing them after birth to cold, starvation or dogs; he reminds his audience that Christians are forbidden murder or abortion. The same abhorrence is voiced by Minucius Felix (*Octavius* 30.2). In the early fourth century, the Council of Elvira condemned the practice (canons 63, 68).

It can, therefore, readily be accepted that Christian concern for the living infant, 'he who is least among you all' (Luke 9.47), would extend, at death, to the careful interment of his body with other Christians, particularly as a belief in a physical resurrection and in the imminence of the Second Coming prevailed. It is likely that Christian teaching on the value of all human life was taken from the Jewish faith; in his study of the rise of the Christian religion, Frend (1984: 413) notes that the Jewish catacomb at the Villa Torlonia in Rome contained the bodies of many infants, each given the same care as adults: '. . . scrupulous care for the dead, however young'.

A further point is that the sacrament of baptism was available also to infants by the fourth century, although adult baptism was still the more common.[16] The early Christians took their profession of the faith very seriously, and preparation could take anything up to three years (Hippolytus, *Apostolic Tradition* 20). The whole of Lent was a period of fasting and intensive preparation, and presumably this preparation would be undertaken by godparents on behalf of their infant godchildren. That the sacrament could also be conferred on infants indicates the Church's acceptance of the very young and even the newly born as worthy of membership of the Church,[17] along with, and equal to, adult candidates.[18] It is a simple matter to transfer this philosophy to the burial of infants, and to provide that, as Christians, they were given in death the same respect as adults.

It is quite likely, too, that only baptised Christians or catechumens were interred in Christian cemeteries.[19] Although baptism of infants became infrequent by mid-fourth century (Yarnold 1978: 95), they could still become catechumens, and it seems they still had the right to be buried as Christians: a Roman Catholic canon law of 1917 states that Christian burial is granted to catechumens, and the Church accepted that catechumens who died would have baptism by desire, the authority being Augustine, *De baptismo contra Donatistas* 4 (Migne 43.173). Such laws are presumed to go back to the early Church, since they do not deal with points which are disputed (E. de Bhaldraithe, pers. comm.). The implication is that the privilege of Christian burial was extended only to baptised Christians. But, in the fourth century, despite access to the catechumenate, this rank was probably regarded 'less as a first preparation for baptism than as admission to second-class membership of the Church' (Yarnold 1978: 96); therefore it is likely that there would have been fewer babies who became Christian, and hence fewer in Christian cemeteries, in the second half of the fourth century.[20] This would go some way to explaining the disproportionately low numbers of neo-natals and very young babies in a cemetery such as Butt Road phase II at Colchester, especially if, as is likely, the growth of this burial ground coincided with the decline of infant baptism, towards the middle of the fourth century.

That then leaves us with the problem of identifying Christian cemeteries. The accumulation of evidence from many parts of the Empire makes it clear that Christians favoured west–east orientation, to the extent that this orientation is not generally disputed as a criterion for identification.[21] It would seem that, when one eliminates burials other than those orientated west–east, sizeable west–east cemeteries exist where no infant or neo-natal burials are found at all; the absence of neo-natal or infant burials would not reflect the Christian belief in the equality of all baptised members of the faith.

Infants are found both in cemeteries where, while they may be given discrete burials, little care is given to them or to others when later interments are made; they are also found in cemeteries where all burials are respected and lie undisturbed by later graves.

The cemetery at Lankhills, Winchester, for instance, contains neo-natals, but there is much intersection of graves, which rules out a Christian identification. An exception is feature 6, which has been proposed as Christian (Macdonald 1979: 430), and indeed the enclosure is noteworthy for the care in which the burials have been placed to avoid intersecting, and for the presence of a neo-natal burial (no. 259) in what may be a family grouping. These same conditions exist in the late Roman cemeteries at Ashton, phase II of Butt Road at Colchester, Icklingham, and Poundbury cemetery 3; that is, that in a west–east cemetery carefully laid out to avoid intersection of graves or disturbance of other burials, the bodies of newborn or very young babies are found given the same burial rites as adults. This, it is proposed here, assists in their identification as Christian.[22] The presence of neo-natals in cemeteries where these conditions do not exist, such as at Dunstable, Bath Gate Cirencester and Lankhills (with the exception of feature 6), does not suggest a Christian identity, nor does the absence of such burials from a fourth-century cemetery.

It is realised, of course, that this cannot be the only criterion applied in the attempt to classify burials as Christian, and in Part 2 of this chapter a number of ranked criteria are developed which make further progress towards such identification. Nevertheless, it would appear that the presence of such neo-natal burials is one reliable guide to the identification of Christian cemeteries from the fourth century to the end of the Roman period.

2: OTHER SUGGESTED CRITERIA

The problems of identification of Christian burials were discussed in Part 1 of this chapter, and it was acknowledged that no one criterion could be used to identify Christian burials. If, however, it is recognised that certain criteria are of far more importance than others, that evidence can be both positive and negative, and that, in a newly approved and promoted religion there may still be the occasional lapse to an earlier rite, then the problem of identification is not insoluble. It is to this end that the criteria in this section have been developed, and this study may be seen as complementary to the previous work on infant burials.

Since all evidence is not of the same value in identification, it is logical that the various characteristics of burial should be ranked.

An obvious example to follow might have been that of Thomas (1981), who evaluates the evidence for Romano-British Christianity and ranks it on a 3–0 scale. Such, however, is the complexity of the task and the number of criteria involved, it has been thought more satisfactory to give initially relative rankings only: the comparative value of each type of evidence is discussed and ranked; a summary is given in Figure 1. In Part 3, it is convenient to convert the criteria to a numerical scale (Figure 2) and to show the cemeteries studied in a rank order (Figure 3). The application of these criteria to specific cemeteries is studied, and essential features for a Christian identity determined. The results are then reduced to Thomas's 3–0 scheme. The various characteristics of pagan burial mentioned in this section are discussed at greater length in a chapter on pagan influence and practices in Romano-British Christianity (below, ch. VI).

The first set of criteria belongs to a group which might be termed Internal Evidence, or Burial Evidence, for Christianity. Only inhumation cemeteries are examined, since, although there is no scriptural objection to cremation, many in the early Church did not favour the practice.[1] It seems that at least by the end of the second century inhumation was the mode of burial favoured by Christians (Minucius Felix, *Octavius* 34.8–12). Moreover, by the fourth century inhumation had replaced cremation as the preferred method of burial in the Roman world generally (Jones 1981). As Internal Evidence, various characteristics of burial and of the cemetery overall, and the place of the cemetery in the wider community are examined and evaluated.

A maximum weighting should be given to any inscription, symbol or object which has an undoubted Christian identity and is found *in situ*. Several inscriptions and symbols will be considered briefly here; a more detailed discussion of the symbols will be found in Chapter V. The first is an inscription from York, a city which has several known burial grounds (Ramm 1971: 187–94), many of them now destroyed, but no certain Christian cemetery: in Sycamore Terrace was a stone coffin, the only known burial in the area, which contained the remains of a woman and also a bone plaque inscribed *S{OR}OR AVE IN DEO* (RCHM 1962: 73(v), fig. 58.H.5). Inscriptions such as this are accepted by scholars[2] as having a Christian identity, and similar inscriptions have been shown in the present work to be Christian (below, ch. V.1). On the lead lining of a coffin lid from Poundbury cemetery 3 was an inscription which has been interpreted as *I(N) N(OMINE TUO) D(OMI)NE*, and given a Christian context, although there are other possibilities (Wright and Hassall 1973: 330); and from another grave a non-functional metal object in the shape of a Y, which is shown to have been a Christian symbol in the fourth century (below, ch. V.3). The phase II cemetery at Butt Road, Colchester yielded a lead coffin, the sides of which were decorated with a cross and circle device and 'S' motifs, and the lid with a zigzag and circle motif and pecten shells.[3] It will be seen that the cross and circle and the zigzag and circle are found on lead tanks which were almost certainly Christian (below, ch. V.2) and, in a discussion of pagan elements in Christianity (below, ch. VI), that the shell was also a known Christian symbol. Finally, from feature 6 of Lankhills cemetery was a platter with an *iota-chi* on the upper side and a stylised fish on the reverse (Clarke 1979: fig. 80, no. 256). The *iota-chi* was one of the earliest Christian monograms, and it has been found on several objects from fourth-century Britain (below, ch. V.1, n.9). Although feature 6 had characteristics which suggest a Christian identity, there were also pagan elements evident.

In evaluation of these inscriptions as evidence, there seems little doubt that, despite the lack of supporting data, the York inscription should be given the maximum weighting: the inscription seems unequivocally Christian, and the burial should be accepted as such. The Poundbury inscription alone, in view of the possibility of other readings, would rank about two-thirds of maximum, but this is improved with the addition of the evidence of the Y-shaped object, perhaps to one level below maximum. With regard to the Colchester coffin, although the cross-and-circle motif has been found with other undoubtedly Christian symbols from fourth-century Gaul, at Colchester there is no such corroborating evidence; nevertheless, because of the combination of symbols on the lead tanks, as evidence for Christianity the coffin would seem to warrant a ranking only one level below maximum. The *iota-chi*, in view of the syncretic nature of the whole of feature 6, would have about the same value as the Poundbury inscription by itself, that is, two-thirds.

On the maximum point on any scale of evidential weighting must come the west–east orientation of the graves in a cemetery, that is, with bodies interred with heads towards the west so that in a sitting or standing position they would face east. The subject has been much discussed,[4] and theories advanced for the adoption of the custom by Christians. The east had special connotations for Christians: the glory of God is seen in the rising of the sun (Isaiah 59.19); at the Second Coming, Christ will appear in the east (Matthew 24.27); in the early baptismal rite, candidates faced west to renounce the devil (Cyril of Jerusalem, *Mystagogic catechesis* 1.4), then turned east to pledge loyalty to Christ (Ambrose, *De mysteriis* 7). Tertullian (*Apologeticus* 16) says that Christians turned to the east to pray, but he accuses the pagans who do so of sun worship. However, while there is evidence to suggest that a west–east burial alignment was adopted by pagans in Britain in the fourth century, perhaps in response to a sun cult (Macdonald 1979: 425–6), there is no doubt that, with the notable exception of the catacombs,[5] it was the favoured orientation for Christian cemeteries throughout the Empire. In any attempt to identify Christian burials this criterion must be one of the first to be applied, and its ranking at the top of the evidential scale is justified.

There are, it is true, examples of known Christian burials not placed west–east, such as at Salona, in Roman Illyricum on the Adriatic coast, where graves are crowded in around the martyrium with no regard for orientation (Dyggve 1951: fig. IV 3). Morris (1983: 17) refers to later non-orientated burials on the site of the pre-conquest cathedral at York; he quotes Faull (1977: 7), who warns that the danger in defining as Christian only unfurnished west–east burials is that, where strong local traditions prevail, Christian burials which do not strictly conform to this rule are likely to be excluded. Nevertheless, the distinction has had to be made, and for this analysis only cemeteries of west–east orientation are studied in detail.[6] They are: Ashton; Brean Down; phase II at Butt Road, Colchester; Cannington; Crown Buildings site, Dorchester; Frilford; Icklingham; Lamyatt Beacon; Lankhills, Winchester (including the enclosure feature 6); Nettleton A; and cemetery 3 at Poundbury, Dorchester.[7] To this list could be added three further sites: Bradley Hill group III, with one north–south burial with hobnails at the eastern edge of a group of twenty-four of west–east orientation; Ancaster, with sixteen of a total of about 240 not west–east – but these, with the exception of two infant burials, were all in the western and less-organised part of the cemetery (D. Wilson, pers. comm.); and Queensford Farm, Dorchester-on-Thames, having, out of 164 excavated, two east-west burials; these, however, do not appear to have been peripheral although one, grave 245 (F66), may still have been later as it was not aligned with adjacent burials.

Ranking with west–east orientation and, it is proposed here, a necessary corollary of this characteristic, was the positioning of these burials to avoid disturbing previous interments. That might suppose the use of either grave stones or markers, the *cippi* of Horace (*Saturae* 1.8.12–13). It has been found (Jones 1984) that gravestones were much more common in the military zones of the Empire than in the civilian; but there is no certain evidence for gravestones and little evidence for markers in what may be Christian cemeteries in Britain. Indeed, one of the few sites in Roman Britain where there is evidence of any markers is the undoubtedly pagan cemetery at Dunstable; and it has been proposed (Matthews 1981: 11) that their presence in that cemetery, where burials were fairly frequent, was more likely to have been to avoid the unpleasantness of uncovering a putrefying corpse than for any other purpose. Even so, a study of the burials from Dunstable shows that, in one instance where markers were noted, a second burial, that of a male about 30, had been placed parallel to and intruding into the excavation of an earlier marked grave of a girl about 10; both skeletons had the same congenital abnormality, which suggests close kinship. In another pair of burials from the same site, although no marker remained, one body had been placed above an earlier one, disturbing the bones a little in the process; the pathology report suggests a close relationship of the male and female, again because of a common hereditary abnormality (Jones and Horne 1981: 40). Such evidence has, up to recent times, been rarely recorded, but examples such as Dunstable, and also Queensford Farm cemetery, where post- and stake-holes were found (Harman *et al.* 1978: 4), are sufficient to show that markers of some kind were known. Perhaps elsewhere the mounds of earth remained visible to allow the grave-digger to avoid other burials. If the soil were stony, as at Cannington, there is every likelihood that this would be so (P.A. Rahtz, pers. comm.). It could not have been the case everywhere.

It had been a law of the Romans that a tomb dedicated to the gods of underworld (*dis manibus*) was inviolate (Gaius, *Institutes* 2.4–6), although an examination of the large cemeteries of the fourth century, such as Trentholme Drive, Bath Gate Cirencester and Lankhills shows that the law had not been complied with in many instances. Nevertheless, there is no doubt that, even in some of the large cemeteries, great care had been taken not to intersect or disturb other burials; this includes cemeteries which it is believed are Christian. That Christians did, in fact, make a point of caring for the graves of the deceased is confirmed by Julian the Apostate (*Ad Arsacium* 429D, Loeb edn) when he claimed that such treatment of the dead by Christians had done much to increase their popularity. In Britain, the evidence for undisturbed burial is not always available. As far as is known, however, cemeteries which were both west–east and contained undisturbed burials included: Ashton, Bradley Hill 3, Brean Down, Butt Road II, Cannington, Crown Buildings site Dorchester, Icklingham, Lamyatt Beacon, Lankhills (feature 6 only), Nettleton A, Poundbury 3, Queensford Farm, and, with some reservation, Ancaster.[8] (Poundbury 3 had one disturbed burial recorded from over 1,000 excavated graves (Green 1982: 70), but this would be statistically irrelevant, and may be ignored.)

Undoubtedly respect for other burials reflected 'Christian fellowship and piety' (Macdonald 1979: 427). Along with west–east orientation, it was probably also related to a prevailing belief in a physical resurrection (Green 1977b: 46). Yet a close study of the relevant texts indicates that official Church teaching did not, in fact, encompass such a belief. Two texts, one from Eusebius (*Historia ecclesiastica* 5.1.61–3) and another from Tertullian (*Apologeticus* 37), show only that pagans, by their complete destruction of the physical remains of martyrs, *thought* that Christians held such a belief. Tertullian accepts that the body decays, but that at the Last Judgement soul and body are reunited before God, and by God. But this is not the reconstituted body from the grave, but a spiritual body, because humans were nothing before they came into being and will become nothing when they cease to be (*Apologeticus* 48.2–6).[9] If many early Christians did believe in the resurrection of the actual body interred – this seems very likely, and is borne out by Justin Martyr (*Dialogue* 80), whose own beliefs seem confused[10] – then it was faulty theology. Cumont (1922: 68–9), in his study of belief in the afterlife, believes that Christians, even if they no longer had a fear of joining the unburied spirits wandering on the banks of the river Styx, were 'still pursued by the superstitious dread that they would have no part in the resurrection of the flesh if their bodies did not rest in the grave'.

The same belief in a physical resurrection would have underlain the practice of placing the body in the grave in a supine and extended position; it is best explained by the need of the dead to rise in immediate response to the reveille of the Last Trumpet (1 Corinthians 15.52).[11] The position of head, arms and hands seemed unimportant, although, in noting that fourteen of the bodies from Cannington had been placed with arms flexed at the elbows and crossed with hands to the shoulders, Rahtz (1977: 58) suggests this might be a specifically Christian trait. Positions for the body other than supine and extended, that is, crouched or prone, are found in pagan contexts.

The crouched position is typical of Iron Age burials in Britain (Whimster 1981: *passim*), and the incidence of such burials in a cemetery dated mainly to the fourth century, such as at Trentholme Drive, where all the children and most of the juveniles were crouched burials (Wenham 1968: 38), suggests some sociological or quasi-religious reason or, as in the handful of cases at Bath Gate, Cirencester, a pathological cause (Wells 1982: 181), or even a return to an earlier, pre-Roman rite. Of the cemeteries listed as west–east without intersection, only Ancaster, Queensford Farm, and Cannington had any crouched burials: at Ancaster, one was crouched and a further four were on their sides with legs flexed; at Queensford Farm there was one crouched, and two others partially so; and at Cannington, three of a total of 570 were crouched. All five Ancaster burials were irregular in other respects: one was north–south, another south–north, one overlay an earlier burial (these three in the western part of the cemetery) and two had grave goods (D. Wilson, pers. comm.). The material evidence, such as it is, suggests that they were late in the burial sequence of the cemetery. At Queensford Farm cemetery, dating from the fourth to the sixth century, the crouched burial overlay two earlier graves, and it could be that similar burials at Cannington cemetery, which was in use from the fourth to the seventh century, were also late.

Prone burials are more complex. In a recent survey of prone and decapitated burials, it was shown that these practices appeared in late Romano-British cemeteries and continued into the Anglo-Saxon period, that they were rather more common in rural than in urban contexts, and that both practices might occur in the one cemetery and in the one burial (Harman *et al*. 1981: 166). The increasing frequency with which prone burials have been reported now discredits the interpretation of the practice as an undertaker's error.[12] At Bath Gate, Cirencester, exactly one-third of all female burials were prone (Anderson, 1987: 9), while at Alington Avenue, Fordington, one prone burial, accompanied by the body of a dog, showed evidence of wounds (Davies *et al*. 1986: 107). The reasons suggested for prone burial are that it was 'the final indignity inflicted on a corpse' for personal attributes or past actions, or, more likely, that it was associated with some belief in an afterlife (Harman *et al*. 1981: 168). Given that Christians appear to have taken care in the laying out of the body to have it ready to face east at the Second Coming, such inhumations would seem to be non-Christian. It is also significant that there was a complete absence of prone burials in all but two of the west–east undisturbed cemeteries analysed for this study. Ancaster had three: the uncoffined remains of a woman with arms outflung, accompanied by a baby in similar position and, elsewhere, another adult in prone position. All three burials occurred in the western part of the cemetery (Wilson 1968: 198 and pers. comm.). Queensford Farm had two: an adult male and a child (Chambers 1987: nos 46, 246), but there is nothing here to suggest these were late in the burial sequence. From this evidence, it seems that the supine, extended position should be given maximum weighting.

Close to the maximum ranking for evidence of a Christian identity is the absence of decapitated burials in a cemetery. Several theories have been advanced for the practice of decapitation, all of which give a completely pagan interpretation.[13] Without entering into this debate, it is pointed out that the practice would be anathema to a Christian who believed in a physical resurrection and who, following the Gospels, believed the same care should be given to the bodies of the dead as was given to that of Christ (described in John 19.39–42), in order to facilitate that resurrection. Care for the dead has already been mentioned as a feature of Christianity. The practice of decapitation was very likely in some way connected with the Celtic cult of the head (Ross 1959; 1967: 62–126). Of all the west–east cemeteries analysed, only two are reported as having decapitated burials – Lankhills major cemetery and Poundbury 3 – although there may also have been one at Queensford Farm.[14] It is of considerable interest that the site which has often been suggested as the most likely of all to have been Christian – Poundbury 3 – had one decapitated burial, and there were three others outside the cemetery bounds (Green

1982: 67). The archaeologist has speculated that there may have been some special significance in the burial in area 3C, that of a woman in whose grave the bodies of two infants were later interred: 'Although perhaps not a martyr and therefore a cult figure, she was more than simply a criminal who had suffered capital punishment' (Green 1982: 74). Perhaps there is also some significance in the fact that the other three decapitated bodies were interred at a distance from the main burial ground.

The evidence presented would suggest a maximum ranking for the absence of decapitated burials; but they were not found in all parts of Roman Britain, nor in some presumably pagan cemeteries such as Butt Road I (C. Crossan, pers. comm.), Frilford (Buxton 1921; Bradford and Goodchild 1939), Ospringe (Whiting *et al.* 1931)[15] and Trentholme Drive, York (Wenham 1968). Therefore this criterion is placed on a level below maximum.

One further condition of the inhumed body should now be examined as a possible criterion for identification as Christian, that is the apparent attempt to preserve it. 'Plaster burials' is a generic term (Green 1977b: 52 n. 1) used to describe inhumations employing various substances which encased or were in contact with a body, presumably with the aim of delaying decomposition. They occurred throughout the western part of the Empire from before the birth of Christ, and the practice was adopted by Christians, particularly in North Africa.[16] The subject has been extensively treated by Green, who believes that not all plaster burials are Christian, but that, 'when they occur in numbers and coincide with other features of Christian burial . . . [this] would suggest such sites are Christian' (Green 1977b: 52). This careful conclusion brooks little argument, but, in the light of more recent excavations, some additional observations may be made.

In the first place, cemeteries exist where there are no plaster burials, yet by other criteria they are probably Christian. Examples here would include Ancaster, Ashton, Bradley Hill III, Brean Down, Cannington, Lamyatt Beacon, Lankhills feature 6, and Nettleton A. To this list could be added a small cemetery not previously mentioned in this study, that in the vicinity of the apsidal building in the Verulam Hills at St Albans (Anthony 1968), designated Verulamium 7 by Lewis (1966). This cemetery of nine or so inhumations, the last in a series of burials in the area beginning with the Belgic period, was placed, as at Butt Road, Colchester, directly over earlier north–south burials. The later graves were west–east and unaccompanied,[17] and a flint tomb enclosed three graves, which, on skeletal analysis, may well have contained members of the one family (Wells 1968: 40). The orientation of the graves, their probable association with the apsidal building thought to be a Christian church, the presence of what is probably a family tomb, and the area's association with St Alban make it very likely that, in its last phase, this was a small Christian burial ground.

Furthermore, while plaster burials were found at sites which, on other grounds, seem to be Christian, such as Butt Road phase II, Icklingham, Poundbury 3, and the Crown Buildings site, Dorchester, they were also found in undoubtedly pagan contexts. A selection will suffice for illustration: there were two such burials at Alington Avenue in Fordington, Dorchester, a cemetery which contained, in addition, three decapitated burials and two burials with dogs (Davies *et al.* 1986; Frere 1986: 417). At Dunstable, there were twelve burials containing quicklime amongst the 112 humans (twelve decapitated), four horses and one dog deposited there (Matthews 1981). At Trentholme Drive, there was one plaster burial (Wenham 1968: 40–1) and one also in the Butt Road Colchester phase I cemetery (C. Crossan, pers. comm.). Bearing in mind that at York, at various sites around the city, more than forty other plaster burials have been found, some of them quite likely Christian (Ramm 1971: 187–92), the one in the clearly pagan cemetery at Trentholme Drive was evidently following a local 'fashion'. Similarly, the one from the earlier phase I cemetery at Butt Road, that of a young woman, may have been following a newly introduced practice, since plaster burials were also found in the later phase II cemetery, and another at Balkerne Gate (P. Crummy, pers. comm.). The same explanation might be given for the examples from Alington Avenue, Dorchester, as there were many plaster burials found in Poundbury 3. The Dunstable cemetery is particularly interesting. An analysis of the group there shows that it comprised one child, five females and six males. The child's grave contained a pottery vase, one of the females was buried with a considerable amount of jewellery, and another had a glass beaker, the only glass found in the cemetery. Of the males, all burials were findless, but one, with evidence of a coffin, was decapitated. This strongly suggests that here, at least, plaster was considered the hallmark of the wealthy, perhaps prestigious burial. *En passant* it also puts a different light on decapitated burials.

Finally, with regard to Green's conclusion that, when plaster burials occur in numbers, there is a probability of a Christian identity, the evidence of Dunstable should be sufficient for the cautious to take into account the second part of his statement, that such burials should 'coincide with other features of Christian burial'. Yet even one or two plaster burials may add to the cumulative evidence for Christianity: despite the fact that no such burials were recorded in the modern excavation at Icklingham (West 1976), the one found in the nineteenth century in a west–east unaccompanied grave (West 1976: 63–4) may have been part of the more recently discovered cemetery, and thus give weight to a Christian identity for the later finds.

From the above, it is clear that the presence of plaster burials does not necessarily equate with a Christian identification for a cemetery in Roman Britain, despite evidence from elsewhere in the Empire advanced by Green (1977b). Therefore, in weighting this kind of evidence, it cannot rank more than one-sixth on any weighted scale (that is, as evidence for Christianity it has only half the value of 'absence of hobnails' or 'absence of coins in the mouth', discussed below).

After consideration of the treatment of the bodies, the composition of the cemetery population should be analysed to determine if there is any feature which may be specifically Christian. In Part 1 of this chapter, the presence of newborn or very young infants in a cemetery was proposed as a criterion for the identification of Christian cemeteries. It is not necessary to recapitulate the arguments advanced, but merely to restate the conclusion that, in a west–east cemetery carefully laid out to avoid intersection of graves or disturbance of other burials, the presence of bodies of newborn or very young babies, given the same burial rites as adults, supports a Christian identification. Such evidence must be weighted. Since there may be cemeteries smaller than those sampled which could be Christian, but which statistically would not contain a neo-natal burial, on an evidential scale this characteristic could not be given maximum weighting, but would rank directly below maximum. Cemeteries in this present study which fit this criterion are: Ancaster, Ashton, Bradley Hill III, Butt Road II, Icklingham, Lankhills feature 6, and Poundbury 3; Cannington is a probable addition, although excavation conditions made it difficult to determine if the neo-natals not in discrete burials were given equal respect with adults (P.A. Rahtz, pers.

comm.). The list might also include, at perhaps one-third of the weighting, two cemeteries with fewer than thirty burials: Nettleton A, where available evidence only indicates 'infant' burials, and Lamyatt Beacon, where the age of the infant buried was between 1 and 2 years.[18]

In an examination of the overall layout of a cemetery, one characteristic of fourth-century sites which may indicate a Christian identification is the presence of family groups in enclosures or mausolea. Toynbee (1971: *passim*), in her study of burial in the Roman world, tells how the rich had their graves, mausolea, columbaria and hypogea on privately owned property away from the burials of the masses. The ordinary Roman was buried in a simple grave tucked in between the grand burials of the rich, or in a communal columbarium or cemetery financed and run by a *collegium funeraticium*, a burial club or guild to which the deceased himself had belonged, as at Dunstable (Matthews 1981: 46–8); such clubs catered for free, freed and slave (Hopkins 1983: 213–16). It would, in a large community, have been of little avail had the members of a family wished to be buried alongside the remains of a deceased relative; unless they had been rich enough to purchase a burial plot, they could not have dictated where their bodies were to be interred. It was to these types of people that Christianity had its earliest and perhaps greatest appeal. It was a religion in which master and servant were brothers (1 Timothy 6.2) and, in early Christian burials, little distinguished rich from poor.

When the Church created its own cemeteries, however, the rich were able to have a special section allocated for family burials. As is seen in the catacombs, the walls of these private chambers were sometimes elaborately decorated. The burials themselves were kept as unadorned as those of poorer Christians, the distinction between rich and poor seemingly one of separation and space rather than of richness of actual burial (Toynbee 1971: 235–42). Above ground, a feature of the cemeteries surrounding martyrial churches came to be similar 'rich' burial enclosures, or even actual structures, placed as close as possible to the grave of the martyr (Dyggve 1951: 71). This trend to enclosures in a cemetery may have merely reflected the natural desire of members of a family to be close to one another in death as they had been in life: the skeletal analyses from Cannington (P.A. Rahtz, pers. comm.) and Verulamium (Wells 1968: 40) give evidence of family members in adjoining graves. However, the examples from Dunstable given above show this was not a sentiment exclusive to Christians. A specifically Christian reason may have been the preservation of family unity, as endorsed by Paul (Colossians 3.18–21). Presumably the practice was connected with the prevailing belief in a physical resurrection and the desire for reunion with loved ones, and, in the case of martyrs' graves, for the whole family to share in the benefits of propinquity. Yet there seems little doubt that it was also a way of displaying wealth or status without transgressing any Church teaching.[19]

In Britain, an examination of the major burial sites of the fourth century has shown the incidence of enclosures such as would indicate family groups of some importance or wealth.[20] While there are none in those which have formed part of this study and have pagan characteristics,[21] they do occur in several cemeteries which fit the criteria so far proposed for a Christian identity: Poundbury 3 (Green 1982: 65), Butt Road II (Crossan, in Crummy 1980 and pers. comm.), Verulamium 7 (the triple grave), and feature 6, Lankhills; Nettleton A is a possibility. The best evidence is from Poundbury 3, where mausolea with painted plaster walls gave indication of both wealth and status; even so, although in some cases they were interred in stone sarcophagi and plaster packed, the burials themselves were unaccompanied.

Another type of 'special' burial is also probably found at Poundbury, and others at Cannington. There appears to have been a singling out of a particular grave, which may then have become the site of a pilgrimage of sorts. At Cannington there were two such focal graves (Rahtz 1977: 58). At Poundbury, the grave of the woman buried with the Y-shaped object (Green 1982: 67, and below, ch. V.3) may have been a focal burial, in an area where access was easier – but this could be said of other burials as well. Another could have been the grave of the decapitated woman with the later addition of the two infants, since this burial is in a densely populated part of the cemetery, and this could perhaps be compared with the crowding of burials around the graves of martyrs. Despite the density of the burials at this spot, there is space around the woman's grave. The evidence is, however, not conclusive.

In weighting the evidence of mausolea and focal burials, it has to be borne in mind that, in the smaller cemeteries, such as Bradley Hill, the whole cemetery population may have been merely one family group. In addition, in two of the larger cemeteries, Ashton and Ancaster, there is no evidence for such enclosures or special graves at all. Nonetheless, since these are features which do not appear in the presumably pagan cemeteries of fourth-century Britain,[22] they must each rank fairly high on an evidential scale, perhaps a little above two-thirds. The evidence of adjoining family burials, based on skeletal analysis alone, cannot rank.

A feature which would be strong indication of Christianity would be evidence in the presumed Christian cemetery of demonstrably different burial rites from those in a contemporaneous cemetery in the same locality, thus indicating two concurrent burial practices. There seems no doubt that, from an early period, Christians were interred alongside fellow believers, and that by the third century recognisable Christian cemeteries existed. In Rome, there is evidence that they were not content to be buried in the company of their pagan contemporaries in roadside cemeteries. Private burial plots were created by wealthy converts[23] to be used by rich and poor alike. When the catacombs of Rome were dug in the second century, Christians were buried in catacombs separate from the earlier Jewish ones and from pagan hypogea (Toynbee 1971: 234 makes the distinction), and contributions to the Church were used, among other things, to bury the faithful poor (Tertullian, *Apologeticus* 39).[24] Hippolytus (*Apostolic Tradition* 40), in the early part of the third century, also wrote of the cemetery under the direction of the bishop (*episcopus*). The third century saw the growth in North Africa of the great Christian burial grounds of Timgad and Tipasa; and Eusebius records that a rescript of Gallienus (Augustus *c.*260) required heathens to leave Christians and their churches in peace, and gave Christians permission to recover the sites of their cemeteries (*Historia ecclesiastica* 7.13.1). A tradition of separate Christian cemeteries had thus been well established.

In Britain, too, evidence from the fourth century of two different burial rites in the same town or *vicus* seems to indicate that Romano-British Christians did not want to be buried with pagans. As yet such evidence is slight, but Poundbury cemeteries 2 and 3 were both fourth-century, the former with north–south burials frequently disturbing other interments, and with grave goods, often footwear and food offerings; the latter was west–east, undisturbed, fewer than 5 per cent with grave goods, and footwear and food 'very rare' (Green 1982: 65). At Ashton there were unorientated burials, including some decapitated, others with hobnails or deliberately broken pots,[25] in individual properties (B. Dix, pers. comm.), as apparently was the custom in a number of small Romano-British towns of the fourth century (Smith 1987: 115–19); there was also a formal west–east cemetery with carefully laid out graves, the bodies unaccompanied by grave deposits. At Lankhills, feature 6 stands out as distinct from the remainder of the cemetery with its careful interments and the inclusion of a newly born infant given equal respect, whereas in the rest of the cemetery there was considerable intersection and disturbance of burials. In contrast to the examples given above, the two cemeteries from Radley also seem to have been contemporaneous; but the first (Atkinson 1952–3) was north–south, the second (Frere 1984a: 302) predominantly so, and there were decapitated burials at each site (D. Miles, pers. comm.). These features would preclude any Christian identification.

There will be situations where it is not possible to apply the criterion of contemporaneous cemeteries of differing rites. There may have been small, newly settled sites where no other cemetery was in use, and where, perhaps, the whole population was Christian.[26] Another situation might exist where a small community converted to Christianity, and thus the burial evidence would appear as sequential, rather than parallel, cemeteries with rites of a different kind. This could quite easily be the case at Bradley Hill or Nettleton, where clearly different burial practices were carried on at different periods and in the final phase, burials were west–east, undisturbed, supine and extended, and separated from earlier burial grounds. Such changes, however, are not in themselves evidence of a change in religious belief: the newly reported cemetery at Radley (Frere 1984a: 302; 1985: 290; D. Miles, pers. comm.), in a site dating from the second to the fourth century, has a series of cremations followed, it would seem, by north–south and, finally, west–east burials. The same sequence is found at Lynch Farm (Jones 1975). In these two cemeteries, the west–east burials were grouped together, but there is nothing to support a Christian identification for them as a group. Rather, the evidence suggests merely a change in fashion for burials. Although it is unlikely, this could have been the case at Bradley Hill and Nettleton as well. Therefore, sequential cemeteries of differing rites cannot be ranked as evidence for Christianity.

On the other hand, the existence of two cemeteries in use concurrently, and employing different rites, is persuasive evidence for Christianity, and it is felt that such evidence must be given maximum weighting on any evidential scale.

The next criterion to be considered is one which has often been held to be positive indication of Christianity, but analysis of fourth-century cemeteries from Roman Britain makes it clear that this is far from the case. In Thomas's archetypal Christian burial, the believer is buried without grave goods, and especially without any that have 'specific pagan connotations' (Thomas 1981: 231). But that is an idealised situation, where traditions of centuries have dictated the conventions to be observed in burying the dead. In Britain, in the fourth century, a new and officially sponsored religion was now being promoted among a people who had already absorbed almost three centuries of Roman *mores* and innumerable generations of Celtic practices. For such traditions to be discarded entirely in the space of a few decades is an unrealistic expectation. In a small community, it would perhaps not be so difficult to indoctrinate thoroughly the newly converted into the total external signs of Christianity. Such a community might be the one at Ashton, or Bradley Hill, Brean Down, Lamyatt Beacon or Nettleton, where there is a complete absence of grave furniture in formal cemeteries of the fourth century and beyond. In the larger, newly christianised community, the best one could hope for would be an elimination of the more offensive pagan practices in burial, for example decapitation, a cessation of the provision of grave goods such as Charon's fee, footwear, animal or fowl offerings (all of which obviously had religious or ritual meaning to a Roman Briton of the period), and the progressive elimination of all objects in graves. Much would depend on the zeal of the converted, the depth of training of the local clergy, and the supervision of the bishop. Attention is drawn here to canon 41 of the Council of Elvira, held in Spain about AD 304, which allowed the pagan shrines of slaves to remain in Christian households, so as to avoid confrontation.[27] Such accommodation must surely have taken place in other parts of the Romano-Celtic world as well, and it is suggested that it would have applied equally to burials of the newly converted in Christian cemeteries.

There is also the problem that the total absence of grave goods does not necessarily equate with Christianity, as has been pointed out (Macdonald 1979: 427–8; Thomas 1981: 231). However, the presence of grave goods in one burial area and the absence of them in another of the same period does indicate a difference in religious rites. The difficulty is to ascertain, when comparisons cannot be made, whether such absence of grave goods is because of religious belief, poverty, or even, in a primitive society, wealth and status (Ucko 1969–70: 267).

It is against this background, therefore, that the absence of grave goods as a criterion for the identification of Christian cemeteries must be evaluated. Ideally, with each cemetery studied, a comparison would be made with both earlier and contemporary sites in the same geographical area but, with the exception of Poundbury, such evidence is not available. All that can be done is to compare examples from roughly the same area or the same period. In the larger cemeteries, such as Poundbury or Butt Road II, the *relative* absence of such goods is perhaps the more appropriate criterion. A study must also be made of the types of grave goods to determine whether there is an absence, or relative absence, of those more likely to offend Christians.

In the larger west–east, supine, extended and undisturbed cemeteries, although none has been recorded as being completely without grave goods, few objects were found. At Ancaster, the only goods reported were one grave group which may have been second- or third-century, a set of bronze bracelets, a comb, a brooch or two and a handful of coins probably originally contained in a leather bag (Wilson, 1968: 197–8 and pers. comm.). The Cannington site was similarly lacking in accompanied burials: fourteen knives, perhaps from later, intrusive burials (cf. Lankhills: Clarke 1979: 377), two (shroud?) pins, two bracelets, a brooch and two beads, the jewellery considered post-Roman (Rahtz 1977: 56 and pers. comm.). Such finds must be regarded as generally inoffensive to Christians, and statistically a figure under 5 per cent would seem to be irrelevant. Unfortunately, there are no cemeteries in the same general geographical location with which to compare those sites. At Butt Road II, of the 664 burials excavated, 8 per cent contained grave goods, compared with the earlier Butt Road I where the figure was 41 per cent (C. Crossan, pers. comm.). Yet this could indicate merely a change in fashion, since the west–east cemetery was the later. It may, in fact, also have been the case at Poundbury: here, the presumed Christian cemetery has 4.4 per cent of graves with grave furniture, and the contemporaneous pagan cemetery about 3.2 per cent, whereas the earlier 'transitional' site C to the south-east had 13 per cent (D. Farwell, pers. comm.).

In the group of smaller cemeteries, only Icklingham and feature 6 of Lankhills had grave deposits. Of about thirty-eight burials at the former site, one had a coin in the mouth and other coins in the fill of the grave, a second had bracelets and beads at the foot of the grave, and another wore a bracelet (West 1976: 71). In the latter were a pot with the remains of a bird, one vessel outside a coffin, a comb, some unworn personal ornaments, hobnails, and, with burial 250, hobnails, three vessels, a box containing a spindle whorl, a jet pin, and a blue glass *tessera*; this grave also contained two platters, one of which was mentioned earlier, bearing an *iota-chi* on the upper side and a fish-like graffito on the reverse (Clarke 1979: *passim*). Feature 6 contained a central burial which was probably pagan, the first grave in an enclosure which was later used for sixteen others, perhaps members of his family who had become Christian (Macdonald 1979: 430). Such interpretation seems reasonable, given the evidence of the grave goods and of the conditions of burial in the enclosure. In view of the relatively few burials in this enclosure, any statistics produced will necessarily be of little value for purposes of comparison. Nevertheless, it is noted that approximately 66 per cent of burials in the major cemetery had grave goods, while in feature 6 the figure was 59 per cent. On the other hand, at Ashton, 11 out of 67, or 16 per cent of the backyard burials were accompanied by grave goods, while there were none at all in the west–east cemetery (B. Dix, pers. comm.).

Although it has been possible to make comparisons at four sites only, it would seem that, in what may be interpreted as a Christian burial ground, there is likely to occur a complete or relative absence of grave goods, but this is not always the case. Moreover, in view of the tendency, as exemplified by Lankhills major cemetery, towards a decline in grave furniture through the fourth century, this is far from satisfactory as a criterion for identification of Christian sites. To confirm this, a study of three late or even sub-Roman cemeteries in Oxfordshire – Frilford, Queensford Farm and Church Piece – reveals that the grave goods here were quite insignificant in number, if not always in type: from Frilford, a coin hoard and other coins in mouth or grave, some glass and a couple of pieces of bronze (Buxton 1921; Bradford and Goodchild 1939); from Queensford Farm, a comb (Chambers 1987: fig. 7); and from Church Piece,[28] an ox mandible (Harman *et al.* 1978: 11). Some of these objects would appear to be completely innocuous, but there is a pagan significance in others. Moreover, there is not sufficient additional evidence to suggest any one of the three is a Christian site. It would seem that 'absence of grave goods' as a general criterion for the identification of Christian cemeteries is unworkable and may, therefore, be discarded.

An analysis of the types of grave furniture is more fruitful. Of the items mentioned above, several have pagan connotations which would have offended orthodox Christian sensibilities. The presence of food implies sustenance for the deceased in life in the netherworld. The Roman practice of holding a *refrigerium* at the graveside, and presumably leaving some of the food behind, had been condemned by Ambrose (Augustine, *Confessiones* 6.2) and Augustine (*De moribus ecclesiae* 34), so we know that the custom of leaving vessels of food or drink in graves was not approved by the Church. Its condemnation by Augustine implies that it was still carried on in his day.

The occasional presence of vessels in graves cannot, therefore, be seen as indicating a pagan identity, although one would expect its occurrence to be rare in a presumed Christian cemetery: at Colchester, in the earlier cemetery, 29 per cent of graves held vessels of pottery or glass, in the later, 2 per cent (C. Crossan, pers. comm.); at Poundbury, two burials were accompanied by pottery in cemetery 2, but none in cemetery 3, although there were three from site C, the 'transitional' area (D. Farwell, pers. comm.). Perhaps the observation by Black (1986b: 225) that 'the burial of pots and other containers as grave-goods seems to have become customary rather than a religious duty' is apposite. As evidence for Christianity, a figure under 5 per cent could rank about half on a weighted scale.

On the other hand, the presence of whole animals or birds implies some sort of sacrifice to the gods of the underworld (*dis manibus*), and it may be that the 'joints' of meat from animals frequently recorded in pagan burials were a form of token sacrifice. Cicero (*De legibus* 2.22) speaks of the sacrifice of a pig at Roman burials, and, at Romano-British pagan sites throughout Britain, whole horses (Matthews 1981) and dogs (Black 1983) are found in burials, as well as joints from these and other common domestic animals (Whimster 1981: 51–2). The ox mandible in a grave at Church Piece follows this tradition. The offering of a cock, one of the attributes of Mercury, messenger of the gods, who escorted the dead to the netherworld, was undoubtedly a Roman pagan practice, and is found once only in the group of cemeteries under discussion: in burial 150 of Lankhills feature 6, which is believed to be the initial pagan grave in the later Christian enclosure. This will be taken into account in the analysis.

There is no other known evidence for the burial of birds or animals in those west–east, supine, extended and undisturbed cemeteries which are the subject of this study, although they do occur in contemporaneous, presumably pagan sites, for example, a dog in Butt Road I (C. Crossan, pers. comm.) and poultry in Poundbury 2 (Green 1982: 62). Undoubtedly such a practice would have been strenuously opposed by the Church, because of the implication of pagan sacrifice, and Christians abhorred any form of sacrifice (Tertullian *Apologeticus* 10.7–8). The absence of bird or animal remains in virtually all west–east cemeteries of undisturbed burials is a good indication that as evidence it should rank high, perhaps three-quarters on an evidential scale.[29]

Another type of grave furniture found at Lankhills feature 6 and elsewhere, and likely to have been opposed by Christians, was footwear. The occurrence of 'hobnail burials' has been frequently noted, but the practice is imperfectly understood. It may have been to provide footwear in case the deceased had to wander in the netherworld for a hundred years (Vergil, *Aeneid* 6.326–30), or for the actual journey to the netherworld, before crossing the River Styx. The practice occurred in both cremation and inhumation burials from as early as the first century: hobnails were found in inhumations at Jordan Hill from that period (Warne 1872), and in cremations at Avisford and Cirencester (Chambers 1978). There appears to be no pattern to the distribution of hobnail burials in Roman Britain, except that the practice may not have been as common in the north: the cemetery at Trentholme Drive has no record of 'hobnails', although the report says over 500 nails from about 5 mm to 75 mm long were found in the remains of cremations at the *ustrina* (Wenham 1968: 25) and many others were found in the cemetery.[30] In the west–east cemeteries under consideration here, hobnails are recorded from Colchester Butt Road II, Poundbury 3 and Lankhills feature 6 only, and some comparison can thus be made with other cemeteries at those locations. At Colchester, in phase I of Butt Road, 16 per cent of burials had hobnails, while in phase II only 0.8 per cent (six burials) had them (C. Crossan, pers. comm.). At Poundbury, it was found that 21 per cent of the graves in Cemetery 2, 6 per cent in site C, and only two graves, or 0.2 per cent, in the presumed Christian section had hobnailed footwear (D. Farwell, pers. comm.). At Lankhills, in the major cemetery, 39 per cent had hobnails, and, in feature 6, so did eight of the seventeen burials, or 47 per cent (Clarke 1979). At Ashton, the trend is very clear: 3 per cent of graves had hobnails in the backyard burials, but there were none whatsoever in the contemporaneous west–east cemetery (B. Dix, pers. comm.).

Therefore, while hobnail burials seem to have been very much a feature of presumed pagan cemeteries, their occurrence on putative Christian sites was very limited. They apparently indicated a pagan view of an afterlife to which the Church did not subscribe; perhaps it was the implication of material needs in the afterlife which the Church found so offensive.[31] Whatever the significance of footwear in burials, the absence of hobnails in a cemetery does appear to be an indicator of a Christian identity. Yet its value must not be overrated, since they may also be absent from presumably pagan cemeteries.[32] There is at least one large pagan site where they were found in very few burials, at Bath Gate, Cirencester; and even Dunstable, which displays many presumably pagan characteristics, has only two hobnail burials in its 112 interments. As evidence for Christianity, therefore, the absence of hobnails cannot rate higher than about one-third, unless there is nearby a contemporaneous and obviously pagan site where the practice continues, in which case it could be double that rating.

The final type of grave furniture to be considered in some detail is the coin, especially the coin in the mouth, or Charon's fee. This subject has been treated at length by Grinsell (1957). In all the fourth-century cemeteries analysed in this study, the incidence of coins in the mouth was very limited, suggesting that the custom was not prevalent in fourth-century Roman Britain. Of those sites, possibly Christian, studied here, only six are known to have had coins of any kind. Ashton cemetery recorded two coins of Constantinian date only loosely connected with an infant burial, and therefore presumably lost accidentally when the burial occurred. Nettleton A yielded one coin of Constantine II in mint condition, found in the fill of grave no. 1 (Wedlake 1982: 91). At Ancaster, the small group of fourth-century coins mentioned earlier was recovered in a late excavation at the site. At Butt Road phase II, five graves contained coins: there were three instances of coins on braclets, two as possible grave deposits, and one definite

71

grave deposit of six coins found on the chest of the skeleton (C. Crossan, pers. comm.). Icklingham produced one coin in the mouth (2 per cent of the cemetery population) and five other coins scattered in the fill of the same grave (West 1976: 71). Finally, from Poundbury there were numbers of coins found in graves: these included two pierced coins, one from the reign of Magnentius, with prominent *chi-rho*, the other of Allectus, another placed in the hand of the deceased, and twelve, or 1.2 per cent, in the mouth (D. Farwell, pers. comm.). Charon's fee was extremely rare; the coin in the hand at Poundbury makes it fairly clear that it was hidden there, so it would seem the practice was opposed by the Church. Green (1982: 70) has noted that some other grave goods seem to have been hidden in shrouds, or in the corners of coffins. Perhaps the placing of a coin in the hand or mouth were covert actions of the relatives of the deceased, to ensure that, if the beliefs of one religion did not help, those of another would – 'double insurance', as Alcock (1980: 59) says. The coin in the mouth at Icklingham may have had the same explanation, or perhaps this was an earlier Christian burial, when such syncretism would have been much more likely. One must bear in mind the canon of the Council of Elvira cited above. (A similar explanation for the grave goods in the earliest part of Poundbury 3 (Green 1982: 66), and for those at Lankhills feature 6 (Macdonald 1979: 430) seems entirely reasonable.)

Placing coins in the mouth was a pagan practice, and its almost complete absence in west–east, undisturbed, supine and extended cemeteries does suggest it could rank high as evidence for Christianity. Since, however, the practice was not widespread in Roman Britain, such absence cannot rank higher as evidence than that of hobnails, unless, of course, there was also a pagan cemetery of the same period where the practice occurred. Moreover, Grinsell has shown that the practice continued for many centuries in various parts of the christianised world. Perhaps this was one of the practices to which the Church was prepared, if it was aware of the practice, to turn a blind eye.[33]

There were other specifically pagan grave goods which might have been dealt with here, but there is a singular lack of any of the eggs, lamps or ritual objects mentioned by Alcock (1980) and Black (1986b: 220–5); even jewellery, the presence of which one would imagine would not have caused the zealous Christian too much heartburn, is quite rare. The occurrence of charcoal with burials is cited by Alcock (1980: 60) as a pagan practice, but it may also have been Christian. Its presence in small quantities in three graves at Lamyatt Beacon (Leech 1973–82) and possibly at Poundbury 3 (Green 1972) is possibly of religious significance, but too few parallels exist to weigh such evidence.[34] Furthermore, for the purposes of the present analysis, only those pagan practices which it is believed would have caused particular concern to Christians have been dealt with, and their absence, or relative absence, assessed as evidence.

There is, however, one type of grave furniture found in pagan burials which, perhaps because it was considered innocuous by the Church, was also present in presumed Christian sites. At Ashton, the backyard burials contained grave furniture, including hobnails, pots deliberately broken, and, interestingly, stones placed at various points along the body. In the west–east cemetery, no pots or nails were deposited, but the placement of stones still persisted. Similar finds have been made at Ancaster and Cannington. This suggests that church officials adopted a policy of abolishing offensive pagan grave goods, but accepted (or connived at) practices that did not contradict any church teaching.

It will have been noted that there has been no inclusion as criteria of two of the features of Thomas's burial of 'popular conception', the presence of coffins or shrouds. Although Christians would have known of the account of the burial of Christ (Green 1977b: 46 and refs) which followed Jewish tradition, in Britain, unguents, shroud and coffin may have been beyond the resources of the average convert. Indeed, at some cemeteries, coffins were rarely used, if at all, as at Ashton (B. Dix, pers. comm.); and at Butt Road II, Colchester, there is evidence for the use of tree trunks for coffins (Crossan, in Crummy 1980: 265), although lead-lined and stone sarcophagi have also been found there. On the other hand, stone and lead-lined coffins have been found at presumably pagan sites even prior to the fourth century. Any evidence for shrouds is preserved only by accident, often in plaster burials, and, while such remains have been interpreted as fragments of shrouds, as at Poundbury (Green 1982: 72), it is also possible that a Roman of rank, even if Christian, may have chosen to be buried in his toga, as described by Toynbee (1971: 44). The wrapping of bodies in some sort of covering was not peculiarly Christian: Stead (1967: 42) records evidence of the wrapping of a body in a bear skin before cremation. In a study of textile manufacturing in the Roman period, Wild (1970) lists those found in Roman Britain; and, although he speaks of the 'linen shrouds from York' (1970: 46), fragments of which were preserved in gypsum, and which were possibly Christian, he also lists other examples from the third century and earlier. Coffins and shrouds are found in both Christian and pagan burials, and are thus of little help in the identification of Christian cemeteries in Britain. These characteristics of inhumation have, therefore, not been ranked.

The main features of burials and of the cemeteries in which they occurred have now been analysed and evaluated. But it is desirable as well to look for possible indirect indicators of a Christian presence in a particular locality, and to consider a group of criteria which might be termed External Evidence, or Christianity by Association; this incorporates the kind of evidence which would also be appropriate when identifying Christian churches. It includes literary references to specific places and archaeological evidence at a site or within about 15 kilometres of it, a distance which would perhaps not be thought of as excessive for a devout Romano-British Christian to travel to give expression to his or her beliefs, or within which the influence of Christianity could reasonably be expected to fall.[35] Literary and archaeological evidence of sufficient importance to warrant a maximum weighting is described first.

The presence by 314 of bishops at London, York and either Lincoln, Colchester or Cirencester indicates the certain existence of a Christian communities there, if not yet of Christian churches. Similarly, the evidence for the martyrdom of Alban seems too strong for Verulamium to be considered lower than the maximum ranking. That these cities had sizeable numbers of Christians in the course of the fourth century, and thus Christian cemeteries, seems a realistic assumption. The eighteen or so lead tanks, some with *chi-rho*, others with symbols which elsewhere have been shown to have Christian associations (below, ch. V.2), point to a Christian presence at or near the sites where they were found. Despite Thomas's belief (1981: 226) that they were portable fonts, it seems highly unlikely that an object which it takes four men to lift could be classed as 'portable'. They are best used as evidence for the locality in which they were found, and additional evidence for Christianity in those areas is generally not lacking (Watts 1988a; below, ch. V.2). Graffiti on sherds, and objects of little intrinsic value incorporating Christian symbols should also be regarded as indicative of a Christian presence in the area of their provenance, rather than as items brought in from elsewhere; as Thomas (1981: 108) suggests, the finds of greater value will have less weight as evidence. The small finds are thus ranked from maximum to one third of maximum, dependent on intrinsic value, certainty of Christian association (in the case of inscriptions), and portability. Objects from four sites, not recorded by Thomas, but germane to this study, are: from Kelvedon, a sherd with *chi-rho* (Hassall and Tomlin 1983: 343) and a presumed candleholder with *iota-chi* (Eddy and Turner 1982); from Colchester, a similar candleholder (Crummy 1983: fig. 207) and a *chi-rho* graffito (Drury 1984: 48); a ring from Stonham Aspal, Suffolk, inscribed ΟΛΥΜΠΕΙ ΖΗCΑΙC flanked by two palm leaves (Mawer 1989); and a pewter plate from Stamford with *iota-chi*, *chi-rho*, crosses of the *crux decussata* type and palm leaves (unpublished, British Museum acquisition no. PRB.1927.1–6,1).

Two further features which come under the heading of Christianity by Association and may be given high ranking are the presence within a reasonable distance of the cemetery of Christian hoards, and of villas with indications of Christian occupation or ownership. Of the two, the villa is probably is the better evidence – virtual proof of Christian ownership and probably residency. The sites are well known: Hinton St Mary, Frampton, and Fifehead Neville in Dorset, and Lullingstone in Kent; and one could assume that any overt religious affiliations of the owner of a villa would have had some influence on the local peasant population. Hinton St Mary and Lullingstone are undoubtedly Christian, and should be weighted the maximum. The identification of the mosaic at Frampton as Christian has been challenged in recent years;[36] however, it will suffice to say that the position of the *chi-rho* in the mosaic and the siting of the building itself do suggest a Christian identity for Frampton as a chapel, if not as a villa. It will also be weighted on the maximum. As for Fifehead Neville, the motifs of its mosaic, a central cantharus surrounded by fish and dolphins (Engleheart 1903), are known Christian symbols, but there is no unequivocal Christian sign such as a *chi-rho*, as at the other three villas; and, although there is also the evidence of the two rings deliberately buried (below), these may not have been hidden by the owners of the villa. On balance, Fifehead Neville as a Christian villa would be about three-quarters of the maximum on an evidential scale.

The hoards at Andover, Canterbury, Corbridge and Water Newton, and the pewter bowl from Caerwent, should be given about the same ranking since they include the *chi-rho* symbol or monogrammatic cross, and all appear to have been deliberately buried.[37] The rings from Fifehead Neville should be slightly less, since they were highly portable.[38] They would rank with the hoards from Dorchester in Dorset, Icklingham and Islip, Northants;[39] these contain objects inscribed with *vivas* or decorated with fish, which may also indicate Christian association, but would be weighted less, perhaps two-thirds, of objects with a *chi-rho*.

Negative evidence for the presence of Christians includes what appears to have been the deliberate destruction of pagan sites and sculptures, and the incidence of pagan hoards. Thomas (1981: 134–6) has dealt with the presumed destruction by Christians of Mithraea, and it is worthy of note that, at the London Mithraeum, there probably occurred both the destruction of a pagan site and the concealment of pagan religious objects. In addition to those mentioned by Thomas, examples of the destruction of pagan sites or artefacts in an area where a Christian presence is known from other evidence include: Lower Slaughter, Gloucestershire, three altars and five sculptures badly damaged, found in a well, probably late fourth- or early fifth-century (O'Neill and Toynbee 1958),[40] and Southwark Cathedral, pagan deities, all with heads off, in the fill of a well built after 270 (Hammerson 1978). Because there is no direct indication of Christian involvement, such evidence would rank about half on an evidential scale.[41]

A similar type of evidence, but of even less value in identifying a Christian presence, is the re-use in a secular context of stones of a religious nature. Bearing in mind Toynbee's cautionary tale (1971: 76) of the cutting down of a tombstone in Ostia for re-use as a seat in a public lavatory, the following are recorded as possible evidence only, and are therefore not weighted: Corbridge, three sculptured stones, one to Urbs Romana, re-used as road material for a military street dated to 369 (Richmond 1943: 175–6); and two examples of the re-using of pagan tombstones in what may have been Christian burials at York (RCHM 1962: 116, nos 33 and 34), and at Ancaster (Wilson 1965: 228).

As there is only the assumption of the involvement of Christians in the destruction or profanation of pagan sites or artefacts, the above examples are worth less as evidence than a special group of sites, three of which Thomas lists briefly, where there appears to have been not only the profanation of the pagan site, but also its re-use by Christians. It may be of significance that, in a study of the christianising of pagan sites, Grinsell (1986: 36) observes that almost all the monuments he had noted as christianised either had been funerary or were believed to have had a religious purpose originally. He suggests that their christianising would seem to imply that they had been regarded as 'monuments of paganism' at the time of such christianising. Such evidence could probably be weighted with Christian hoards in the identification of cemeteries, that is, at three-quarters of maximum. The sites are listed here, but as each involves what may be interpreted as a likely Christian church or chapel, the presentation and interpretation of the evidence will be delayed until Chapter IV, on the identification of churches. The sites are: Brean Down, Chedworth, Icklingham, Lamyatt Beacon, Nettleton, Uley and Witham.

The deliberate concealment of pagan religious objects might also seem to indicate a Christian presence, but much depends on the date of deposition. Unfortunately, this cannot always be determined. The most spectacular of the pagan hoards is the recently discovered Thetford Treasure (Johns and Potter 1983), which, though it has what appear to be Christian elements, must be interpreted as a deposition by pagans.[42] It was buried in the late fourth century, possibly as the result of the activities of Christians in the surrounding district. The treasure from the London Mithraeum was possibly hidden before the attack on the temple by Christian zealots. The Hockwold diadems and crown were found with other objects from the late Roman period (Anon. 1957: 211, pl. ix; Toynbee 1964b: 338)[43] and could conceivably have been hidden from Christian iconoclasts, as could the Cavenham Heath ritual crowns (Layard 1925: 258). Both hoards were found near known Christian centres of the fourth century and are within 15 kilometres of Thetford. From Felmingham (Gilbert 1978), another hoard, noteworthy for its syncretic elements, and dating to about the mid-third century, could have been buried much later. Gilbert believes that its deposition may well have been the direct result of the growth of Christianity in the area. From Willingham Fen comes a further collection of ritual objects (Rostovtseff 1923), but there is little to date this hoard, except its similarity to that from Felmingham.[44] Since the deposition of pagan religious hoards might be for various reasons other than the presence of hostile Christians in the same locality, as evidence for a Christian presence it cannot rank more than about one-third on an evidential scale. The Willingham Fen hoard cannot be weighted.

So, too, must be the fate of the last of the pagan ritual hoards, from Barkway (Page 1914: 149; Toynbee 1964b: 328) and Stony Stratford (Page 1908: 11). The concealment of the two collections of ritual objects may have been connected (Page 1914: 149), and since they did not appear to have great intrinsic value, it could be that they were hidden by their custodians from hostile Christians. Equally, they could have been votive deposits. There is, however, no evidence of dating, nor is there any positive evidence as yet of a Christian presence in the vicinity. These hoards are recorded but not weighted.

The hoards listed above have all come from the eastern part of Britain. In a slightly different category is a series of pagan altars and religious sculptures from Gloucestershire, all apparently in an undamaged state when deliberately concealed. They were found at Bisley, Stroud, Tideham Chase, and Ashcroft, Cirencester, and it has been suggested that '[the] deposit was occasioned by the general acceptance of Christianity in the fourth century' (Clifford 1938: 299). But, attractive as this theory is, especially as there is evidence for Christianity in this part of Britain, there is no conclusive dating for the burial of the sculptures. They are, therefore, recorded but not ranked.

It remains now to summarise the weighting for the various types of evidence. When applying the criteria to a particular cemetery, it is felt that the external evidence is of less importance than the internal, and that it should therefore be given half the value of internal evidence. The criteria and their relative importance for identifying Christian cemeteries are set out in Figure 1.

3: APPLICATION OF THE CRITERIA

In Parts 1 and 2 of this chapter, evidence for the identification of possible Christian cemeteries in Roman Britain was presented. Such evidence is of two kinds: internal, that is, relating to the burials themselves and the context in which they occurred, and external, relating to the immediate locality in which the cemetery was found, or within 15 kilometres of it. Criteria for identification were then devised, discussed and ranked on a comparative evidential scale. Those criteria have now been applied to specific sites (Figure 2), and there is a clear indication that, while the highest-ranking cemeteries have features which the lower-ranked

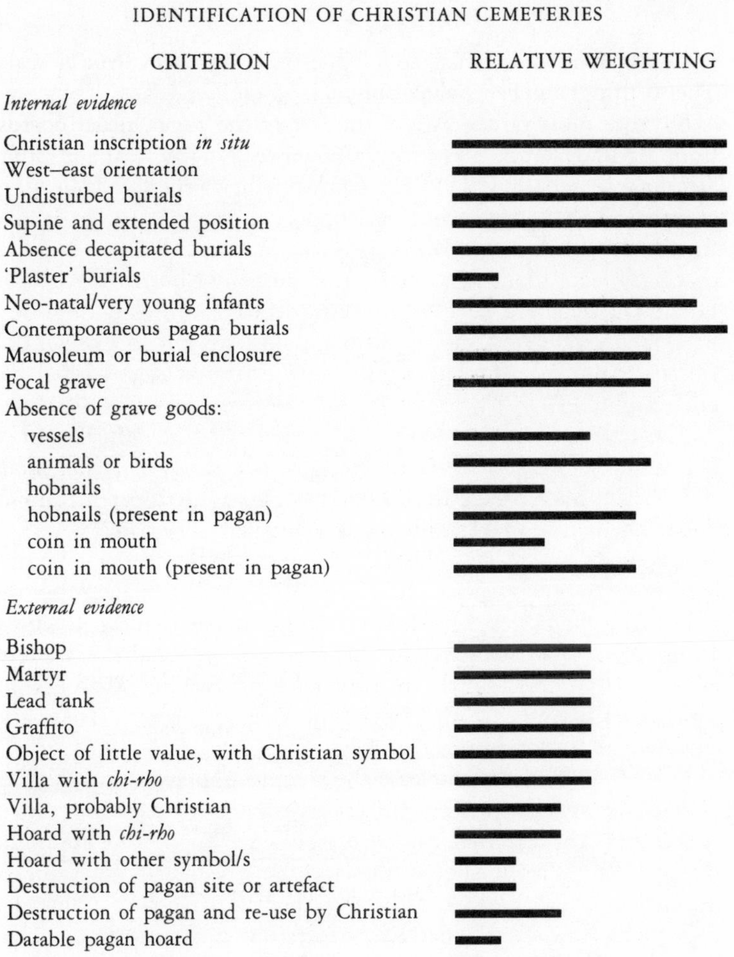

CRITERION   RELATIVE WEIGHTING

Internal evidence

Christian inscription *in situ*
West–east orientation
Undisturbed burials
Supine and extended position
Absence decapitated burials
'Plaster' burials
Neo-natal/very young infants
Contemporaneous pagan burials
Mausoleum or burial enclosure
Focal grave
Absence of grave goods:
    vessels
    animals or birds
    hobnails
    hobnails (present in pagan)
    coin in mouth
    coin in mouth (present in pagan)

External evidence

Bishop
Martyr
Lead tank
Graffito
Object of little value, with Christian symbol
Villa with *chi-rho*
Villa, probably Christian
Hoard with *chi-rho*
Hoard with other symbol/s
Destruction of pagan site or artefact
Destruction of pagan and re-use by Christian
Datable pagan hoard

Figure 1 Criteria for identification of Christian cemeteries and relative weightings

ones do not possess, certain features are common to all cemeteries believed to be Christian. Moreover, when a comparison is made with the cemeteries thought to be non-Christian, that combination of 'essential' characteristics is absent from all the putative pagan sites examined. It is therefore possible to propose criteria which it seems are necessary and those which are highly desirable for the identification of Christian cemeteries in Roman Britain, and, on this basis, to identify probable Christian cemeteries among those already excavated.

Cemetery	Date of cemetery (century)	No. burials excavated (c = plus cremations)	Internal Evidence															
			Christian evidence *in situ*	West–east orientation	Undisturbed burials	Supine extended position	Absence decapitated burials	'Plaster' burials	Neonatal/very young infants given equal respect	Contemporaneous pagan burials	Mausoleum or enclosure	Focal grave	Absence grave goods					
													Vessels	Animals or birds	Hobnails or	Hobnails in contemporaneous pagan cemetery	Coin in mouth or	Coin in contemporaneous pagan cemetery
			10	10	10	10	9	2	9	10	7	7	5	7	3	6	3	6

Site	Date	n												
Alington Ave Fordington	2–4?	58c		?			9					5	7	3	?
Ancaster	4	231	8	10	9		9		9			5	7	3	3
Ashton (private property)	2–4	60		10	10		9		10			5	7	3	3
Ashton (formal cemetery)	4	180	10	10	10		9	??	10			5	7	3	3 6
Bath Gate Cirencester	3–5	450c	10	10	10	2	9	9	10		7	5	7	3	3
Bradley Hill Group III	4	25	10	10	10	2	9	9	10			5	7	3	3
Brean Down	5+	10					9	?							
Butt Road Phase I Colchester	3–4	110c	10	10	10	2	9	9	10	7		5	7	3	3
Butt Road Phase II Colchester	4	664	10	10	10	2	9	9	10			5	7	3	3
Cannington	4–7	570	10 9	10	10	2	8	?	10			5	7	3	3
Crown Bldgs Dorchester Dorset	4	50	10	10	10	2	9		10	7		5	7	3	3
Dunstable	4	112	10	10	10	1	9	9	10			5	7	3	
Frilford	4	95						3							
Guilden Morden	BC–4	120c	10	10	10		9	9	10	7		5	7	3	3
Icklingham	4	38	10	10	10		9	9	10			5	7	3	3
Lamyatt Beacon	5+	16	10	10	10		9								
Lankhills Feature 6	4	17	6												
Lankhills (major cemetery)	4	400c	10	10	10		9	3	10			5	7	3	3
Lynch Farm Peterborough	3–4	50c		10	?		9	?	?	?		5	7	3	3
Nettleton A	4	15	10	10	10		??	3							
Ospringe	1–4	53c	10		10	2	9	9	10	7		5	7	3	3
Owslebury	BC–4	70			?	?				2	4				
Poundbury Camp 2	3–4	121c 9	10	10	10	3	9	3	10	7		5	7	3	3
Poundbury Camp 3	4	1028	5	10	3	2	9	9	10	2		5	7	3	3
Queensford Farm	4–6	164	10	10								5	7	3	3
Radley I (1945)	3–4	35	10	10			9					?	?	??	3
Radley II	2–4	47c	10	10		2	9	9	10	7		5	7		
Trentholme Drive York	2–4	250c													
Verulam Hills Period III	4	9	10	10	10		9	3	10	7		5	7	3	3

Cemetery	Bishop	Martyr	Lead tank	Christian graffito	Object of little value with Christian symbol	Villa with *chi-rho* or	Villa probably Christian	Hoard with *chi-rho* or	Hoard with other symbol/s	Destruction of pagan site or artefact	Destruction of pagan and re-use by Christian	Datable pagan hoard	Total – internal evidence	Total – external evidence	Total
	5	5	5	5	5	5	4	4	2	2	4	2			
Alington Ave Fordington						5			2				2	7	9
Ancaster													63	0	63
Ashton (private property)			5					4					23	9	32
Ashton (formal cemetery)			5					4					79	9	88

External Evidence

Bath Gate Cirencester	2				1							12	5	17
Bradley Hill Group III												66	0	66
Brean Down					5	5						57	12	57
Butt Road Phase I Colchester	2				5	5						24	12	36
Butt Road Phase II Colchester	2				5	5						84	0	96
Cannington												72	7	72
Crown Bldgs Dorchester Dorset							5	2				69	5	76
Dunstable		5										8	0	13
Frilford												44	0	44
Guilden Morden									2			7	11	7
Icklingham			5							4		64	0	75
Lamyatt Beacon										4		60	4	60
Lankhills Feature 6										4		74	4	78
Lankhills (major cemetery)										4		19	4	23
Lynch Farm Peterborough												27	4	31
Nettleton A										4	4	60	4	64
Ospringe				5						4		12	9	21
Owslebury							5					27	0	27
Poundbury Camp 2							5	2				3	7	10
Poundbury Camp 3							5	2				95	7	102
Queensford Farm												47	0	47
Radley I (1945)												28	0	28
Radley II												13	0	13
Trentholme Drive York	5				5							14	10	24
Verulam Hills Period III		5										74	5	79

Figure 2 Analysis of evidence for Christian cemeteries, and relative weightings

Twenty-nine burial sites have been analysed, if Lankhills feature 6 is accepted as a separate 'cemetery'. Most of the sites contained more than thirty graves. They are not all fully reported, but generally sufficient data have been made available to enable comparisons to be made. The conditions of excavation of one site, however, allowed examination of only some of the burials, and that *in situ*; for this study the evidence, now destroyed, of the Crown Buildings site at Dorchester (Green *et al.* 1982) has not been referred to in detail, although an analysis of the cemetery has been made on the available material and the site is also included in the rank-order summary (Figure 3).

To apply the criteria to particular sites, it has been found practical to convert the relative rankings to a numerical equivalent, using a scale of 10, and to discount the weighting when the evidence falls short of the ideal. It is a system which, it is admitted, does have its shortcomings, but it is emphasised that the final 'score' is less important than the combination of particular criteria.

In consideration first of those cemeteries which have the highest ranking, that is, Poundbury cemetery 3, Butt Road Colchester phase II, Ashton, Verulam Hills Field period III, Lankhills Winchester feature 6, Crown Buildings site at Dorchester, Icklingham and Cannington, it may be seen that, on internal evidence alone, Icklingham has the lowest rating; yet this is a site which also has an apsidal building and associated small stone structure confidently identified as a church and baptistery (West 1976), and two lead tanks decorated with *chi-rho*.

The features common to these eight sites are: west–east, undisturbed, supine and extended burials, an absence of decapitated bodies and of grave goods of animals or birds. All these cemeteries except Lankhills feature 6 have an absence of hobnails. Neo-natal or very young infants are present in all but the incompletely recorded Crown Buildings site at Dorchester and the small burial ground at Verulamium. The latter contained nine graves and, since the absence of infant burials is not unexpected (for reasons outlined in Part 2 of this chapter) especially if the cemetery was in use from the middle to the later part of the fourth century, the absence at that site of such burials may be disregarded.[1] As regards the absence of grave goods, all sites recorded fewer than 5 per cent of graves with vessels (the figure proposed as the acceptable maximum in the analysis), with the exception of Lankhills feature 6, which had 12 per cent; but this is

Cemetery	Internal evidence	External evidence	Total
Poundbury Camp 3	95	7	102
Butt Road II Colchester	84	12	96
Ashton (formal cemetery)	79	9	88
Verulam Hills Period III	74	5	79
Lankhills Feature 6	74	4	78
Crown Bldgs Dorchester (D)	69	7	76
Icklingham	64	11	75
Cannington	72	0	72
Bradley Hill Group III	66	0	66
Nettleton A	60	4	64
Ancaster	63	0	63
Lamyatt Beacon	60	0	60
Brean Down	57	0	57
Queensford Farm	47	0	47
Frilford	44	0	44
Butt Road I Colchester	24	12	36
Ashton (private property)	23	9	32
Lynch Farm Peterborough	27	4	31
Radley I (1945)	28	0	28
Owslebury	27	0	27
Trentholme Drive York	14	10	24
Lankhills (major cemetery)	19	4	23
Ospringe	12	9	21
Bath Gate Cirencester	12	5	17
Dunstable	8	5	13
Radley II	13	0	13
Poundbury Camp 2	3	7	10
Alington Ave Fordington	2	7	9
Guilden Morden	7	0	7

Figure 3 Summary of evidence for identification of Christian cemeteries in rank order

actually only two graves out of a total of seventeen, and one of the vessels was marked with a Christian symbol, which has been recorded in the analysis as such. Because of the small number of burials in feature 6, the figure of 12 per cent is not significant. The absence of coins in the mouth is noted from all but two sites, Poundbury 3 and Icklingham, two sites which, paradoxically, have the greatest likelihood of a Christian identification. This is examined further below, in a discussion on pagan influences (ch. VI).

Other characteristics which are features of this group of cemeteries but are, with one exception, not found in the lower-ranked sites include the incidence of inscriptions which are probably Christian, mausolea and focal graves, and 'plaster burials'. Of these, the inscriptions from Poundbury (the *I(N) N(OMINE TUO) D(OMI)NE* on a coffin lining) and Lankhills feature 6 (the *iota-chi* and stylised fish on a platter) have been discounted because of the possibility of other interpretations of the Poundbury inscription, and of the syncretic nature of the whole of feature 6; the symbols on the lead tank from Colchester are discounted as there is no other indisputable evidence for Christianity from Butt Road phase II cemetery. Mausolea or enclosed group burials were found at Poundbury 3, Butt Road II and Verulam Hills Field, and feature 6 at Lankhills was a separate enclosure from the major cemetery; focal graves seem to be present at Cannington, less certainly at Poundbury 3. Plaster burials were found at Poundbury 3, Butt Road II, and Icklingham, but, as has been explained, such evidence is not necessarily indicative of Christianity and has been given a low weighting. The final and, it is believed, very important special feature of four sites in this group is the evidence in those cemeteries of a burial rite different from that in others which were contemporaneous. At Dorchester, a cemetery contiguous to Poundbury 3 displayed what are seen as pagan characteristics; at Ashton, burials on private property differed from those in the formal west–east burial ground; in Lankhills feature 6, practices were not the same as those of the surrounding Lankhills major cemetery; and at Verulam Hills Field, the small cemetery there revealed different rites from burials found outside the wall of Verulamium (Wheeler and Wheeler 1936: 136–7).

A group of lower-rated cemeteries will now be examined: Bradley Hill group III, Nettleton A, Ancaster, Lamyatt Beacon, and Brean Down. It is unfortunate for this part of the analysis that only one site here has thirty or more burials excavated: Ancaster, with upwards of 230. Bradley Hill has twenty-five. Nevertheless, common features stand out clearly: all burials are west–east, undisturbed, supine and extended and have an absence of decapitateds and of any kind of grave goods; that is, there are no vessels, animals or birds, hobnails, or coins in the mouth. There were neo-natal burials in the two largest cemeteries and, of the smaller sites, Nettleton A and Lamyatt Beacon recorded the remains of 'infants'. All that is known from Brean Down is that 'children' were amongst the ten recorded burials there, but, since a good deal more of the site had eroded into the sea, and soil conditions had been responsible for the considerable decay of the skeletal remains found (ApSimon *et al*. 1961), the possibility of retrieval of any more evidence from this site seems remote. As was done in the case of the cemetery from Verulam Hills Field, above, the absence of neo-natal burials in cemeteries with fewer than thirty inhumations is disregarded.

It will now be useful to compare the first two groups of cemeteries. Of the internal evidence, the main difference is an absence of special features such as mausolea or focal graves, or of a contemporaneous pagan cemetery. Poundbury 3 is by far the largest cemetery and it has the greatest number of these features. Yet the special features are common to few sites, whereas there are other, more basic characteristics which are present in all thirteen cemeteries. It is noted that two of those sites which appear less certainly Christian, Bradley Hill and Nettleton A, have, on internal evidence, at least as reasonable a chance as Icklingham of being Christian: the criteria are almost identical, but Nettleton A lacks evidence of neo-natal or very young infant burials. At this site, however, the cemetery was not completely uncovered (Wedlake 1982: 90–2) as it was subsidiary to the main excavation of the shrine of Apollo. Bradley Hill also has more in common with the higher ranking cemeteries, but it suffers in overall ranking because as yet there is no known evidence for Christianity from that part of Roman Britain. Even Ancaster, which also ranks fairly low, has virtually all the features of Bradley Hill, except that there has been a discounting for the sixteen burials which were north–south and the five not supine and extended. They were (with the exception of two infant burials) in the less-organised western part of the cemetery, possibly of an earlier or later period, as it would seem was the one north–south burial from Bradley Hill. Brean Down has lost much evidence for its cemetery to the sea, yet even here the burials have features which are common to the larger and better-preserved sites of the higher-ranked cemeteries.

It could be argued that external evidence is irrelevant in such an analysis. Although this kind of evidence cannot be seen to be as important as that of the cemeteries themselves, it should not be ignored. In future years, sites such as Ancaster, Bradley Hill and Cannington may have as strong claim to a Christian identity as those at Ashton, Colchester, Icklingham, Poundbury and Verulamium. Meanwhile, the internal evidence alone is sufficient to show that the whole thirteen cemeteries have features in common which set them apart from other fourth-century burial grounds in Britain.

The remaining sixteen cemeteries may be considered as a group, as none of them fits the criteria considered essential for a Christian identification. They are a mixed group, and include sites with combinations of features which come close to those of the cemeteries discussed above. When the first criterion of west–east burial is applied, Alington Avenue, Ashton (private), Bath Gate, Butt Road I, Dunstable, Guilden Morden, Lynch Farm, Ospringe, Owslebury, Poundbury 2, Radley I and II, and Trentholme Drive are eliminated. The second criterion of undisturbed burials eliminates Frilford and Lankhills major cemetery; the criterion of a presence of neo-natals eliminates the last site, Queensford Farm. The same exercise may be performed on one or any group of the presumed pagan cemeteries in this study, using the common criteria in any order, with the same ultimate result. It is quite clear that when these criteria are applied, the process eliminates sites which do not have a Christian character.

To summarise the results of this study, it has been found that certain characteristics form the basis for a set of criteria which may be applied to a cemetery, resulting in a reasonably certain identification as pagan or Christian. There are, in addition, other criteria which may be applied which will also assist in such identification. In a cemetery of, say, thirty or more inhumations, those criteria deemed essential for a Christian identity are: burials west–east (that is, with head to the west), undisturbed by other interments, lying supine and extended, in a cemetery in which neo-natal or very young infants are also buried and given equal respect with adults, and with an absence of decapitated burials, and of grave goods of vessels, animals and birds, and hobnailed footwear. It is also desirable that there be an absence of coins in the mouth, or Charon's fee, although this may not be important. There are other criteria which may be applied, such as a Christian inscription *in situ*, the existence of a contemporaneous pagan cemetery, or the presence of a mausoleum, a focal grave, or plaster burials, but not all these features, or any at all, may be present; and all are not of the same value as evidence, particularly plaster burials. Finally, the cemetery must be seen in its broader context, and its environs considered for potential Christian influence. Although not of equal importance, all factors should be considered.

It is obvious that, in assessment of the features of each site, a numerical total is not the best indicator of possible Christianity. The actual numerical conversions have been used as a guide only. What is important is that the cemetery being studied show those characteristics which fit what is considered the essential criteria for a Christian identification. In this analysis, the application of those criteria has resulted in the following cemeteries from Roman and sub-Roman Britain being proposed as Christian (that is, a classification of 3 on Thomas's 3–0 scale):[2] Ancaster, Ashton, Bradley Hill group III, Brean Down, Butt Road phase II Colchester, Cannington, Crown Buildings site Dorchester, Icklingham, Lamyatt Beacon, Lankhills feature 6, Nettleton A, Poundbury 3 Dorchester, and Verulam Hills Field St Albans. The location and plans of these sites, with the exception of Brean Down and the Crown Buildings Site, Dorchester,[3] appear in Figures 4–12.

ANCASTER .

ASHTON .

.ICKLINGHAM

COLCHESTER .

VERULAMIUM.
.NETTLETON

BREAN DOWN
.

LAMYATT BEACON
CANNINGTON .   .WINCHESTER (LANKHILLS)
.SOMERTON
(BRADLEY HILL)

DORCHESTER .
(POUNDBURY)

Figure 4 Distribution map of probable Christian cemeteries in Roman Britain

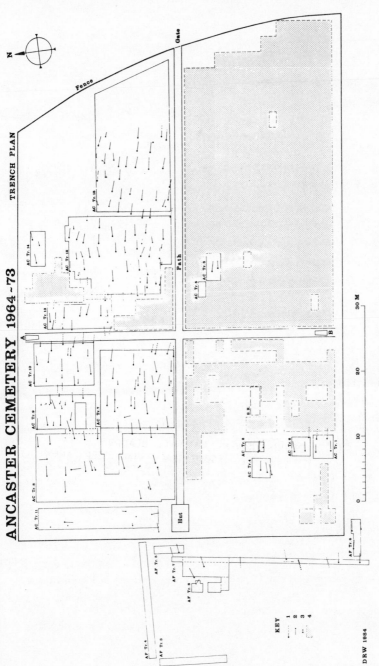

Figure 5 Ancaster cemetery

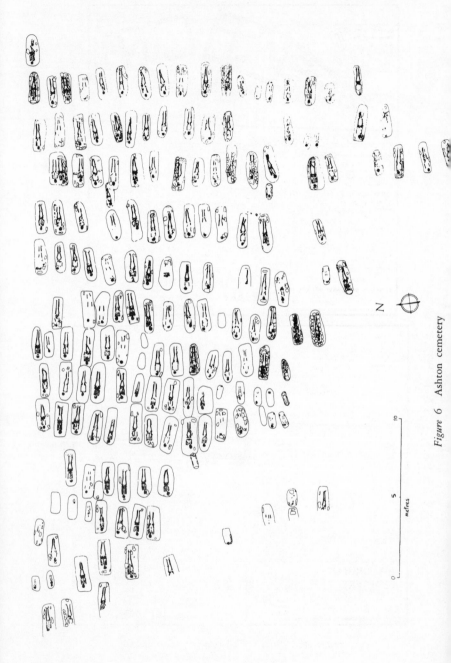

Figure 6 Ashton cemetery

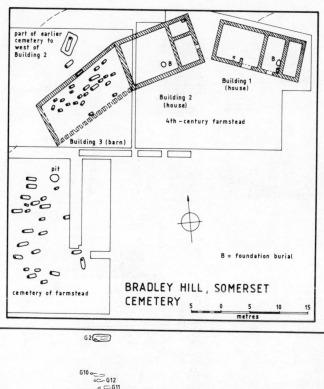

part of earlier
cemetery to
west of
Building 2

Building 3 (barn)

Building 2
(house)

○ B

4th-century farmstead

Building 1
(house)

B ○

pit

cemetery of farmstead

B = foundation burial

BRADLEY HILL, SOMERSET
CEMETERY

5   0   5   10   15
metres

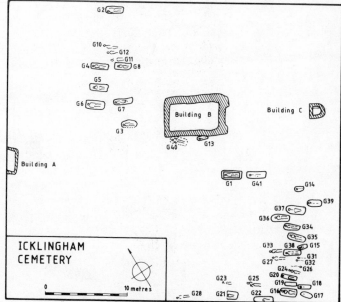

G2

G10
G12
G11
G4   G8
G5
G6   G7
G3

Building B

G40   G13

Building C

Building A

G1   G41
G14
G39
G37
G36
G34
G35
G33   G38   G15
G27   G31
G32
G24   G26
G20
G23   G25   G19   G18
G28   G21   G22   G16   G17

ICKLINGHAM
CEMETERY

0   10 metres

Figure 7(a) Bradley Hill cemetery (after Leech)
  7(b) Icklingham cemetery (after West)

93

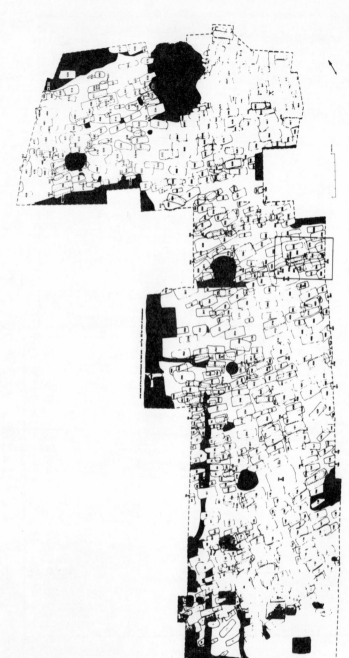

Figure 8 Butt Road, Colchester cemetery, phase II

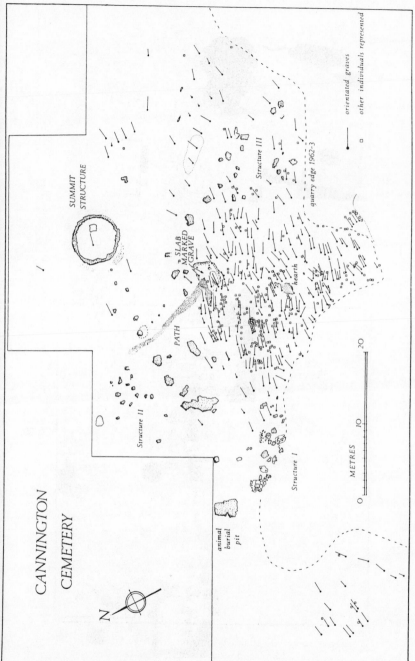

Figure 9 Cannington cemetery

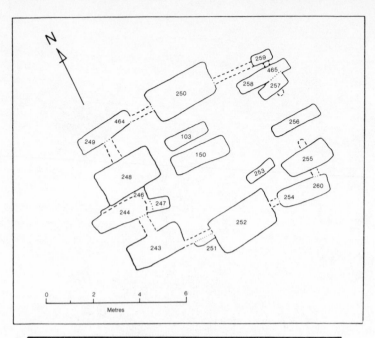

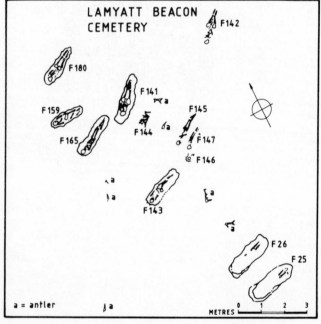

Figure 10(a) Lankhills, Winchester cemetery, feature 6
10(b) Lamyatt Beacon cemetery (after Leech)

96

POUNDBURY

Figure 11 Poundbury Camp, Dorchester cemetery

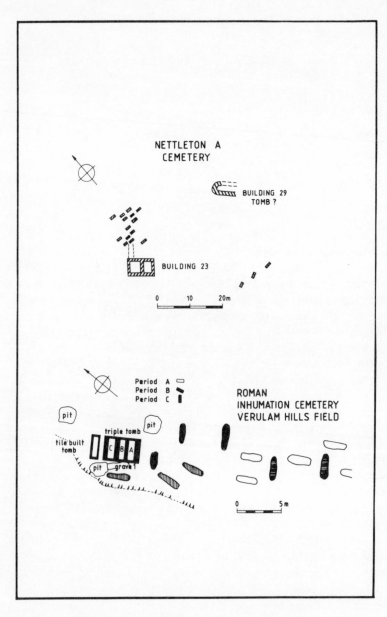

Figure 12(a) Nettleton A cemetery (after Wedlake)
12(b) Verulam Hills Field cemetery (after Anthony)

IV

IDENTIFICATION OF
CHRISTIAN CHURCHES

1: SUGGESTED CRITERIA

In order to assess the extent of Christianity in Roman Britain, it is
necessary to identify not only Christian cemeteries but also religious
structures. Thomas (1981: 143–201, 213–20) went some considerable way in this process but, while he identified several very
likely or probable churches and baptisteries, he did not in every
case set out clearly the criteria for such identification. In this
chapter, the features of presumed Christian churches are examined,
and a set of ranked criteria devised which, it is believed, will assist
in the identification of Christian religious buildings in Roman
Britain.

The difficulties in recognising churches of fourth- and fifth-
century Britain are considerable. There was no single architectural
model for their construction after the Peace of the Church. The
basilical plan was favoured by Constantine or his architects, and
employed in four of his earliest churches (the Church of the
Nativity at Bethlehem, the Church of the Holy Sepulchre,
Jerusalem, and St Peter's and St John Lateran at Rome);
undoubtedly it was adopted in the more romanised parts of the
provinces, or adapted to the simpler apsed style without aisles.
But, as Ward-Perkins (1954: 80) points out, frequently the earlier
house churches – that is, a suite of rooms in a private house set
aside for Christian liturgical use – would have sufficed for some
further time before being replaced by purpose-built churches. In
Britain, there may have been some loss of religious momentum in
the reign of the apostate Julian; and paganism was generally
tolerated by subsequent Christian emperors until Theodosius.
With the withdrawal of the Romans early in the fifth century,

therefore, it is quite likely that in many of the christianised parts of Britain, house churches continued without ever having been succeeded by recognisable church buildings. Such appears to have been the case at Lullingstone, where, although the villa was abandoned, the suite of rooms generally accepted as a house church or chapel continued in use for some years.

Another type of church, found in northern (Celtic) Italy, was the rectangular building without any trace of an apse. This type of church was common around Aquileia until about the sixth century (Radford 1968: 27). It may have been the model for the small, rectilinear, 'oratory' type churches from Ireland and Scotland of the seventh century (Thomas 1981: fig. 18; Rennie 1984: fig. 15) and for the earlier rectilinear buildings, presumed churches, in the south-western areas of Roman Britain, to be dealt with later in this chapter. The small, square mausoleum was also adapted to a place of Christian worship in various parts of the Empire and became the cemetery church or, if the remains of a martyr were deposited therein, a martyrial church. Radford (1968: 20) points out that there was a different architecture and a different liturgical tradition in 'congregational' and 'cemetery' churches, and it was only late in the fourth century that the two traditions began to merge into the one standard architectural form.

One further style of church is relevant to this study: the octagon, with internal chambers in a cruciform. The plan was known to have been favoured in the East as early as the fourth century (Gregory of Nyssa, *Letter to Amphilocius*).[1] An example from Roman Britain may have been the octagonal structure at Nettleton, formerly a pagan shrine (Wedlake 1982); this building is discussed below.

The problems of identification are at once apparent. Churches are of several architectural types: basilical or simple apsidal, rectangular or polygonal, and the house church, which could be two, three or more rooms in a private residence. Yet all these could be found in a pagan or secular context. The basilical plan was that of the judiciary building found in the forum, but the simplified plan, without the aisles, was also used in Britain in pagan religious buildings: Lewis (1966: figs 63, 73, 75, 71, 74) illustrates two *scholae* from Corbridge and a possible one from Silchester, a temple from Benwell and a well shrine from Housesteads 1. The basilical plan was employed for the London Mithraeum (Grimes 1955 and pl. XLIII), and was also used in other parts of the empire for various cults and for some synagogues in Galilee (Krautheimer 1965: 20). In Britain, the octagon was not common, but Romano-Celtic temples or shrines built on this plan are known. Examples include the structure at Chelmsford (Drury 1972), and the presumed house shrine at Stroud (Smith 1978: 127). On the other hand, the simple rectilinear building was so common a shape that it would be impossible to identify as a Christian building without some corroborating evidence; and even when the plan was employed in a mausoleum, the problem is to prove that any burial there, if it remained at all, was Christian. Similarly, the identification of a group of rooms in a private residence as a house church would be virtually impossible without supporting evidence.

The shape of the building alone is thus of limited help in determining a Christian identity. It can, nevertheless, be a pointer, and, as potential evidence for Christianity, it will be evaluated below.

A further difficulty encountered when attempting to identify fourth-century buildings as Christian churches is that, for this period, there was as yet no preferred orientation. This is illustrated by the four Constantinian churches referred to above. Two were west–east, that is, with entrance to the west, and apse to the east, the others east-west. It is true that Tertullian said that Christians turned to the east to pray (*Apologeticus* 16), but evidently this did not come to be the accepted orientation for Christians in churches until somewhat later. Churches with entrance to the east were, apparently, quite common in the late fourth and early fifth century (Paulinus of Nola, *Epistulae* 32.13).[2]

Size is also not a good indication of a church. There was little place for the great basilical buildings of Rome in rural-based Britain, except perhaps for London; but there is faint hope of discovering now what presumably had been the major church in the British provinces. The sizes of the putative churches of Britain vary enormously (see below, Figure 29a), with some of the smaller rural ones barely large enough to hold celebrant, altar and the 'two or three gathered . . . together'.

Since, therefore, the plan, orientation and size of the buildings cannot be of much assistance, it is necessary to look for other features which may be common to all, or several sites, in order to produce a set of workable criteria for identification of structures as probable Christian churches. To this end, the various features are discussed and their relative value as evidence assessed and placed on a weighted scale, with a discounting when the evidence does not exactly fit the criterion. A summary of evidential weightings is given in Figure 13. Thomas's classifications of intra-mural (con-gregational),[3] extra-mural (cemetery), and house or estate churches are used. The evidence is classified as Internal, that is, relating to the building itself and its immediate location, and External (evidence for Christianity within about 15 kilometres of the site). The discussion includes buildings mentioned by Thomas, as well as sites proposed by others subsequent to his publication. In the second part of this chapter, an analysis of various buildings is made by application of the criteria developed (Figure 14). It has been found convenient in that analysis to convert the relative weightings to a numerical equivalent. Finally, the sites discussed are ranked on Thomas's 3–0 scale of probability (Figure 15).

At the outset, it is essential that a building proposed as a Romano-British church be dated to a period when such identification is reasonable. Immediately some sites are eliminated. The apsidal building at Flaxengate, suggested by Thomas (1981: 168–9) as a possible church, is now thought to have been from the age of Diocletian (M. Jones, pers. comm.).[4] The building in the grounds of St John's Abbey, Colchester, seen by Thomas (1981: 174) as a Roman mausoleum with an apse and nave added later, has been identified as Saxon (Webster and Cherry 1973: 140), and the archaeologist does not believe there is any discernible difference in the style or materials in the foundations of the building (P. Crummy, pers. comm.). The rectangular east–west building to the west of and unaligned with the main structures at Cox Green Villa, near Maidenhead, proposed by Rodwell (1980a: 220) as a Christian church, may be rejected on several grounds: the outbuilding was apparently added in the late Antonine period; there is no evidence whatever for any religious use, pagan or Christian; and, finally, if a forge was built on the far side of the villa at the peak of its prosperity in the third and fourth century, then it would seem most unlikely that a church would be located alongside it. The suggestion is that the building was for cattle stalls (Bennett 1962: 66).

At the maximum level on any weighted scale should be the presence of Christian evidence *in situ*. The best examples of this are the Christian mosaics from Hinton St Mary and Frampton, and the wall paintings from Lullingstone. There are several mosaics in Britain which could be Christian, but few which, on other evidence, might have belonged to a house church. One possible site is the villa at Woodchester, the mosaic of which illustrates the Orpheus myth, and this could be weighted about one-third of the others. The evidence from Chedworth suggests a Christian presence, but the stones were not actually *in situ*. Although it is an attractive suggestion by Thomas (1981: 220) that the nymphaeum, on being christianised, may have used as a baptistery, there is to date little archaeological evidence to support the existence of a house church there; and, since baptism was followed by the Eucharist, this would suppose the existence of some form of church. The site is far from fully excavated, but, on present evidence, the Chedworth stones could rank at best only about one-half on a weighted scale.

The evidence for Nettleton octagonal building as a church is not quite conclusive: the eight-chambered shrine was converted to a cruciform, and the walls of this chamber painted with motifs interpreted by Wedlake (1982: 63) as St Andrew's crosses with a central roundel, the design on which is unknown. If this interpretation is correct, the building may have been used as a Christian church, since that form of the cross was known by the fourth century (Watts 1988a; below, ch. V.2). As evidence for Christianity it would have to rank about two-thirds on a weighted scale.

The other site where there is the probability of Christian evidence *in situ* is at Richborough. Here, a silver strainer was found and, within another 50 metres or so, a bronze pronged instrument (Bushe-Fox 1949: pl. XCIX 126, 127). Objects of this type are believed to have been used in the early Mass (Watts 1988b; below, ch. V.1 and Appendix); the presence of the strainer on the actual site, and of the other object only a short distance from what Brown (1971) has convincingly demonstrated to be the remains of a church, enhances this identification. There is, however, no *chi-rho* or other Christian symbol on these objects, so, although found in a non-domestic context, as evidence for Christianity they are ranked only about three-quarters.

The next criterion with maximum weighting deals not with finds at a site, but with their absence. One of the most basic characteristics one would expect of a purported religious site would be the general absence of contemporary domestic, industrial or agricultural features. This does seem to state the obvious; but in buildings which do not necessarily suggest themselves as churches to begin with (that is, those not of the basilical or apsidal plan), it may be difficult to separate the secular from the sacred. The earliest churches had been in houses and the two main sacraments employed everyday objects. The Eucharist was, after all, a meal; the Baptism, a form of bathing. In the days before Christian architecture for both church and baptistery stabilised into a form readily recognised, experiment and local innovation probably prevailed.

Unfortunately, some of the sites which have been suggested as possible churches have not been fully explored or reported, so this negative evidence is not always available. Of the buildings analysed here, Nettleton building 23 has evidence of what may have been food preparation in the basement room of the simple rectangular structure (Wedlake 1982: 75–7); but the building and this room in particular are closely associated with an adjoining west–east cemetery, and the room may have been used to prepare food for the *refrigerium* taken at the graves of departed relatives there, despite Church disapproval.[5] The building at Butt Road, Colchester (Colchester 9) had, beyond its western end, a tile hearth which may have been contemporary with the building (Crossan, in Crummy 1980: 266); but it is now thought more likely to have belonged to a later period, when the presumed church was no longer in use. This area of the excavation was very disturbed, and stratigraphy poor (C. Crossan, pers. comm.).

Two other buildings at Colchester might be examined here. A large fourth-century basilical building at Culver Street had been thought to be a possible church (Crummy 1984: 70), in view of the plan of the structure and the changed use for the site. In the light of more recent excavations in the vicinity of the building, however, it is now interpreted as a grain store, possibly under some official jurisdiction, since it was constructed beyond the existing street alignment. A corn-drying kiln was found nearby, and the area between the building and the city walls was, in the late fourth century, given over to agriculture (P. Crummy, pers. comm.). This site is, therefore, eliminated from a discussion of possible churches. It has also been suggested (Rodwell and Rodwell 1977: 30) that St Martin's, Colchester, may occupy the site of a late Roman church: in Insula XI an 'Anglo-Saxon' burial was reported, and also Roman pots. Since, however, intra-mural burial was forbidden under Roman law, and since the pots do not appear to be funereal (P. Crummy, pers. comm.), it can only be concluded that this was a domestic site and the burial indeed Anglo-Saxon. St Martin's is thus rejected.

A corollary of an absence of non-religious features is that, at a Christian site, there should be an absence of pagan features or artefacts. At two sites which appear to be related, pieces of deer antler were found: at Brean Down (ApSimon 1965), in the ambulatory and annexe of the temple and in the late levels of the rectangular building, and, at Lamyatt Beacon (Leech 1986: 266–7, 271–2), sealed by the rectangular structure and also scattered about the cemetery area. Leech suggests the antler pieces were cult objects, perhaps attributes of a god of the Cernunnos type. He appears to have abandoned an earlier suggestion (1980: 335) that they had any connection with the cemeteries or the later rectangular buildings; in the final report on Lamyatt (1986) he merely associates the finds with the earlier Romano-Celtic temples. An examination of the plans of the sites makes such an interpretation reasonable, although deposition in the fourth century and later is possible.[6]

More specifically, if pagan features had existed at a site, they should subsequently have been christianised or purged, profaned, destroyed or discarded. Literary and archaeological evidence shows this occurred elsewhere in the empire: Zonaras (13.12) tells of how Christians had robbed the temple of Asclepius at Aegae of its columns and incorporated them into a church; and Dyggve (1951: fig. I.9) illustrates the relief of a Nike rather crudely replaced by a cross at the western gate of Diocletian's palace just outside Salona.

There are several examples from Roman Britain. The earlier (pagan?) site at Icklingham had been sealed with a layer of chalk before the construction of an apsidal building and a cemetery of west–east graves; a piece of carved stone, possibly from a temple, was found beneath the layer of chalk, in a pit (West 1976: 69–71). At Uley, votive material was removed from the Romano-Celtic temple and a small building was erected incorporating pieces of a limestone statue of Mercury, apparently deliberately broken; another later (possibly apsidal) structure used an altar to Mercury in its construction, with a second altar employed as a step (Ellison 1980: 313–14).[7] An altar to Silvanus and the *numen Augusti* at Nettleton was profaned to build the furnace in building 18, an industrial extension, after the decline of the shrine of Apollo from about 330 and the probable takeover of the site by Christians (Wedlake 1982: 110). At Chedworth, the site of a pagan temple, an altar had been buried close by a nymphaeum, the stones of which were now inscribed with Christian symbols (Fox 1887: 335), and another small portable altar was inscribed with what may also be seen as Christian symbols (Goodburn 1979: pl. 12.8, 9; below, ch. V.3). At Witham, an artificial lake was drained and its votive contents consigned to a midden. By the edge of where the lake had been, an octagonal structure, possibly a font, was erected, making use of the spring which had previously supplied the lake; at the same time, a small, rectangular stone building was constructed some 40 metres away, on the site of an earlier presumed Romano-Celtic temple (Turner 1982: 21–8 and pers. comm.).[8] A similar situation seems to have occurred at Lamyatt Beacon: most of the votive finds from the temple were found in the destruction debris of some of the structures there, suggesting that they were 'thrown out after the religious use of the temple had ceased' (Leech 1980: 336); from this it could be deduced that the discarding of these objects was a deliberate act. At nearby Brean Down, the late-fourth-century rectangular building aligned east–west was constructed using stone from the adjacent north–south Romano-Celtic temple, perhaps deliberately razed (ApSimon 1965: 226).

Less conclusive evidence of destruction of a pagan feature is that from the site of the apsidal building in the Verulam Hills Field, designated Verulamium 7 by Lewis (1966). Here two fragments were found of what is thought to have been a life-sized bronze statue of a deity, possibly Cupid; one piece was about 5 metres to the south of the building, the other in a ditch 10 metres or so to the south–west (Anthony 1968: 49–50). There were no industrial or domestic features at the site, only a series of burials which ended with a group of fourth-century west–east graves. In the same category would be the building at St Paul-in-the-Bail, Lincoln, where it was reported that, in one of the later levels, fragments of a marble inscription, indicating a temple of the Imperial cult, were found (Hassall and Tomlin 1979: 345). Since they were not in the Roman levels of the building, such evidence is not conclusive. As indicators for Christianity, these examples would have a weighting of only about one-third of that given for those in the preceding paragraph. At Lullingstone (Meates 1955), it may have been that the sculptures of the 'deep room' had been toppled at the time the room above was converted to house church, but the sequence is not altogether clear; the evidence here cannot be weighted.[9]

In any evaluation of these features of a site, it is realised that, although the absence of pagan evidence would be an essential criterion for the identification of Christian buildings, churches would also have been built on sites that had no prior religious associations (and this would apply particularly to new cemetery churches). Moreover, many buildings have been excavated, the purpose of which is completely unknown. On balance, therefore, the absence of pagan evidence could by itself rank only one-half the maximum. Since not every Christian church could have been built on an earlier pagan site, the purging or destruction of pagan evidence, although a fairly conclusive pointer to a Christian identity, should not rank on the maximum, but perhaps at three-quarters.

All the sites above have in common that they appear to have had religious predecessors, and this leads to one of the most important features of Romano-British religion generally: the 'tradition of sanctity' (Lewis 1966: 50) which extends from the prehistoric Celtic cults through, though not necessarily in an unbroken sequence at any one site, to Romano-British Christianity and beyond. The question of religious continuity of sites is one that has been touched on by various scholars in passing (above, ch. II; their views are now collated here for convenience), but, as far as is known, there has been no major study of the topic with regard to Roman Britain. Lewis (1966: 129) included earlier sacred sites among probable favoured locations for Romano-Celtic temples; at that date, however, he found no evidence for Celtic structures. Writing at about the same time, Ross (1967: 2), in her work on the Celts, suggested that careful excavation of Romano-Celtic shrines and temples could reveal Celtic structures, thus bringing Britain more into line with archaeological finds from Europe. By 1984 that evidence had been found, and Henig (1984b: 22, 37) observed that just as 'a line of continuity in worship and ritual links Romano-Celtic religion with its past', so too temples often replaced earlier Celtic structures or marked a sacred place where no building had hitherto stood. Wait (1986: 181) has now been able to find evidence of continuity of religious tradition on twelve sites, and he suggests others which might reveal a similar continuity. He also notes that, of the Celtic religious sites he had examined, 60 per cent had remained in use into the Roman period (Wait 1986: 173).

On the question of religious continuity into the post-Roman and

Anglo-Saxon period, scholars are divided,[10] but there is a growing body of evidence to suggest that Christianity did not die out in the mid-fifth century, to be re-introduced by Augustine 150 years later. Although Lewis (1966) could find no clear evidence in Britain for such continuity, as early as 1953 Toynbee (1953: 2) had pondered whether there might be a link between Romano-British house chapels and some later Saxon churches. This line of research has not been followed up, but a fairly recent study of mediaeval churches on Roman buildings by Morris and Roxan (1980) works from the premiss that the villas which remained into the sub- and post-Roman period acquired a later manorial hall or manorial centre, and it was this which came to have an associated church, rather than that the villas themselves contained embryonic churches. The authors do, however, make the point that 'the position of a church in the landscape is seldom fortuitous, still less the outcome of some spontaneous burst of pious energy' (Morris and Roxan 1980: 183). It is proposed here that one of the reasons for establishing a Christian church at a particular site was, consciously or unconsciously, to preserve that tradition of sanctity noted by Lewis; and some of the evidence for that continuity into the sub- and post-Roman period is preserved at the sites of presumed Romano-British churches.

Their pagan predecessors are dealt with first, and it may be observed, before commencing this part of the analysis, that the identification of Romano-Celtic temples and Iron Age sacred sites is as problematical as is that of Christian churches. There has, however, been a recent thorough study of Romano-Celtic shrines by Wait (1986: 156–90) in which he establishes realistic criteria for their identification. Application of these criteria may call some sites into question, but the identification of those referred to in the present study is generally not a matter of contention.

Lewis (1966) lists a number of Romano-Celtic temples on Celtic sacred places, and others have been published since 1966. A selection of sites will suffice to illustrate this. Examples of temples above Celtic buildings are: Frilford (Bradford and Goodchild 1939: 11–15), Hayling Island (Downey *et al*. 1980), Thistleton 1 and 2 (Wilson 1965: 207), Muntham Court (summarised in Lewis 1966: 83–4) and Maiden Castle (Wheeler 1943; Drury, 1980). At these last two sites, there appeared to have been some hiatus: at the former, the site of the Iron Age building had been levelled before the construction of its Romano-Celtic successor; at the latter, there appears to have been a gap of 300 years, but, with all the space on the hillfort available, the Romano-Celtic circular temple was placed exactly over the site of the previous Iron Age shrine, that is, it seems the tradition of sanctity remained. Temples over sacred water sites included those at Carrawburgh (Smith 1962) and Housesteads (Birley and Birley 1962). Colchester 2 at Sheepen was probably built beside a sacred tree or grove, since it was off-centre in its *temenos* (Hull 1958: 230); Chelmsford 3 was built on the site of some unknown sacred focus which required an artificial mound (Drury 1972); and the publication of the site at Harlow reveals that the earliest sacred focus there was probably a stand of trees, followed in succession by an Iron Age and a Romano-Celtic building (France and Gobel 1985).

There is, therefore, a clear trend for the building of religious structures above earlier sacred sites, implying the dominance of a new religion over an old (or, at least in the case of the pragmatic Romans, an acceptable syncretism). The tradition was maintained when Christianity became an approved and, finally, the official religion of the Empire: two archaeologists working in the Middle East could remark over a hundred years ago, 'The fact that Christian churches were originally built on the sites of heathen temples [as at Rome, Constantinople and Jerusalem] is too well ascertained to need more than a passing notice' (Conder and Kitchener 1883: 427–8). Dyggve (1951: 8–9) refers to the same occurrence at Athens, and Lewis (1966: 145) notes that at least eight Romano-Celtic temples in Europe had been replaced by Christian churches on the same site. This phenomenon is observed throughout the later history of the Church, when missionaries from the Old World sealed the victory of Christianity by siting churches over pagan temples in the New World; examples abound in the countries of Latin America. Ross (1967: 45) comments that 'any study of the sequence of religions shows that an intrusive cult tends to superimpose itself on the actual physical sites of the earlier beliefs'.[11] Moreover, in Britain, the process was not only the replacement of one religion by a more dominant one, but also the replacement of a less developed form of religious architecture by a more sophisticated type: it is known that Romano-Celtic temples replaced primitive Iron Age shrines, and that many Norman churches were founded on earlier, simpler Saxon ones. The gap in knowledge is, therefore, in terms of years, quite small. By analogy, it should follow that the Christians of Roman Britain tended to build their churches on Romano-Celtic sites, and that Romano-British churches were succeeded, at least to some degree, by Saxon ones, or by monastic establishments which had begun to make their appearance in Britain in the fifth century.

Although this study is concerned primarily with the Roman period, the following sub-Roman period naturally is of relevance, since the whole Romano-British culture did not come to an immediate halt with the withdrawal of the imperial forces; and nowhere is this more evident than in the study of churches and cemeteries. The evidence for continuity of religious tradition is as yet slight, but there are indications from recent excavations that Christian buildings were built on pagan sites, and that this continuity was preserved after the Roman period. The outstanding example of this is at a site which has yet to be published fully – Uley, in Gloucestershire. There appears to be a copy-book sequence of religious occupation from Iron Age to the seventh or eighth century AD . The site contained an Iron Age building which possibly had a sacred tree as its focus, and was associated with votive pits and ritual infant burials; a Romano-Celtic temple; and two successive buildings re-using pagan altars and pieces of fragmented pagan statuary, with associated structures which may have been baptisteries. These appear to have been Christian buildings, surrounded by an enclosure bank (Ellison 1980 and pers. comm.).[12] Another example extending into the late Roman period comes from Witham, in Essex. An Iron Age enclosure featured a circular building which was succeeded by a probable Romano-Celtic temple and then a small rectangular building with associated octagonal structure, interpreted as a church and baptistery. In its last phase, the site appears to have resumed a pagan character, with the supposed Christian structures defiled and destroyed (Turner 1982 and pers. comm.).

Four other sites may be examined. At Nettleton, the shrine of Apollo seems to have been abandoned about 330, and the octagonal, eight-chambered building converted into a cruciform church. It is likely that the first Romano-Celtic building marked an earlier Celtic sacred spring (Wedlake 1982: 10), and there appears to have been a continuing religious tradition at the site after the Christian phase, about 370. There are marked similarities between two further sites, Brean Down and Lamyatt Beacon, but both suffer from the loss of evidence, Brean Down to erosion and the sea, Lamyatt Beacon to treasure hunters. There is no evidence for Celtic shrines at these sites, but the prominent location of both may be significant. Both sites were dominated by a square Romano-Celtic temple, aligned north–south, and built, in the case of Brean Down, about 340, and of Lamyatt Beacon, sometime after 300. Towards the end of the century a second, small, rectangular building was erected at each site, aligned east–west; at Brean Down at least, the stone of the temple was robbed for the construction of the later building. These buildings may have continued in use into the fifth century. Cemeteries have been found near both, and the west–east orientation, the supine, extended and undisturbed nature of the burials and the complete absence of grave goods or of any pagan indicators suggest a Christian identity (see above, ch. III). On the limited radio-carbon samples taken, the burials date from the sixth to the eighth century, and so do not appear to be contemporaneous with the rectangular buildings. Nevertheless, both sites give a good indication of the continuity of religious tradition, at least from Romano-Celtic into the post-Roman period, especially as it will be proposed below that the association of burials with a religious structure was likely to be an indication of a Christian identity. Finally, the presumed house church at Lullingstone (Meates 1955) should be considered. It was placed, perhaps not by accident, above the 'deep room' of the villa, a household shrine whose contents may have been treated with scant respect, if not deliberately defiled.

A tradition of religious continuity may be viewed from two directions; it follows that, if Romano-British Christian churches had religious predecessors, some, at least, most likely had Saxon successors. Generally this has been beyond the scope of the present work; nevertheless, of the sites studied in some detail, it would seem that several revealed such a continuity, although Morris and Roxan (1980: 187) remind us that a religious focus can creep about at a site. The example of Uley has been mentioned above. St Pancras, Canterbury, has been shown to have had Roman origins, and Thomas (1981: 170–4) has argued persuasively that this site is the Roman church mentioned by Bede (*Historia ecclesiastica* 1.26). The apsidal building in the forum at Lincoln, the earliest church on the site of St Paul-in-the-Bail, is another excellent example, the only doubt here being whether the original building was Roman or sub-Roman. It will be argued below that it is Roman in date. At Richborough, a Saxon church, St Augustine's Chapel, was built about 100 metres from the late fourth-century Roman church, still within the confines of the old Roman fort (Bushe-Fox 1928: 37–40).[13] The villa at Woodchester with its Orpheus mosaic, mentioned above as a possible house church, is known to have had a pre-conquest church on the site (Morris and Roxan 1980: 185, 203), which also may suggest the preservation of a tradition of sanctity there. The presumed house church at Lullingstone villa seems to have been succeeded at some later period by a church which used a Roman mausoleum in its construction. However, there is no certainty that the church was Saxon (Taylor and Taylor 1965: 401–2).

Two sites for which there is almost-certain literary evidence of the existence of churches in the Roman period, but which have not yet yielded the archaeological evidence, are the cathedrals at Canterbury and St Albans. The Roman church at Canterbury is mentioned by Bede and Eadmer; the cathedral is on the old Roman street alignment, and supposedly on the site of a Saxon church (Brooks 1977: 493), thus presumably over the successor to the Roman church; Lewis (1966: 114), however, argues that the Saxon bishop Odo only rebuilt the roof and walls of the church he inherited, and therefore the building beneath the present cathedral is, or was, the original Roman. The site of the cathedral of St Alban is, as Thomas (1981: 180) rightly observes, the most likely location of the martyrial church in Roman Britain visited by Germanus in 429. Current excavations are down to Roman levels, with the discovery of burials (Frere 1984a: 304), but as yet no evidence of the Roman church described by Bede (*Historia ecclesiastica* 1.7). The location of a Roman cemetery at this site, some distance removed from the town and the main Roman roads leading into it (the usual place to find Roman cemeteries), lends supports to the view that this is the site of Alban's burial, and of the original martyrial church.[14]

Other churches which may have had Roman antecedents, but for which little information is available, are: St Botolph's, Colchester (Rodwell and Rodwell 1977: 37; Crummy 1980: 274), a twelfth-century priory, built on a Roman cemetery; St Mary's, Silchester, which is on the old Roman street alignment, and may occupy the site of a Romano-Celtic temple (Boon 1974: 155); and St Bride's in Fleet Street, London, on a Roman extra-mural cemetery which extended into the Saxon period (Toynbee 1953: 13). To these may be added a group suggested by Rodwell (1980a: 238) in view of their location above ancient Roman fora, and thus possibly on the site of earlier forum temples: All Saints, Colchester; St Michael's, St Albans; All Hallows, Gloucester; York Minster; Sts Peter and Paul, and St Mary de Stalls, Bath; and St Peter Cornhill, London. In another study, Morris (1983) includes many of those listed above, plus a number of others: one of the most noteworthy is the minster at Wells (his figs 8, 9), which now appears to have been built on a sub- or post-Roman mausoleum.

The occurrence of a pagan predecessor or a Christian successor must now be ranked on a weighted scale. In view of the undoubted connection between Celtic and Romano-Celtic and between Saxon and Norman sites, and the widespread evidence for Christian adoption of pagan sites, it would seem that any connection between Romano-Celtic and Christian, and Romano-British Christian and Saxon, should rank on the maximum. Yet not all Romano-British churches would have had both, or even one, of these links. There would obviously have been other reasons for establishing a church on a particular spot, such as the needs of the community at the time, commemorating a holy place the reasons for which in the passage of time were forgotten, or even something as mundane as the availability of land. The evidence for such continuity should, therefore, rank just below maximum.

It will have been noted that one of the features common to many of the sites discussed or listed above was proximity to a cemetery. Lewis (1966: 6, 135) does make the observation that it was not unknown for cemeteries to be located near temples, but he also notes that the occurrence of such burials was 'unusual' (cf. Macdonald 1979: 425). Examples he proposes are the temples at Frilford, Jordan Hill, Lancing Down, Weycock and Worth. Leech (1980) mentions Henley Wood and Woodyates. Before consideration of possible Christian sites, it will be useful to examine these pagan sites for such a connection.

At Frilford, besides the temple and the cemetery, there was a settlement which began in the Iron Age and moved a little to an area beyond where the temple was found (Bradford and Goodchild 1939: 26). A more recent field survey has now shown considerable occupation areas to the north and south of the cemetery as well as that beyond the temple, and a road between cemetery and temple *temenos*. From the plan, it would seem that the position of temple, settlement and cemetery reflects a normal settlement pattern, and it has been suggested that there is a likely association of temple with the newly discovered amphitheatre (Hingley 1982:

309 and fig. 5), rather than with the cemetery, some 200 metres away. The third- to fourth-century temple at Henley Wood was surrounded by a *temenos* ditch and part of this covered with a rubble causeway, which was in turn cut by (?)west–east graves of a subsequent inhumation cemetery from no earlier than the late fourth century (Wilson 1965: 219; 1970: 296; Leech 1980: 349). It appears here the cemetery clearly post-dated the temple, and the disregard for the *temenos* may suggest a disregard for the religion represented by the temple. The site at Jordan Hill, which has attracted attention for almost two hundred years, has generated many confused and conflicting accounts,[15] but it seems that there was an inhumation and cremation cemetery dating probably from the early Roman period to the end of the second century. There is also evidence for a villa, with coins of Carausius and Constans. On the top of the hill was a square Romano-Celtic temple which dates to the fourth century (Lewis 1966: 51). The relationship between cemetery and temple is at best indistinct: the burials were said to be '300 yards' from the temple (Oliver 1923, quoting Medhurst, who found it in 1845); and it seems that there was a time lapse of at least a century between the last of the burials and the construction of the temple.

The uncertainties of the Jordan Hill site are at least as great as those associated with Lancing Down. At this latter site there is a Romano-Celtic temple which Lewis (1966: 51) dates from about AD 100–250, and a cremation cemetery whose date is unclear: Wait (1986: 412) describes the cremations as 'Romano-Celtic'; Bedwin (1981) writes of late second-century cremation *cemeteries*; Whimster (1981: 389) sees the cremations as 'pre-conquest'; Lewis (1966: 6) writes of a Belgic cemetery which was apparently sacred, probably basing this description on a suggestion by Frere (1940: 167) that 'in the absence of stratified evidence . . . the evidence of Bronze Age and Iron Age sepulchral pottery does seem to hint at the existence of a sacred site before the Roman period'.[16] This does not, however, solve the date of the cemetery. All that can be said of Lancing Down is that there may have been a correlation in time between temple and cemetery, but it is more likely that the burials were pre-Roman, and the siting of the temple was to continue the tradition of sanctity of the Iron Age site, rather than to have any connection with the cemetery, had it been realised it was there.

For the last three sites, Weycock, Woodyates and Worth, the information is sparse. Woodyates may have had a temple, but it has not been found (RCHM 1975: 55) and it is supposedly associated with a cemetery of east–west burials within a square enclosure. Weycock (Cotton 1956–7), and Worth (Stebbing 1937) temples were not only near cemeteries but also near settlements. The association of temple and cemetery is not proven, and is probably, like the Frilford site, part of a normal settlement pattern, unconnected with religion.

The purpose of this rather lengthy excursus has been to illustrate the point that there was no tradition of an association of burials with shrines or temples in pre-Christian Roman Britain.[17] In her study of the Celts in pagan Britain, Ross (1967: 39) notes only some evidence of graves as foci for ritual; she does not say that Celtic graves and burial grounds themselves became shrines, or that it was a Celtic custom to build them there. There is evidence that cemetery enclosures were known in the pre-Roman period: Black (1986b: 205) documents some with European parallels,[18] and others are discussed by Jessup (1959); dry-stone enclosures were found in the cemetery at Jordan Hill (Warne 1872: 229), a feature which, since it does not appear in later pagan Romano-Celtic cemeteries in the area, may have been a local pre-Roman tradition. But there is no hard evidence for a cemetery–shrine link in the pre-Roman period, nor is there for a cemetery–temple link after the Roman occupation. That is not surprising, in view of the fact that, in Roman times at least, such an association would have been most irregular, as it was believed that corpses would pollute a site.[19] This is not to say that there were no buildings in Roman cemeteries; the mausoleum was a well known and readily recognised feature of Roman burial grounds, but a mausoleum was not a temple. A study of Romano-British burial grounds suggests that they were few, and, in the fourth century, were built mainly in private burial areas (below, ch. VI). In all the putative pagan cemeteries of Roman Britain, there is no known example of a building of a religious nature clearly associated with the burials. Thus, if religious structures were not found in the cemeteries of Roman Britain before the Christian period, it is proposed that the presence of non-domestic, non-industrial or non-agricultural buildings in association with cemeteries of the fourth century and beyond is an indicator of the Christian identity for both the building and the cemetery.[20]

There is a considerable body of evidence to support this view. It is to the presumed extra-mural churches that we should turn, and first to the apsidal buildings. The church of St Pancras, Canterbury, is situated outside the walls of Roman Durovernum Cantiacorum, close to both a Romano-British inhumation and a Christian Saxon cemetery (Brooks 1977: fig. 1). This is entirely in accordance with the archaeological evidence for the building: the phase II church had burials within the chancel by the seventh century, contemporaneous with some of the early Saxon burials in the cemetery (Jenkins 1976: 4). The building designated Colchester 9, at Butt Road, Colchester, was located about 150 metres south-west of the *colonia*, and activity on the site continued from about 320–40 to the fifth century (Crummy 1980: 274). Immediately to the east of the building was a fourth-century west–east cemetery, overlying an earlier north–south one. The later cemetery had characteristics which indicate a Christian identity, while the earlier one had features which are generally recognised as pagan (see above, ch. III). There are indications that the building may have been a martyrial church (Crossan, in Crummy 1980: 265–6). At Icklingham, the purging of the site with the layer of chalk was followed by both the erection of the apsidal building and the commencement of a cemetery of west–east, supine, extended, undisturbed and generally unaccompanied graves, which included at least one neo-natal burial. These features point to a Christian identification for the cemetery (above, ch. III), and the stratigraphy and location of the cemetery and building make it certain they were associated. A church identification cannot be doubted, even without the corroborating evidence of lead tanks with *chi-rho* and a structure confidently identified as a baptismal font. The apsidal building known as Verulamium 7, in the Verulam Hills Field, is less certain. It was located in an area where burials from the Belgic period to the fourth century were found. The latest of these burials, a group of nine or so west–east, supine, extended, undisturbed and unaccompanied graves were located some 150 metres down the slope from this building, and, although there is no reason to believe they were not associated with it, there is not the close relationship of building and cemetery noted above. Of the building itself, the archaeologist notes an absence of all domestic features, and, while not committing herself on its identification, says, 'The only fact which might suggest that this building was a Christian shrine is that it stands near the cemetery' (Anthony 1968: 50). This association and identification have not been challenged.

116

Of the rectangular structures, the stone building no. 23 from Nettleton, having a lower level which opened on to a path leading directly into a cemetery, was very probably a cemetery chapel. As was observed earlier, this lower room may have been used for the preparation of the *refrigerium* or meal celebrated at the tomb of the deceased on anniversaries of birth or death, a Roman pagan practice which was known to have continued into Christian times. A parallel is found on the Continent: Radford (1968: 31) notes that at Xanten, in the Rhineland, there was a small two-celled rectangular building over the burials of 'martyrs' dating to about 385, and that from the beginning meals were eaten here. The Nettleton cemetery had characteristics which point to a Christian identity, and the path connecting the building and cemetery makes their association undoubted.

Brean Down and Lamyatt Beacon rectangular buildings will be considered together, since they have very similar features. The evidence is not so clearcut here. The cemeteries with which they were apparently associated[21] displayed features which could identify them as Christian, and therefore it was proposed in Chapter III that they were Christian burial grounds. Yet they do not seem to have been contemporaneous with these presumed churches or oratories. The date of the abandonment of neither building has been indicated, but a well-constructed stone building could stand for a hundred years or so, particularly if it were in reasonably regular use. The association of a Christian cemetery with a ruined church seems less easy to accept, although there may be something in Leech's suggestion (1986: 273) that perhaps these cemeteries 'were deliberately sited close to what was known to have once been a sacred place'. Unfortunately much of the evidence has been lost, but, on balance, it is felt that these two buildings would have been Christian, and the presence of the cemeteries enhances such identification.

There are three sites which require separate treatment because they do not fit the pattern of any of the above examples. The first is that of the cathedral at St Albans. It has previously been proposed as most likely of Roman origin, and one might assume it would have been one of the earliest places of Christian public worship built after the Peace of the Church. Current excavations have revealed Roman inhumations and cremations. This is one case where it would not be surprising to find Christian burials amongst pagan, since it would have been extremely unlikely that there would have been any Christian burial ground in Britain at the time of Alban's martyrdom, although such cemeteries evidently existed at Rome (Hippolytus, *Apostolic Tradition* 40). Even on the evidence so far published, there seems little doubt that the present church is the descendant of the first martyrial church at Roman Verulamium. It may have been built amidst a pagan, rather than Christian, cemetery; alternatively, Alban's burial may have been the first at this site, with a wholly Christian cemetery growing up around it.[22]

The second site is Stone-by-Faversham, in Kent. Thomas (1981: 183–4) has set out a brief history of the building and in his summary says, 'The missing link is any real evidence of a later or sub-Roman use of [this structure] to house a Christian burial.' What Thomas seems to have missed is the possible connection between this building and Ospringe cemetery, less than 700 metres away, and with the later west–east burials around the mausoleum. The presence of a mausoleum in Roman Britain suggests, on the current evidence, a private, and probably pagan, burial connected with a villa, or a private enclosure within a general cemetery, such enclosure having a likely Christian identity (see below, ch. VI). No evidence has yet been produced for a villa in the vicinity of the building, but there is a cemetery. This cemetery of cremations and inhumations dated from the second to the fourth century, and seems to have been pagan. There is, however, just the possibility that part of it may have been taken over for Christian burials. The report by Whiting *et al.* (1931) is sketchy, and there was no plan of the cemetery published. But, if one can go by the date of the excavation of the various burials and their grouping together in the report, there appears to have been a number of west–east burials, including a small group of seven or more generally unaccompanied inhumations in Area E of the cemetery (Whiting *et al.* 1931: 33–7). There was no evidence of decapitation, or of prone burial (although it must be pointed out that the skeletal remains of the cemetery were generally in a very poor state of preservation). These inhumations might have been, as in Lankhills feature 6, a small number of Christians buried as a discrete group in a pagan cemetery. There can be little doubt that there were Christians at Ospringe by the late fourth century. It is barely 15 kilometres from Canterbury, where there has been found considerable evidence for Romano-British Christianity.

The above sample is, however, far too small for definite

conclusions to be drawn. The lack of evidence in the cemetery forces a reconsideration of the Stone-by-Faversham church itself. Three points may be noted: there appears, on pottery evidence, to have been Saxon activity in the area from the earliest Saxon period (Fletcher and Meates 1969: 284; 1977: 70); the floor of the mausoleum seems to have been repaired by these early Saxons (Fletcher and Meates 1969: 280); and perhaps most importantly, 'many' west–east burials over a considerable period and at different levels were made on both the north and south sides of the Roman building (Fletcher and Meates 1969: 282). The first two points suggest that there was probably not the gap of three or more centuries inferred by Thomas (1981: 184) between Romano-British and Saxon use. In fact, the excavators, commenting on the clay surface within the later nave area, suggest that 'there might have been a space for worshippers immediately west of the mausoleum, dating back perhaps even to the days of St Augustine's mission' (Fletcher and Meates 1977: 69), that is, that the building may have been first extended early in the seventh century. There is then the question of why this building, if a pagan burial site, was the focus of so many later west–east and presumably Christian burials over such a long period.[23] One interpretation of the evidence is that, if Christian burials were found in the vicinity of Christian religious buildings, as has been proposed in this study, it is likely that the original Roman mausoleum on the site of the Chapel of Our Lady of Elwarton at Stone-by-Faversham was for a Christian burial.

The final site to be considered with regard to the association of cemeteries and churches is that of St Paul-in-the-Bail, Lincoln. The site has produced a series of structural foundations, the earliest before 450, and probably of Roman, rather than sub-Roman, date. This early building is unusual on two counts and it is these unusual features that make dating difficult. The first is that it is sited in the forum of the *colonia*; the second, that a burial with a medial radio-carbon date of AD 370 was found within the building, on the chord of the apse. There does not appear to be any doubt that the building was a church: the continuity of use of the original rectangular outline, illustrated by Colyer and Gilmour (1978: 104), and the continued use of the site for a church, would seem to confirm this.

The location of the church does seem to be unusual for Roman Britain. Towns thought to have a temple *on* the forum were mentioned above. It is the only known British example of a religious building *in* a forum, although on the Continent parallels for temples in fora do exist: Goodchild (1946) and Duval (1961) illustrate sites where the temple is placed in as prominent a position in the forum as is the church at Lincoln. The major difference between the continental and the British sites is that there the forum enclosures are larger, and therefore the temples occupy proportionately less space than does the Lincoln church. Questions arise: would the civil authorities of late fourth-century Lincoln have had sufficient devotion to Christianity to build a church in such a prominent position? Would they have countenanced an intra-mural burial in this church? Finally, why was the burial there? These questions will be dealt with first; an alternative sequence of events will then be offered, which also raises questions.[24]

Given the parallels of temples within fora from the Continent, there cannot have been any legal bar to the erection of a church in much the same position. With imperial promotion of Christianity, it is possible that civic-minded *curiales* would have accepted the challenge to emulate the imperial church-building programme, and if, as seems highly probable, Lincoln had been a bishopric since early in the century, the religion cannot have been seen, some half-century later, as a passing fad, especially as it had official endorsement. One further point: Vitruvius (1.7.1), writing on the location of temples, said that an elevated position overlooking the city should be reserved for the patron gods of the city and for the Capitoline Triad, while a temple to Mercury should be built in the forum, or, as for Isis and Serapis, in the public square. Once the religious allegiance of the emperor had been transferred to the Christian faith, it would seem appropriate to build a church in as prominent position in the *colonia*. There is, therefore, no reason why a church should not have been built in the forum at Lincoln during this stage of the Roman occupation.

As to the second question, the legality of the intra-mural burial, it has been shown in Chapter III that Roman law was strict in its adherence to the clause of the Twelve Tables forbidding such a practice. However, exceptions were known: Trajan's remains were buried under the column in the forum he built (Dio Cassius, 68.16; 69,2); Cicero (*De legibus* 2.23.58) tells how Publicola and Tubertus were given the privilege of intra-mural burial, and that this right was retained by their descendants; others, such as Gaius

Fabricius, were exempted from the law because of their personal merit. Plutarch (*Quaestiones Romanae* 79; *Publicola* 23) also mentions Fabricius and Publicola, adding of the latter that he was buried, by express vote of the citizens, within the city, on the Palatine, overlooking the Forum. In her study of Roman burial practices, Toynbee (1971: n. 158) relates that Gaius Julius Celsus Polemaeanus, founder of the library at Ephesus, was given the privilege of being buried in it. Evidently the rule could be waived in special cases.

There is an example from the later Christian period which may provide the answer to the third question and the key to the puzzle: Sozomen (*Ecclesiastical History* 5.19) records that Gallus Caesar, in an attempt to stifle the pagan oracle of Apollo at Daphne, near Antioch, ordered the burial of the martyr, Babylas, at the temple site. The burial at Lincoln must have been a 'special' case; it may well have been that of a martyr, since this was the period when it began to become fashionable to import sacred relics. If this were so, no 'ordinary' intra-mural burials would have been permitted in addition; and such a situation would have held firm until probably some time after the Roman withdrawal (J. Drinkwater, pers. comm.). This accords with the evidence: the second burial, outside the church, has a date of 450.

An alternative sequence of events is possible: that the church was built some little time after the withdrawal of the imperial forces, and that the AD 370 burial on the chord of the apse, possibly of an early bishop or even yet of a martyr, was a translated one. But the question arises: would there have been the impetus, or the resources, to erect such a building in a period when the economy was returning to subsistence, and Christianity was losing its hold? It would seem, after careful consideration of the implications of the alternative, that the first is the more acceptable; it is proposed, therefore, that the building on the site of St Paul-in-the-Bail was of Roman date.

This then brings us to the question of the association of cemetery and church at the Lincoln site. It will be noted that only one external burial was made before the original building decayed, but burials still went on over the ruins. When the small Saxon rectangular structure was erected, the inhumations continued. There cannot be any doubt of the connection of the cemetery with the original building, and this reinforces the identification of this and all the subsequent buildings on the site as Christian churches.

The association of cemeteries with religious buildings must now be evaluated as a criterion for identification as Christian. The combination of contemporaneous burials and building would normally occur only in extra-mural sites in the Roman period, and should, it is felt, be given the maximum ranking on an evidential scale. A combination involving only later burials still preserves the tradition of sanctity, but would rank slightly less, perhaps a little above three-quarters.

After a discussion of St Paul-in-the-Bail, it is appropriate to look at apsidal foci as possible Christian indicators. The placement of the altar in an early apsidal Christian church was usually on the chord of the apse or just into the nave. This came to be seen as the holiest place in the church, and the location for the tombs of martyrs or for reliquaries with some remains of a martyr. If the tomb was below ground level, the altar was placed over the burial. If above ground, it became the altar. The authority for such burials was probably *Revelation* 6.9: 'And when he had opened the fifth seal, I saw under the altar the souls of them that were slain for the word of God, and for the testimony which they held.'[25] In buildings without a projection of some kind, it would be less easy to recognise the site of the altar, although, if the church at Aquileia may be taken as a guide, a semi-circular *synthronon* for clergy marked the place before which the altar stood (Radford 1968: 28). In the third-century house church at Dura-Europus, however, the altar appears to have been placed against a wall (Gough 1973: fig. 24), and in a small sixth- or seventh-century oratory-type church at Ardnadam in Argyll, Scotland, the base for the altar is against the eastern wall (Rennie 1984: fig. 15). Perhaps much depended on the size of the building.

In Roman Britain, there is no such feature in the presumed rectangular churches, although it could be suggested that the 2.1 m × 0.9 m masonry structure against the eastern wall of the mausoleum at Stone-by-Faversham (Fletcher and Meates 1969: pl. LVIb) served the purpose of an altar behind a central burial in the earliest (Roman?) phase of the building as a church. This study will, however, concentrate on apsidal structures. The burial at St-Paul-in-the-Bail has been discussed above. It may have been the body of a martyr, an early bishop or even a saintly lay person. Such were the people whose remains were venerated, to the disgust of Julian the Apostate (*Against the Galileans* 335C, Loeb edn). At Colchester 9, it has been proposed (Crossan, in Crummy 1980:

265–6) that the feature just into the nave, below the apse, was a pair of burials: one was north–south, the other east–west, located on the southern side of the nave, with space left, presumably for other burials, on the opposite side of the building; a skull, found in an earlier excavation (Hull 1958: 245–8), is thought to be that of the north–south burial. The whole feature suggests that the church was a *martyrium*. At Silchester, the apsidal building has a square geometrical mosaic arranged in a cruciform just below the chord of the apse, and this, it is thought, marked the position of the altar, possibly originally made of wood, then later replaced by stone (Frere 1975: 293). Finally, the mosaic at Frampton, a possible estate chapel, has on the chord of the apse a *chi-rho*. It has been proposed that use of this symbol in a group of mosaics whose motifs include Cupid and Bacchus, Neptune and dolphins, Bellerophon and the Chimaera and a central cantharus in the apse merely indicates that the owner had a 'heterodox approach to religion, and treated Christ here no more nor less than as a pagan god' (Henig 1986: 164); but it would seem more likely that the prominent position of the *chi-rho* in relation to the three rooms which make up the suite emphasises the Christianity of the site. This point will be taken up below, in a discussion of the shape and layout of house churches.

As evidence for Christianity, these apsidal features are not of equal importance. A burial here must rank at the maximum, since it was a peculiarly Christian practice, and continued into relatively modern times. A mosaic feature which is not unequivocally Christian, such as the Silchester example, (but may, of course, be interpreted as a disguised cross)[26] could be ranked at two-thirds; possible evidence for an altar, at the same level.

The ground plans of purported churches are now studied, in an attempt to detect any trend in Romano-British church architecture. As was stated earlier, the most common plan for the Christian church was that taken from the secular basilica, and this layout was adopted, adapted and added to throughout the Empire. In Britain, there were several possible churches built on the true basilical plan. The building at Silchester has the additional feature of quasi-transepts, which Frere (1975: 293) says are 'specific indications of church architecture', a fact which those who argue against a Christian identity for the building[27] are apt to overlook. As yet the Colchester 9 building is not fully published, but preliminary reports suggest it, too, had aisles and a narthex, and that the apse may have been an addition (Crossan, in Crummy 1980: 266 and pers. comm.). At St Albans, Verulamium 6 is a late Roman basilical building with rectangular, rather than semi-circular, projections, one at each end (Wheeler and Wheeler 1936: 122–3 and pl. XXXV).

The simple apsidal plan seems to have been more common in Britain, and, although it was used for the quasi-religious *scholae*, there is no suggestion that such buildings were, in fact, churches. They are eliminated from this discussion. One intra-mural apsidal building which was a probable church was the first structure on the site of St Paul-in-the-Bail at Lincoln. Extra-mural examples include St Pancras at Canterbury, the small structure at Icklingham, and Verulamium 7 at St Albans. To this list the building at Richborough should be added, because although its apsidal feature is only conjectured, Brown's (1971) continental parallels are apsidal, and his case is convincingly argued. Building 8 at Uley (Ellison 1980: fig. 5.3) has a rectangular projection, similar to those of Verulamium 6. Finally, the cathedral church at Canterbury may have had Roman origins, and, if Lewis (1966: 114) is correct, Eadmer's description of the church restored by Bishop Odo suggests a western apse. This would have conformed to the church plan which seemed more common in urban than rural areas of Britain: of the ten buildings referred to above, basilical or simple apsidal, only two, Uley 8 and Icklingham, may be classed as rural.

The rectangular buildings are, without exception, from rural areas: Uley 7 and Witham, which, although intra-mural, were situated in religious complexes that were rural, and the extra-mural structures at Brean Down, Lamyatt Beacon, and Nettleton building 23. The problem of identification of the rectangular churches was recognised by Radford (1968: 31) in his discussion of the 'hall' at Abodiacum in the Rhineland, which was also a church: 'These buildings seldom show Christian characteristics. Their function as churches is established either by a continuous Christian tradition, or by their association with inscriptions or other objects.' Unfortunately, the objects and inscriptions are, to date, notably absent from presumed Christian sites in Roman Britain; the evidence for 'continuous Christian tradition' is, as shown above, one criterion for identification of these sites.

This leaves two other buildings which have formed part of this study, Stone-by-Faversham and Nettleton Octagonal. The Stone building was built as a mausoleum, and, even if adopted as a church, cannot be considered to be a purpose-built church. The Nettleton building, if it was a church, is, so far as is known, unique to Britain, in that it was converted from a pagan shrine. Wedlake (1982: 63, 104) sees the converted cruciform shape as resembling that of the fifth-century oratory of St Lawrence (known as the tomb of Galla Placidia) at Ravenna. For identification of the Nettleton building as a church, much hinges on whether the well-known, and not necessarily contradictory, instructions of Pope Gregory to Augustine and Ethelbert (Bede, *Historia ecclesiastica* 1.30, 32) were a new papal initiative, or if Gregory was following a policy of his predecessors. Socrates (*Historia ecclesiastica* 4.24) implies that the conversion of temples was official policy even in the fourth century, and archaeological evidence suggests the re-use of pagan or secular buildings was not unknown two or three centuries before Augustine: at Salona, on the Adriatic Coast, an early oratory may previously have been a pagan water shrine, and another rectangular one, pre-dating the Peace of the Church, used a private baths suite erected a hundred years before (Dyggve 1951: 23–4, fig. II.7). The use of a pagan shrine for a church at Nettleton would thus not be unique in the fourth century.

The plan of proposed churches must be assessed as evidence. In view of the widespread use by the Church of the basilical or simple apsidal shape, it must be seen to be a pointer to a Christian identity. Despite the fact that the plan was not exclusive to Christian buildings, it would seem that any fourth-century building with such a layout would have a fairly good chance of being Christian. However, as weighted evidence, the apsidal shape could rank only one-half; the rectangular church would be impossible to identity, and therefore could not be weighted at all, unless there is some internal feature which marks *synthronon* or altar.

House churches are a special category, and their layout is dealt with separately. There are few models. Nevertheless, if the example from Dura-Europus (Gough 1973: fig. 24), a certain house church, and that from Lullingstone (Meates 1955: fig. 13a), an almost-certain one, are examined, common features emerge. The complex at Dura included a baptistery, but since not every church had a baptistery, this is not an essential characteristic. Moreover, it is likely that some baptisms in private houses took place in bathrooms (Davies 1962: 314). Both sites had a vestibule, and an ante-room, the purpose of which would have been similar to the narthex in a church, that is, where catechumens were relegated during the administering of the Sacrament, and where they were instructed in the faith. The chapel proper was off this ante-room. At Dura, this room had a focus: a platform, presumably for an altar, against a shorter, eastern wall. The situation at Lullingstone is not so clear: the west wall as one enters the chapel was covered with a mural depicting *orantes*; on each of the two shorter walls, perhaps the back and front of the chapel, a *chi-rho* was painted (Meates 1955: fig. 13; Wright 1970: 312). Both suites of rooms were cut off from the rest of the building, and had their own entrances.

From this description, it should be possible to extrapolate what are probably the essential or highly desirable features of a house church. There seemed to be the need for two rooms, since only the baptised were admitted for the actual Eucharist. It also seems significant that the suite of rooms could be entered without having to come from somewhere in the adjoining building, and that the whole suite was separate from the rest of the house. As part of the chapel proper, a religious focus also seems desirable. It is realised, of course, that these are architectural features only, which could well be replicated in a totally secular context. Nevertheless, it is a starting point for the recognition of possible house churches, as opposed merely to houses owned by Christians.

But, because of this, the weighting of such evidence should be reduced by half. The availability of two or more adjoining rooms and some kind of focus, apsidal or otherwise, would rank on this half-level. A location separated from the rest of the building would seem important, but it would also be possible to have doors which could be locked to achieve the same effect, and this would not always be detectable archaeologically; this feature therefore cannot rate. A separate entrance would probably be important if the church were to serve a wider circle than just the residents of the associated house or villa; in view of the few complete plans available, however, this type of evidence could, as yet, rate only about one-quarter.

The plans of possible Romano-British house churches will now be examined and tentative conclusions reached; further discussion will be delayed until the following section. The sites are: Caerwent House XXII N (Ashby *et al.* 1911: 411–12; pl. LVII), Chedworth (Goodburn 1979), Frampton 'villa' (Farrar 1957), Hinton St Mary

(Painter 1968: 1976), Littlecote (see above, ch. II n. 18, for references), St Mary de Lode at Gloucester (Bryant 1980), and Woodchester (Clarke 1982: fig. 1).

The Caerwent house had a suite of rooms which was not accessible directly from the street. There may have been an entrance at the side of the building. A block of four rooms seems to have been converted to one smaller room (vestibule?), a room with a rough stone slab floor (baptistery?), another almost-square room (narthex?) which opened into the largest rectangular room (chapel?), into whose eastern end an apse had been inserted.[28] The floor of this apsidal room had a pavement of red brick *tesserae*, with the apse covered in what was probably a red, white and blue mosaic, the report suggesting a 'finer pavement' for this area. Dating on coin evidence is the fourth century, with activity to the second half of that century. This site has all the architectural features which seem to be desirable for a house church.

The purpose of the complex at Chedworth has recently been called into question (Webster 1984) but, as yet, there is little to suggest it was other than a villa. The site is not fully excavated, and the many sequences of construction make identification of a suite of rooms as a possible house church hazardous at best. Rooms 24a, 25 and 25a could have constituted such a house church, and the dating seems to have been late third or early fourth century (Goodburn 1979: 22 and fig. 3). Room 25, the apsidal room, ceased to be heated in the later period. There does not, however, appear to have been any separate entrance to these rooms, nor is there evidence for any mosaic or other feature in the apsidal room, although there was a mosaic in room 25a adjoining. There is no recorded connection between the *chi-rho* stones found at the site and these rooms, so the possibility that these rooms constituted a house church here is fairly remote.

The building at Frampton is a more likely prospect. Over the years it has consistently been referred to as a 'villa', but is very likely not one (Farrar 1957). The low-lying position and the absence of outbuildings normal for a villa suggest it may have had another purpose. No plans are available, as the site has been lost, but the mosaic gives a good indication of the layout of the suite. It was, apparently, a semi-detached structure of a smaller rectangular room (narthex?) opening onto a larger, squarish one (chapel?), and at right angles to this larger room, an apse with a cantharus as its central motif and a *chi-rho* on the chord. The motifs of the mosaics have been much discussed, but Toynbee's interpretation (1968) seems the most realistic. In view of Farrar's findings, it may, in fact, have been an estate chapel.

The Hinton St Mary villa, famous for its mosaic which is generally accepted as a portrayal of Christ, with a *chi-rho* behind the figure, had two rectilinear mosaics, and again Toynbee's interpretation seems to fit the evidence: the smaller room, with Bellerophon and the Chimaera, was probably the narthex; the larger room, the chapel. Although there was no apse here, there does appear to have been wear on the mosaic beyond the Christ roundel away from the 'congregation' area, which may have been where the priest stood, behind a portable altar, facing the congregation (Toynbee 1968: 185). The two rooms cannot, on the available evidence, be said to be cut off from the rest of the building, since the whole villa site has not been plotted (see Painter 1968: fig. 1). Nevertheless, a house church is still a possibility.

The Littlecote site is far less certain as Christian, although the arrangement of the two-room mosaic is in the form of a rectangular and a triple-apsed room, which Smith (1978: 134) says is exactly like a church at Binbirkilise in Turkey in its dimensions; but that small chapel is dated to the fifth or sixth century (Ramsay and Bell 1909: 25, 79–80). The Littlecote building appears separate from the associated villa, so could well have had a religious function. However, the mosaics, which have been variously interpreted, do not seem to be Christian.

St Mary de Lode, Gloucester, has been suggested as the site of a church or mausoleum from the sub-Roman period (Bryant 1980: 4), and, indeed, this is a very reasonable proposal since the site continued in use as a church in the ninth and tenth centuries, on the alignment of the original Roman buildings. It may be that the predecessor to the sub-Roman structure was a house church. Although the plan of this early period (period 2) has not been fully traced, it does seem that adjoining rooms would have made the existence of a suite for a church a possibility, and their decoration does not preclude such identification. Moreover, there is an 1825 record of a mosaic with decoration of a wreathed border surrounding figures of fish (Bryant 1980: 6), and, although this pavement was not found during the 1978–9 excavations, Bryant has proposed that the room would have adjoined those already plotted. There is insufficient archaeological detail to ascertain if any suite of rooms would have had a separate entrance, as the site is still occupied by a church.

The layout of the villa at Woodchester, with its great Orpheus pavement and ante-rooms on each side (Clarke 1982: fig. 1), could readily be adapted to a house church, and the date proposed for the mosaic, the early part of the fourth century, probably before 325 (Cookson 1984: 50), would suit the use of the Orpheus motif as a crypto-Christian symbol. It is a great pity that the central roundel had been destroyed at Woodchester, since the displacement of Orpheus from the normal focal position in the mosaic would seem to have had some special significance. With regard to the layout, as there are no plans available, there is no way of determining whether any suite of rooms which could be used as a church had its own entrance.

Floor plans have been studied as a means of recognising Romano-British churches; orientation should also be examined as a possible aid to identification. It was pointed out early in this chapter that the Constantinian buildings were both east–west and west–east; and there were some which were south-north. Of the buildings analysed here whose orientation is known, there seems to be an overwhelming preference for east–west or west–east: only one, at Witham, is north–south, and its entrance may have been from the west (Turner 1982: fig. 17). There are several which do not align on the cardinal points, however. It seems that, since Christian churches did not finally settle down to a standard west–east orientation until the end of the fourth century, orientation as a criterion for identification would be hazardous, and is, therefore, best not ranked.

Of the evidence classified as internal, a final feature which may assist in identification is the existence of a baptistery or a baptismal font in association with a purported church. At two sites only, Icklingham (West 1976) and Richborough (Brown 1971), has the identification of a font been universally accepted. At Icklingham, the structure was apsidal in shape, with a step taking up part of the basin; at Richborough, it was a hexagon. However, there may have been others at as many as six further sites, and these will be dealt with in order of probability of a Christian identity.

The almost-square structure at Silchester (Frere 1975) is accepted by many scholars as a font, and the re-interpretation of the archaeological evidence by Thomas (1981: 214–15) is persuasive. One further point could be added. There has been little emphasis in any discussion of the Silchester site on the fact that there are two structures here, the second, smaller one being generally interpreted as a soakway. In view of the fact that footwashing appears to have been part of the baptismal ceremony in the Celtic areas of the Empire as well as in those areas where the Eastern Church dominated, it is proposed here that the second structure could have been for this part of the baptismal rite. A similar arrangement could have been at Witham, where an octagonal structure is located next to a 'sump', but there is a also a soakway to the east. It appears, however, that the sump was filled in the final Roman phase of the site, when the presumed font was enclosed in a wooden box about 2 metres square, and the outsides of this frame packed with clay (Turner 1982: 21–2). It may have been that the footwashing ritual in the baptism ceremony ceased in the later part of the fourth century,[29] or that the number of converts dropped to a size where it could be carried out by the officiant who had also performed the baptism. (See below, chapter V.2 for a discussion of the baptismal rite in the fourth century.)

At Uley, the later presumed-Christian building, no. 7, has what the excavator originally thought was an irregular apsidal extension to the north-west (Ellison 1980: 314); however, she now believes that this was part of a D-shaped or apsidal baptistery (A. Ellison, pers. comm.). If this was the case, it may be worth while looking at another structure at the Uley complex, no. 3, which is contemporaneous with the earlier presumed church. This is a four-sided feature in the shape of a half-hexagon, with two shorter wings flanking two longer sides. Ellison has not postulated a purpose for this structure; if, however, there was a baptistery with the later church, building no. 7, it is a reasonable assumption that its predecessor also had one.

The site at St Paul-in-the-Bail, Lincoln, has been discussed at length above. One feature that was not mentioned in that discussion was the existence of a Roman well of elaborate and sound construction and an adjoining small room situated on the forum, where one would expect to find shops (Jones *et al.* 1982: 368–9). These features were immediately adjacent to the original apsidal building in the forum, and it could well be that they formed the water supply and the room for a baptistery associated with the first church on the site. The construction of the well pre-dated the presumed church (M. Jones, pers. comm.), but the siting of the church may have been influenced by the presence of an existing source of water for baptisms.

The last two sites, Caerwent house XXII N, and Chedworth villa, could also have had baptisteries. In the Caerwent building, in the suite of rooms proposed as a house church, room 1 with its rough stone floor could readily serve this purpose. There is also, as 'external evidence', the fact that house VII N, where a pewter bowl with *chi-rho* was found hidden under the floor (Boon 1962), was only about 100 metres from the building XXII. It is possible that a house church in this position would not have lacked a congregation, and an associated baptistery, candidates. There is, however, no Christian evidence at the site itself, nor is there any structure which might be interpreted as a font. The rooms could have had a multitude of other purposes. At Chedworth, as has been mentioned, the nymphaeum may have been converted to a baptistery, and Christian evidence does exist at the site. It remains to find convincing evidence of an associated church or chapel.

In an evaluation of the evidence for baptisteries, it is thought that, where no doubts exist, that is, at Icklingham and Richborough, the maximum ranking should be given. Where some doubt does still exist, the evidence should be discounted: Silchester a level below maximum; Witham and Uley, until the final reports of those sites are published, at about three-quarters; Lincoln, perhaps one-half, since the identity of the church is not doubted; Chedworth, one-quarter; Caerwent cannot rank.

At Uley, the later presumed Christian building, no. 7 in the Interim Report, has what the excavator originally thought was an irregular apsidal extension to the north–west (Ellison 1980: 314); however, she now believes that this was part of a polygonal baptistery (pers. comm.).[30]

A consideration of external evidence which may also assist in the identification of churches will be brief, since this was carried out in some depth in the previous chapter on the identification of Christian cemeteries, and the reasons for the inclusion of various features and for the weightings were given there.

The literary evidence of the attendance of British bishops at the Council of Arles, while indicating a Christian presence in London, York and probably Lincoln, cannot be taken necessarily to indicate the existence of churches in 314, although it is likely, and much more so in the later part of the century. As evidence it would rank one level below maximum. Bede's accounts of churches at Canterbury and St Albans should be taken at face value (cf. Thomas 1981: 131–2) and given the maximum.

The remaining evidence will be weighted at the same level as for cemeteries. Objects with Christian symbols warrant the maximum ranking: the lead tanks, graffiti on sherds, objects with little intrinsic value incorporating Christian symbols (with a discounting for more valuable portable items) and Christian villas; Christian hoards with *chi-rho* or similar, three-quarters; hoards with less explicit Christian symbols, one-half; destruction of pagan artefacts or sites, one-half; with re-use by Christian, three-quarters; and datable pagan hoards, one-third.

The evidence, both internal and external, for buildings which have been proposed as Christian churches has now been analysed, assessed and ranked on an evidential scale. As with the study on cemeteries, external evidence is considered to be of less value than internal and will be weighted at half that of internal. The various criteria and their relative value in the identification of churches are summarised in Figure 13.

2: APPLICATION OF THE CRITERIA

As part of the process of identifying fourth- or early-fifth-century structures as churches, the first section of this study was devoted to an examination of the internal and external evidence, and characteristics common to some or all proposed churches were indicated. These were then discussed and evaluated as evidence, and a set of ranked criteria was developed. The criteria have now been applied to those sites which have been suggested as Christian. While the numbers involved are small, and may not closely reflect trends in the fourth century, the results themselves may be seen as a guide to identification; for instance, although there are only two features which are common to all sites, there are several common to more than half. If the buildings are classified as intra-mural, extra-mural and house churches, certain dominant features emerge within each category; and if a division into urban and rural sites is made, other predominant features are revealed. Therefore, while it is not possible to give a long list of characteristics which would virtually guarantee a Christian identity for a fourth- or fifth-century building, it is possible to indicate some features which are deemed essential, others which are highly desirable, and others again which are useful, in attempting the identification of Romano-British Christian churches. Various sites, and their likelihood of a Christian identity, are proposed at the end of the chapter.

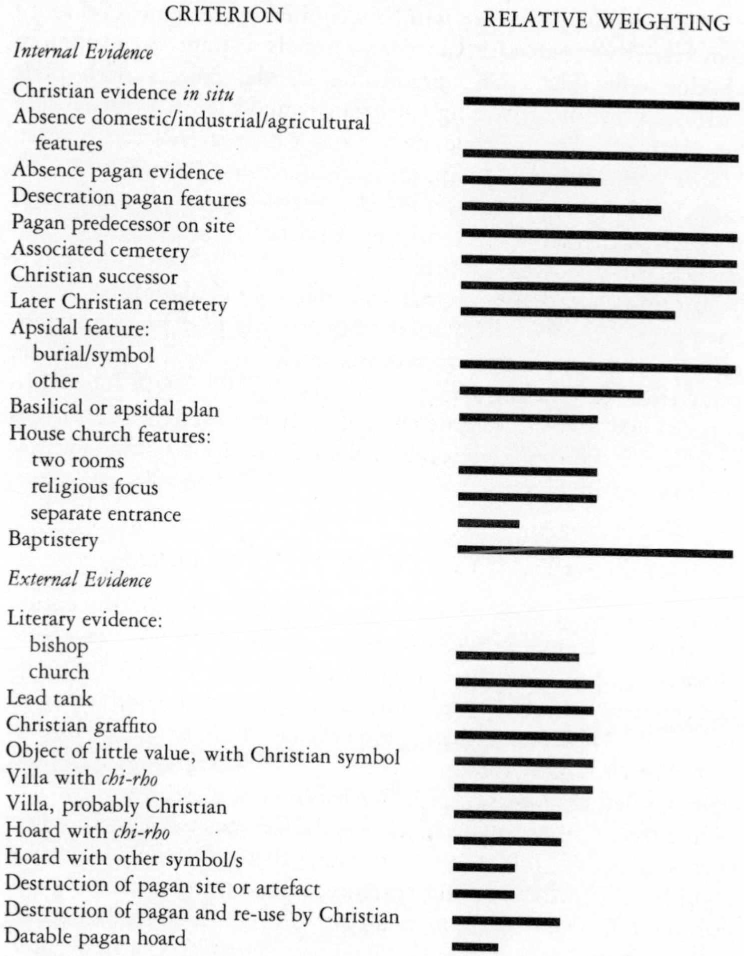

CRITERION   RELATIVE WEIGHTING

Internal Evidence

Christian evidence *in situ*
Absence domestic/industrial/agricultural
  features
Absence pagan evidence
Desecration pagan features
Pagan predecessor on site
Associated cemetery
Christian successor
Later Christian cemetery
Apsidal feature:
  burial/symbol
  other
Basilical or apsidal plan
House church features:
  two rooms
  religious focus
  separate entrance
Baptistery

External Evidence

Literary evidence:
  bishop
  church
Lead tank
Christian graffito
Object of little value, with Christian symbol
Villa with *chi-rho*
Villa, probably Christian
Hoard with *chi-rho*
Hoard with other symbol/s
Destruction of pagan site or artefact
Destruction of pagan and re-use by Christian
Datable pagan hoard

Figure 13   Criteria for identification of Christian churches, and relative
weightings

In Part 1, five sites which had been suggested by different
writers as possible Christian churches were eliminated; thus only
sites which are fourth- to fifth-century and have the possibility of a
Christian identity have been considered in detail. In the
examination of the results of this survey, it is felt that internal
evidence should be the yardstick by which the possible Christianity
of a site is measured, although the total of internal and external

Site	Approximate date of building	Shape (✓ with square projection/s)	Orientation (entrance first) ✓ entrance uncertain)	Approximate internal size (metres)	Urban or rural	Christian evidence *in situ* [10]	Absence dom. indust. or agric. features (* presumed) [10]	Absence pagan features (* presumed) [5]	Desecration pagan features or [9]	Pagan predecessor on site (✓ not weighted twice) [9]	Associated cemetery [10]	Christian successor or [9]	Later Christian cemetery (✓ not weighted twice) [8]	Apsidal burial or symbol (* presumed) or [10]	Other apsidal feature [7]	Basilical or apsidal plan (* presumed) [5]	Two rooms [5]	Religious focus [5]	Separate entrance [2]	Baptistery [10]
Intra-mural																				
Canterbury Cathedral	4?	Apsidal?	E–W?	—	U		*	*		?		9	<			5				?
Lincoln St Paul-in-the-Bail	4	Basilical	W–E	c.16 × 7.6	U		10	5	3	?		9	<	10		5				

House church — columns: Two rooms, Religious focus, Separate entrance

Site	Date	Plan	Orientation	Dimensions (m)	Type	1	2	3	4	5	6	7	8	9	10	11	12	13	14
Nettleton Octagonal	330–60	Cruciform	SE–NW	dia. 7.0	R	6	10	5	9	<	9	5		7		*			10
Richborough	4–5?	Apsidal?	W–E?	17.0 × 9.0	U?	7	10	5	?	?	?	9	?				2	2	9
Silchester 9	mid 4?	Basilical	E–W	10.3 × 7.5	U		10	5	9	?	9	9	8				5	2	7
Uley building 7	5	Rect.^	SE–NW	4.7 × 2.6	R		10	5	9	<	9	9	10				5	2	3
Uley building 8	380	Rect.^	NE–SW	3.7 × 3.0	R		10	5	9	<	9		10				5	?	
Verulamium 6	4	Basilical^	SE–NW^	14.0 × 11.6	U		10	5			9		?				5	2	9
Witham	330–60	Rect.	N–S^	3.4 × 1.9	R		10	5	9	<	9		7	?			5	2	
Extra-mural																			
Brean Down	370	Rect.	W–E	3.8 × 2.3	R		10	5	9	<	9	5	<				5		
Canterbury, St Pancras	late 4	Apsidal	W–E	12.8 × 8.0	U		10	5	9	<	?	9	8				5		
Colchester 9 (Butt Road)	320–5th	Basilical	W–E	22.6 × 6.2	U		10	5	5	?	9	?	10		8	10	5	2	10
Icklingham	350	Apsidal	W–E	6.3 × 4.0	R		10	5	9	<	5	?	10				5	?	
Lamyatt Beacon	300+	Rect.	W–E	3.0 × 2.0	R		10	5	9	<	9	?	?		8		5	2	
Nettleton building 23	330+	Rect.	SE–NW^	6.7 × 3.6	R		10	5	9	<	5	<	10		<		5	2	
Stone-by-Faversham	4	Rect.	W–E	4.0 × 3.6	R		10	5	9	?	9	?	?		<		5	?	
Verulamium St Alban	–	–	–	–	U		*	*		3		?	10				5	2	
Verulamium 7	4	Apsidal	SE–NW	13.4 × 8.0	U		10	5	3	3	?	?	7	?			5	?	
House/Estate church																			
Caerwent XXIX N	4	4 rooms			U				9								5		
Chedworth	4	3 rooms?			R	5			<					<			5	2	
Frampton	mid 4?	2 rooms			R	10			9		9						5	5	
Gloucester St Mary de Lode	4?	–			U	3											5	?	
Hinton St Mary	mid 4	2 rooms			R	10											5	5	
Littlecote	4	2 rooms			R												5	2	
Lullingstone	350–400	3 rooms			R	10			9		?			<			5	5	?
Woodchester	4	–			R	3			9		9						5	?	1

Site	Literary evidence: bishop	Literary evidence: church	Lead rank	Christian graffito	Object of little value with Christian symbol	Villa with *chi-rho* or	Villa probably Christian	Hoard with *chi-rho* or	Hoard with other symbol/s	Destruction of pagan site or artefact	Destruction of pagan and re-use by Christian	Datable pagan hoard	Total internal evidence	Total external evidence	Total
	4	5	5	5	5	5	4	4	2	2	4	2			
Intra-mural															
Canterbury Cathedral	4	5		5									14	14	
Lincoln St Paul-in-the-Bail								4					42	4	46
Nettleton Octagonal													30	0	30
Richborough				5						2			37	7	44

Silchester 9					5				36	5	41
Uley building 7	2								40	1	41
Uley building 8			5						41	1	42
Verulamium 6				5					20	2	22
Witham				5		5			33	10	43
Extra-mural											
Brean Down	2								32	0	32
Canterbury, St Pancras		5	5	5		4	1		37	14	51
Colchester 9 (Butt Road)			5			4	1		40	12	52
Icklingham					5			2	45	11	56
Lamyatt Beacon									32	0	32
Nettleton building 23								4	30	4	34
Stone-by-Faversham		2	5			4			24	11	35
Verulamium St Alban		5							19	5	
Verulamium 7		2			5				30	2	32
House/Estate church											
Caerwent XXIX N				5					9	5	14
Chedworth									20	0	20
Frampton							2		22	2	24
Gloucester St Mary de Lode									17	0	17
Hinton St Mary							4		20	4	24
Littlecote									9	0	9
Lullingstone									31	0	31
Woodchester									17	4	21

Figure 14 Analysis of evidence for Christian churches, and relative weightings

evidence indicates the likelihood of such identity, given the locality of the site. In view of this, one structure which, on internal evidence, has only a possibility of being Christian, will not form part of this discussion: the Verulamium 6 building, which was described only very briefly by Wheeler and Wheeler (1936: 122–3). It will also be noted that, for two other sites, the cathedrals at Canterbury and St Albans, certain Roman features are presumed (marked * in the analysis) but since the actual Roman buildings have not yet been discovered, they have not been given totals, and are not ranked in the summary. Even without this evidence, however, the two buildings presently on the site have every probability of Roman antecedents. One further note on the analysis to follow: the evidence from putative house churches is not generally included in the discussion; they form a special group, with their particular criteria for identification, and will be dealt with separately. As was proposed in Part 1, the relative weightings have been converted to a numerical equivalent. A summary in rank order, which also gives totals for internal and external evidence, follows the analysis (Figures 14, 15).

Characteristics common to all buildings are at once apparent. The first is the absence of all contemporary domestic, industrial or agricultural features. Possible domestic features at Colchester 9 and Nettleton 23 have been discussed and suggested explanations advanced. No other site showed any such evidence. It is felt this should be the first criterion applied in identification of a church. Equally important for a Christian identification is the absence of any overtly pagan features. This was noted at all the seventeen suggested churches in this study, if the probable votive antler pieces at Brean Down and Lamyatt Beacon are accepted as belonging to an earlier religious structure.[1] Should pagan features have existed at a site, they should be seen to have been desecrated. Absence of domestic and pagan features are, therefore, proposed as essential criteria in the identification of Christian churches.

A highly desirable characteristic would be evidence of religious continuity at the site. It is noted that eleven of the seventeen sites analysed had either a pagan predecessor or a Christian successor or both. Of the others, Richborough and Icklingham should probably also be added here, the former because of the presence, less than 100 metres away, of an early Saxon chapel, and the latter in view of the purging of the site before construction of the presumed church; Nettleton 23 could share the pagan predecessor of

Site	Internal evidence	External evidence	Total	Ranking 3–0 scale
Intra-mural				
Lincoln St Paul-in-the-Bail	42	4	46	3
Richborough	37	7	44	3
Witham	33	10	43	3
Uley building 8	41	1	42	3
Silchester 9	36	5	41	3
Uley building 7	40	1	41	3
Nettleton Octagonal	30	0	30	2
Verulamium 6	20	2	22	1
Canterbury Cathedral	14	14		
Extra-mural				
Icklingham	45	11	56	3
Colchester 9 (Butt Road)	40	12	52	3
Canterbury, St Pancras	37	14	51	3
Stone-by-Faversham	24	11	35	2
Nettleton building 23	30	4	34	2
Brean Down	32	0	32	2
Lamyatt Beacon	32	0	32	2
Verulamium 7	30	2	32	2
Verulamium St Alban	19	5		
House/Estate church				
Lullingstone	31	0	31	3
Frampton	22	2	24	2
Hinton St Mary	20	4	24	2
Woodchester	17	4	21	1
Chedworth	20	0	20	1
Gloucester St Mary de Lode	17	0	17	1
Caerwent XXIX N	9	5	14	1
Littlecote	9	0	9	1

Figure 15   Summary of evidence for identification of Christian churches in rank order

Nettleton Octagonal building, since its construction probably occurred at the same time as the conversion of the octagonal interior into a cruciform; and, while Verulamium 7 has no evidence of a pagan antecedent on its site, the presence of fragments of a possible cult statue suggests a temple or shrine nearby, perhaps in the area of extensive occupation indicated by Anthony (1968: 9) to the west of the ditched enclosure, near Watling Street. This could leave only two sites with no religious connection either before or after the Romano-British Christian period, and it is paradoxical that the identification of the two buildings, Silchester 9 and Colchester 9 (Butt Road), as churches can hardly be doubted. Thus it is clear that, even though it is highly desirable for purposes of identification that a Romano-British church have a religious predecessor or successor, it is not essential.

It will be noted that there is a close correlation between the existence of later Christian churches and cemeteries. This is to be expected, as one of the characteristics of the Saxon church was the accompanying graveyard. In order not to inflate the value of these criteria, however, where both features are found at a site, they are treated as one criterion only.

If the sites are classified as rural and urban, it is seen that most of those which had pagan predecessors come from the country, with only St Paul-in-the-Bail and Verulamium 7 as possible urban examples. Moreover, in every case but one, where there has been a pagan predecessor there appears to be evidence for some sort of desecration or purging of the site or its artefacts. The Verulamium 7 building may have replaced a pagan temple associated with a settlement nearby, but proof of this would require further excavation. It would, of course, be possible for a desecrated pagan object to be found on a site which was some distance removed from the source of the object, but this seems improbable. It is reasonable to assume that these two features of a Christian site would be found together; but, in order not to exaggerate the importance of these criteria, since some sites had neither pagan predecessor nor Christian successor, when the two occurred, they were also taken as one.

Although most of the sites with pagan predecessors were rural, it is also seen that, of those sites with later Christian successors, four of the six examples are urban, if Uley is taken as one site only. The pagan revival, from about 360 on, saw a resurgence of temple building in the rural areas. The dates of the demise of some presumed rural churches coincide with this revival of paganism: Nettleton Octagonal, Witham and perhaps Nettleton 23 and the rectangular buildings at Brean Down and Lamyatt Beacon did not survive the new wave of paganism. The more romanised towns, insulated from such influences, appear to have resisted. With the departure of the Romans, it seems that, as Bede records for Canterbury (*Historia ecclesiastica* 1.26, 33), Christianity held on in the towns, or, at least, sufficient folk-memory was retained for the tradition of sanctity to live on at Christian sites. Uley is exceptional in that the site does not appear to have been christianised until about 380, when the pagan influence was lessened by the actions and legislation of the more militantly Christian emperors after Valentinian I. The site may reflect the first wave of monasticism which arrived in the south-west in the fifth century.

As regards the shape of the building, ten of sixteen (this excludes St Albans) were probably basilical, apsidal, or with variations such as the squared projection at Uley 8. Although orientation was not ranked as a criterion, it is noted that ten of these sixteen buildings were oriented either west–east or east–west. Thus, an apsidal plan and west–east or east–west siting would also seem to be highly desirable, but not essential, features for a church.

If the buildings are classified as intra-mural and extra-mural, it is found that five out of ten intra-mural and four out of eight extra-mural are apsidal. However, if they are classified as urban or rural, all seven buildings in the towns are apsidal, but only two of nine in the country. The pattern is clearly that apsidal is the preferred shape for urban churches, whether intra- or extra-mural.

The opposite side of the coin will be, of course, that there are fewer apsidal buildings in the country; there will thus be more instances of a plan less readily identifiable as a church. The rectangular shape is found only in rural areas. This may reflect the degree of sophistication, or lack of it, of Romano-British Christians in rural districts, and the relative slowness at which *romanitas* penetrated those areas. It is especially interesting to note that the first Uley building had a type of apse, but the second, which Ellison (1980) dates to the early fifth century, was, apparently, rectangular. When one is seeking churches in country areas, therefore, particularly in the south-west of Britain, it is as well to look for the rectangular structure as for the apsidal.

It is noted that all extra-mural buildings had either contemporaneous, presumed Christian, Romano-British cemeteries or later Saxon Christian ones, or both. This would be expected, since Roman law forbade intra-mural burial, while the presence of Saxon Christian burials around churches, even within former Roman towns, is well attested. It would be possible for an extra-mural Romano-British church not to have an associated or later cemetery, but the evidence suggests this is far from the norm. This seems to be one characteristic which is highly desirable for the identification of extra-mural churches.

Unique to churches, and useful indicators of a Christian identity, are apsidal burials, and baptisteries or fonts, although such features are not found at many sites. There is, too, the problem of recognition of a baptismal feature, as the site at Silchester 9 has shown only too clearly.

To summarise the above, the features considered essential for identification of Christian churches in Roman Britain are: an absence of domestic, industrial or agricultural evidence and of evidence of any pagan activity; if pagan features are present, they should be seen to have been desecrated or profaned in some way. Characteristics which make the identification highly likely are: evidence of religious continuity at the site, either before or after the Romano-British Christian period; and a building of basilical or simple apsidal plan, orientated west–east or east–west. In the town areas, the apsidal plan may be the more common; in the country, particularly in the south-west, a rectangular shape may occur. For extra-mural sites, a fourth-century cemetery with Christian attributes associated with a structure is a likely indicator that the structure was a Christian church; similarly, a later Saxon Christian cemetery may indicate an earlier Romano-British church in the vicinity. On intra-mural sites, a Saxon Christian cemetery may also point to an earlier church. Finally, useful indicators of a church include the apsidal burial or, to a lesser extent, the apsidal feature, the presence of a baptistery or font, and the defiling of a pagan site or artefact, but this last is of little help unless it can be seen that the site or object had been reused in a Christian context.

As regards house churches, it is difficult, because of the small number of sites, to detect trends, but in Part 1 of this chapter, two known house churches were used to indicate desirable features. This seems to have been reasonably successful, for, in applying the criteria to a set of seven sites, two which are usually assumed to be house churches, Frampton and Hinton St Mary, rank well, despite the absence of full excavation details. Plans were studied with criteria deemed highly desirable for a house church, that is, a suite of at least two rooms for liturgical use, one of which has a religious focus or provision for it, and the whole to have a separate entrance apart from the building to which it may be attached. It was found that Caerwent house XXII N, Frampton, Littlecote and Lullingstone had these features, Hinton St Mary and Woodchester two of the three, while there is insufficient evidence from Chedworth and St Mary de Lode, Gloucester. But such a layout could also have been found in a totally secular context, so it was necessary to look for specific evidence of a Christian presence as well. Such evidence was lacking at Caerwent, Littlecote, St Mary de Lode and Woodchester. Its presence at the other sites indicates the Christianity of the owners of the buildings, but by itself does not prove that the rooms in which the symbols were found were house churches, although when found *in situ*, as at Frampton, Hinton and Lullingstone, it is certainly a useful indicator. Furthermore, if the Lullingstone site can be a guide, the criteria of pagan predecessor or Christian successor may be applied, with useful results.

In addition to internal evidence, external factors should also be taken into account for assessment of the likely Christianity of a site. Though of less value, such factors do help to relate the site to its geographical setting and the overall distribution of Christian evidence.

It is now possible to identify the likely churches of Roman Britain. In his study of Romano-British Christianity, Thomas (1981) classifies sites on a scale of 3–0: 3, nearly certain; 2, reasonably probable; 1, possible; 0, chronologically irrelevant or dubious. In this present analysis, sites which were considered chronologically irrelevant or dubious were eliminated from the discussion. The summary has produced a numerical total made up of both internal and external evidence, but that total may now be converted to Thomas's scale of probability. Results will be given showing firstly, Thomas's rating, and then, in italics, the suggested rating as a result of this analysis. Where the site was not evaluated by Thomas, this will be indicated by an asterisk (*), and where a site was not ranked in the present study, it will be indicated by two asterisks (**). The suggested churches are as follows:

Intra-mural churches: Canterbury Cathedral (3) (**), St Paul-in-the-Bail, Lincoln (*) *(3)*, Nettleton Octagonal (*) *(2)*, Richborough (3) *(3)*, Silchester 9 (3) *(3)*, Uley 7 (*) *(3)*, Uley 8 (*) *(3)*, Verulamium 6 (1) *(1)*, Witham (*) *(3)*.

Extra-mural churches: Brean Down (*) *(2)*, Canterbury St Pancras (3) *(3)*, Colchester 9 (Butt Road) (*) *(3)*, Icklingham (3) *(3)*, Lamyatt Beacon (*) *(2)*, Nettleton 23 (*) *(2)*, St Alban's Cathedral (3) (**), Stone-by-Faversham (*) *(2)*, Verulamium 7 (3) *(2)*.

⊙ = 3 SCALE

• = 2 SCALE

LINCOLN ⊙

ICKLINGHAM ⊙

COLCHESTER ⊙
WITHAM ⊙
ULEY ⊙   VERULAMIUM .
• NETTLETON   ⊙ LULLINGSTONE
• BREAN DOWN   ⊙ SILCHESTER   ⊙ ⊙ (RICHBOROUGH
                                  CANTERBURY
• LAMYATT BEACON
HINTON ST. MARY •
FRAMPTON •

Figure 16   Distribution map of almost-certain and probable Christian churches in
Roman Britain

House churches: Caerwent House XXII N (*) *(1)*, Chedworth
(*) *(1)*, Frampton (3) *(2)*, Hinton St Mary (3) *(2)*, Littlecote (3)
(1), Lullingstone (3) *(3)*, St Mary de Lode, Gloucester (*) *(1)*,
Woodchester (*) *(1)*.

The distribution of 3- and 2-scale structures and plans of those
considered almost certainly Christian (3-scale) are set out in
Figures 16–19.

144

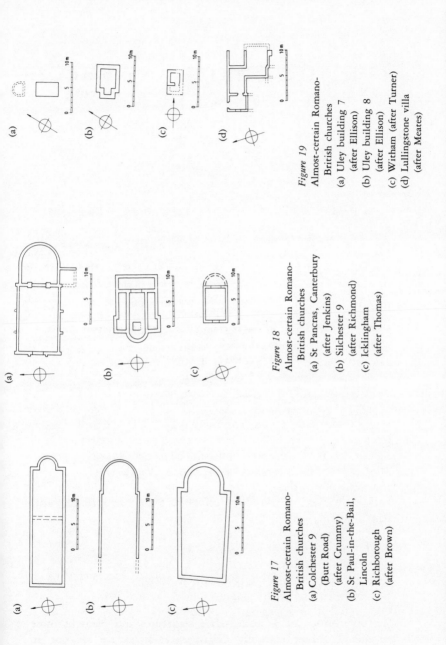

Figure 17
Almost-certain Romano-British churches
(a) Colchester 9 (Butt Road) (after Crummy)
(b) St Paul-in-the-Bail, Lincoln (after Brown)
(c) Richborough

Figure 18
Almost-certain Romano-British churches
(a) St Pancras, Canterbury (after Jenkins)
(b) Silchester 9 (after Richmond)
(c) Icklingham (after Thomas)

Figure 19
Almost-certain Romano-British churches
(a) Uley building 7 (after Ellison)
(b) Uley building 8 (after Ellison)
(c) Witham (after Turner)
(d) Lullingstone villa (after Meates)

V

FURTHER CHRISTIAN SYMBOLS
AND INSCRIPTIONS

1: A REAPPRAISAL OF THE THETFORD TREASURE[1]

To gain as complete a picture as possible of Romano-British
Christianity, a study must also be made of various inscriptions and
symbols. Toynbee, Thomas and other writers have dealt with many
of these. This chapter is, therefore, devoted to three detailed
studies only: Part 1, an important hoard of inscribed utensils from
Thetford; Part 2, a group of lead vessels from various parts of
Roman Britain, the decoration and use of which have, until now,
not been thoroughly discussed; and Part 3, two (unrelated)
artefacts with rare symbols from Chedworth and Poundbury.

At Gallows Hill, Thetford,[2] a rich hoard of late Roman gold
jewellery and silver utensils was found in 1979. The conclusions of
the scholars who subsequently published the Thetford Treasure
(Johns and Potter 1983)[3] have far-reaching ramifications for the
identification of Christian objects in the Roman world. Hence it is
essential that these conclusions be closely examined in the light of
the available evidence. A reappraisal of the Treasure will, it is
believed, reveal a Christian component in this predominantly
pagan hoard.

The Treasure comprises eighty-one items: twenty-two gold
finger rings, twenty-one other items of gold jewellery, one
unmounted gem (these contained in a shale box with lid), together
with thirty-three silver spoons and three silver strainers. Of the
spoons, thirty-two were engraved with a mixture of pagan and
what could in another context be considered Christian symbols or
inscriptions. The pagan element related to the ancient Latin god
Faunus, either by that name or given a Celtic epithet, such as *Dei
Fau{ni} Medugeni* 'of the god Faunus Medugenus [the Mead

Begotten]' (Figure 20a); the jewellery appears to have iconographical links with this deity. The cult was of a Bacchic type popular in the fourth century, especially as a counter-influence to Christianity (Johns and Potter 1983: 52; Hutchinson 1986: 108–9).

Summarising their research, Johns and Potter see the spoons as part of the ritual plate of a sanctuary for the worship of Faunus. They regard the jewellery as a jeweller-merchant's stock, and offer three possible solutions: that it comprised regalia specially commissioned for the cult; that the jeweller-merchant, a devotee of Faunus, incorporated some of his religious beliefs into his creations and kept his wealth in a (presumed) sanctuary or temple; or that, ignoring all iconographical references, the jewellery was but the stock of a jeweller-merchant located in a wealthy part of Roman Britain, a stock stolen and hidden with silver looted from the sanctuary.

In view of what may be shown to be a definite Christian element in the hoard, another hypothesis is now proposed: that the whole was a cult treasure, kept for safe keeping at a temple or in the hands of someone associated with the cult. The jewellery was a votive offering to Faunus, either specially commissioned by the various members of the sect for this purpose or, in one or two cases, the gift of a devotee's personal property. The spoons and strainers were in some instances owned and previously used by members, the others made and intended for use in a ritual honouring Faunus. To explain the Christian element, it is suggested that the owners of the spoons with fish-and-plant, *uti felix* and *vir bone vivas*, plus Agrestius, Auspicius, Ingenuus, Persevera, Primigenia, Silviola and perhaps Restitutus,[4] were lapsed Christians. The accession of Julian (360–3) and the return to paganism must have been a stimulus for nominal or half-hearted Christians to revert to the pagan cults; and the policy of religious toleration of the Christian Valentinian I (364–75) would have ensured at least security for such cults well into the second half of the fourth century, perhaps until the decree of Theodosius in 391, which closed all temples and banned pagan cults.

Julian's association with Britain had begun in 355: he became Caesar in charge of Britain and Gaul, where his policies gained him popularity with soldiers and civilians. As Augustus, he openly promoted paganism (Ammianus Marcellinus 22.5.2) by restoring and rebuilding temples, and fostering the worship of pagan gods in the provinces. The Christian church lost its privileged position, and, while its members were not persecuted, they were at least

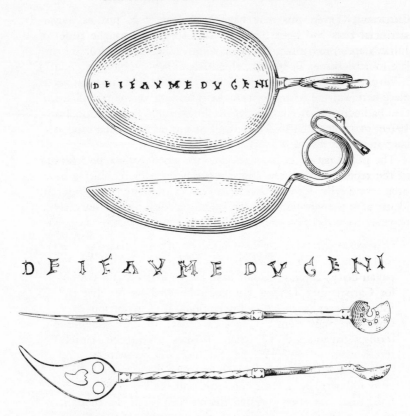

Figure 20 Thetford Treasure (after Johns and Potter)
(a) Spoon 54: *DEI FAV{NI} MEDVGENI*
(b) Strainer 49 with pronged terminal

discriminated against. It is suggested therefore that, at Thetford in provincial Britain, a small group of disaffected Christians renounced their faith and formed their own exclusive pagan cult, choosing to worship an ancient Latin god, Faunus, whose very antiquity was probably an attraction;[5] this deity might then have been conveniently conflated with a similar rustic god worshipped there in earlier times (Henig 1986: 166).

That the cult of Faunus was still practised in parts of the empire in the fourth century is likely, but it does seem that even by the early Empire there was considerable uncertainty about the ritual involved (Johns and Potter 1983: 50–1). With the advent of

Christianity, even this may have been forgotten, just as pagan sacrificial rites had been forgotten in Cappadocia by the time of Julian's apostasy (Julian, *Ad Aristoxenum* 375C, Loeb edn). By the late fourth century in Britain, therefore, it was probably necessary to invent a ritual. A model was close at hand. Perhaps what took place here was the reverse of the 'christianising' of the nymphaeum that had occurred at Chedworth (Richmond 1959b: 22; Goodburn 1979: 24), where the structure itself may even have been used as a baptistery (Thomas 1981: 219–20).

The pagan nature of the Treasure as a whole cannot be refuted; in the report, indeed, the links between the various objects have been masterfully deduced. There can be no argument with a pagan identity for the jewellery and the Faunus spoons. The authors have, however, rejected any possible Christian connections:

> It is worth observing that the Thetford fish, associated as it is with a set of spoons directly related to the worship of the pagan deity, Faunus, cannot have been intended as a symbol for Christianity. Despite the common assumption that the fish, together with *vivas* inscriptions is a reflection of a Christian component, it is clear that, in iconographical terms, pagan and Christian themes could be closely interwoven, at any rate in the northern provinces. . . . Notwithstanding the inscription on spoon 69, namely *Silviola vivas* followed by a cross, and the fish on spoon 67, (both finds that, were they isolated discoveries, might be thought to have Christian connotations), the whole set of spoons can safely be regarded as exclusively devoted to the celebration of pagan ritual.
>
> (Johns and Potter 1983: 40, 71)

If these conclusions are accepted, it then follows that no fish-and-plant, *vivas* and cross or fourth-century *vivas* inscription can be identified as Christian without corroborating evidence; this is to negate much of the scholarship on Christian symbolism of the past fifty years or more. Moreover, it does seem that in the Thetford Treasure evidence for Christianity has not been recognised; and, it is argued, other indicators are present which, while not so definite, still point to a Christian identification for this part of the hoard.

The first of these indicators is the fish-and-plant inscribed on spoon 67 (Figure 21a); this, it is proposed, is a fish-and-palm motif. The fish itself is a well-known Christian symbol,[6] and Thomas (1981: 89, 92) gives those known from Roman Britain. A

Figure 21 Thetford Treasure (after Johns and Potter)
(a) Spoon 67: fish and plant
(b) Spoon 69: *SILVIOLA VIVAS+*

Christian identity may not always be certain, for example, in the case of fish on platters. These are fairly common, and their presence on what may be considered ordinary domestic tableware does not necessarily equate with Christian ownership (Liversidge 1959: 9). Yet there is a fish on both a spoon and a platter in the Traprain Treasure (Curle 1923: pls XXVI, XXVII) and on a platter in the Appleshaw, Andover, pewter (Read 1898: fig. 9); in these two hoards a *chi-rho* symbol is also present. Fish on platters do occur without such supporting evidence: on a pewter dish in a set of plate from Icklingham (Liversidge 1959) and on a plate in a newly found pewter hoard from Islip, Northants.[7] But in both cases the fish was the only decoration in the sets of tableware. It is perhaps also significant that Icklingham has a known Christian presence – of church, baptistery and cemetery (West 1976) – while Islip is only a few kilometres south of Water Newton and Ashton, the latter the site of a fourth-century and almost certainly Christian cemetery (see above, ch. III).

The palm branch is frequently depicted on Christian monuments, the palm tree less frequently. It represented victory (Origen, *Commentary on John* 21), justice (Psalm 92.12) or martyrdom (Revelation 7.9–17) and occurs not only on funerary inscriptions, such as those found in the catacombs (e.g. Cabrol and Leclerq 1920–53: vol. 3.2, fig. 3362 s.v. *'croix et crucifix'*), but also on objects such as lamps and rings where a conscientious Christian might follow the injunction of Clement of Alexandria to give evidence of his faith (*Paedagogus* 3.11.59.1). In Roman Britain the palm by itself is not attested as a Christian symbol, but it is found in other probable Christian contexts, apart from its association with the fish. It accompanies the inscription *ama me* on a ring from Carlisle (Dalton 1901: no. 64), and Thomas (1981: 151) believes it is the palm, rather than the sentiment, which suggests Christianity; this ring was found with another, inscribed with a *chi-rho* (Charlesworth 1978: 123). On a Late Roman ring from Stonham Aspal in Suffolk, the Greek inscription ΟΛΥΜΠΕΙ ΖΗCΑΙC ('Olympis, may you live long'; the equivalent sentiment in Latin is *vivas*) is flanked by two palm-like devices (Mawer 1989);[8] by the fourth century such inscriptions (discussed below) were often used in a Christian context. There is a palm between two birds, presumably doves, on a late Roman ring from Moore Park near Verulamium (Henig 1987); and on a ring from Fifehead Neville a monogrammatic cross is surmounted by a dove and two palm branches (Middleton 1882). Even more positive evidence for a Christian identification is the unpublished pewter plate found at Stamford, referred to in Chapter III, on which a rather crude design of a central *iota-chi*[9] surrounded by a series of five crosses of the *crux decussata* form and a *chi-rho* is interspersed with a palm-like pattern similar to that found on 'votive leaves' (Toynbee 1978) and in the Water Newton Treasure (Painter 1977b).

The fish-and-palm combination is known in Christian iconography: Cabrol and Leclerq (1920–53: vol. 7.1, figs 6058, 6065, 6101 s.v. 'ΙΧΘΥΣ') illustrate two inscriptions where the pictorial fish becomes the Greek ΙΚΘΥC in one case, ΙΧΘΥΣ in the other – both with palm branches, and a fish-and-palm platter. Four early-Christian engraved gems in the British Museum bear both symbols, three in combination with other Christian emblems such as shepherd's crook, dove or anchor (Dalton 1901: nos 34, 35, 39); the fourth is engraved with a wreath of two palm branches encircling the word ΙΧΘΥΣ (no. 9). More conclusive for a study of these symbols in connection with religious ritual objects, however, is the presence of a fish on the bowl, a palm on the reverse of a spoon in the Canoscio Treasure, a set of Christian eucharistic plate (Giovagnoli 1935: 315 and fig. 6).[10] The fish-and-palm has been found elsewhere in Roman Britain: on a similar spoon of unknown provenance (Potter 1982) and on five engraved glass fragments, possibly from the same Cologne workshop, found at Caerleon, Chesters, Colchester, Corbridge and Silchester, and identified as Christian (Charlesworth 1959);[11] their provenance does not preclude such identification. Separately the two symbols were pagan or secular motifs as well (below, ch. VI); it does seem, however, that the combination fish-and-palm was not a pagan symbol, and Johns and Potter (1983: 121) themselves say they have no explanation for the plant on spoon 67. A Christian identity for the spoon must therefore be a real possibility.

Further evidence in the Treasure for Christianity is the *SILVIOLA VIVAS* + inscription on spoon 69 (Figure 21b). It is the Greek cross which first commands attention. This form of the cross has not previously been attested in Roman Britain, and it could be inferred from Thomas's study of Romano-British Christianity that it was unknown until early in the fifth century (Thomas 1981: 91 and fig. 3). That is far from the case: the equal-armed cross was found in one of the earliest parts of the catacomb of Callistus, the crypt of Lucina (De Rossi 1864: vol. I, pl. XVIII), and dates at least from the beginning of the third century (Northcote and Brownlow 1869: 229) or even mid-second century (Cabrol and Leclerq 1920–53: vol. 3.2, col. 3056 s.v. '*croix et crucifix*'); the Montanist heretics of Asia Minor in the late second and early third centuries used the Greek cross instead of the letter *chi* on their funerary inscriptions (Gough 1961: fig. 10 lines 4–5); and Sulzberger (1925: 371–5), in his authoritative work on crosses and Christian monograms, while proposing that this form of the cross was rare in the third century, does allow local exceptions. That the Greek cross was employed by the following century cannot be doubted, and its appearance on a late fourth-century spoon inscribed *SILVIOLA VIVAS* is even less surprising, in view of both the name and the sentiment expressed.

The words *Silviola vivas* appear on two spoons, 68 and 69, the latter with a cross. Hassall identifies the name as a diminutive of Silvius/a, derived from *silva*, and thus a suitable name for a devotee of Faunus. As he notes in his analysis of the personal names from the Treasure (Hassall and Tomlin 1981: 389–93), research on the Latin cognomina has revealed only one instance of Silviola: on a Christian inscription from Rome (Kajanto 1965: 368).[12] It would, it seems, be an equally appropriate name for a fellow-Christian at the far end of the Roman Empire, especially when one of her associates also carried a name known only in a Christian context: Persevera.

Spoon 61 (Figure 22a) is inscribed *PERSEVERAVITVIVAS*. Hassall has suggested that this equates with *(qui) perseveravit vivas* 'to him who has persevered, long life to you', but there is a grammatical inconsistency here with the use of the third and second persons, so this reading is suspect. More satisfactory is the suggestion by Jackson in the monograph (Johns and Potter 1983: 46) that the inscription is an engraver's error, the correct reading being *Persevera uti (=ut) vivas*, 'Persevera [I wish] that you may live long'. A search for the name Persevera reveals Perseverandus and Perseverantius: both are known only in a Christian context, and Kajanto (1965: 135) reminds his audience that, for early Christians, the virtue of perseverance was emphasised.[13]

A final point regarding the other personal names: all are known in Christian as well as pagan inscriptions (Kajanto 1965: 290, 310, 314, 318, 356).

This leads to a consideration of features of the other inscriptions: *uti felix*, *vivas*, and *vir bone*. All of these are found elsewhere in fourth-century Christian contexts.[14] Undoubtedly such inscriptions were common in the pagan world: a second-century brooch from Canterbury was engraved *VTERE FELIX* (Hassall and Tomlin 1980: 413), as was a belt fastening of unknown date found at South Shields (Sherlock 1984: 84). Pairs of third-century fiddle-shaped spoons have been found with one word of this inscription on each. Sherlock has suggested that, while the use of *utere/uti felix* on all kinds of objects probably began in the first or second century, by the time Christianity was widespread it could also have had a religious significance. Certainly a fragment of a lead casket from East Stoke boasted a *chi-rho* along with its inscription (Wright 1955: 147),[15] and spoons from the Continent are found

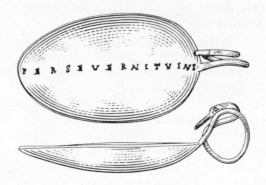

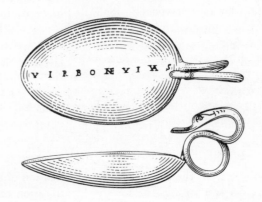

Figure 22 Thetford Treasure (after Johns and Potter)
(a) Spoon 61: *PERSEVERAVIT VIVAS*
(b) Spoon 60: *VIR BONE VIVAS*

bearing *VTERE* + *FELIX* (Milojčić 1968: 139). The cross
between the words must surely have had some religious
significance. Similarly, a religious significance for the inscription
on spoon 59 is enhanced by the presence of an 'ivy leaf' between
the *uti* and *felix*. These ubiquitous symbols have been found to
occur only on votive or dedicatory inscriptions, or on gaming
tables (Cabrol and Leclerq 1920–53: vol. 5.1, col. 1464 s.v.
'*feuilles de lierre*').[16]

Still more common than *utilutere felix* are *vivas* inscriptions, and these, too, had a pagan origin: the back of a large altar found at Maryport is inscribed *VOLANTI VIVAS* (*RIB* 812). Even so, it does seem that, by the fourth century, *vivas* inscriptions (and the equivalent Greek, on occasion latinised as *zeses*) had been widely adopted for Christian use, perhaps overtaking *utere felix* (Sherlock 1984: 85). One of the best-known associations of *vivas* and Christianity is in the Mildenhall Treasure, where two spoons are inscribed *PASCENTIA VIVAS* and *PAPITTEDO VIVAS* respectively, and three others the *chi-rho* monogram (Painter 1977a: nos 27–31). At Corbridge, a silver cup inscribed *DESIDERE VIVAS* was found in the same area as another piece with a *chi-rho* (Haverfield 1914: figs 2 and 3); and at Canterbury, a spoon inscribed *PIVM VIVAS* was probably part of a set which included two bearing the monogrammatic cross (Johns and Potter 1985: nos U.3, U.1, C.5). The association may be even more positive: a spoon in the Traprain Treasure bears two graffiti of *vivas* and *chi-rho*, thus an unequivocal Christian combination (Sherlock 1973: 206), and several examples of *vivas in Deo* are known in Roman Britain.[17]

One other inscription, the *vir bone vivas* on spoon 60 (Figure 22b), should be noted. The *vir bone* is paralleled by *viribonism* on a spoon from Canterbury (Hassall and Tomlin 1981: n. 110),[18] and this item was part of the hoard which included two monogrammatic crosses and probably *pium vivas* (above).

It will be seen, therefore, that the combination of *vivas* with the Greek cross is a strong case for the identification of spoon 69 as Christian; the *vivas* and *uti felix* inscriptions are also readily identifiable as Christian in a fourth-century context, particularly when associated with other objects bearing known Christian symbols such as fish-and-palm and the cross. This identification is supported by the presence in the Treasure of three silver strainers.

In their comments on the strainers 47, 48 and 49, Johns and Potter point out that similar utensils are found in several late Roman hoards, and it is noteworthy that many of the examples cited are from hoards where a Christian element is present, even if a Christian identity for the hoard itself has not been established.[19] One strainer from a pagan site is listed: from the London Mithraeum, but in shape it does not resemble those found at Thetford.

That strainers had a liturgical purpose is indicated by their presence in the eucharistic sets from Water Newton (Painter 1977b), Canoscio (Giovagnoli 1935) and Hama (Diehl 1926). The strainer in the Traprain Treasure (Curle 1923: no. 111 and pl. xxviii) is also from what does seem likely was part of a set of church plate.[20] Another silver strainer, similar in shape to no. 48 in Thetford, but with a comma-shaped terminal like 49 (Figure 20b) and a suspension ring, has been found at Richborough (Bushe-Fox 1949: pl. XCIX, 126). It is surely more than a remarkable coincidence that this object was found on the site of a building which has in more recent times been convincingly demonstrated to be a Christian church (Brown 1971). The use of these utensils in the liturgy for straining the communion wine has already been suggested (Toynbee 1953: 22). Recent research on the early Mass[21] has shown that, by the fourth century, they indeed had a place in the ritual: as the subdeacon was intoning the epistle he held the strainer suspended from his finger; it was then used later in the service to strain the wine. The small strainer was used to remove bread from the chalice in an early rite of consecration; a similar use has been ascribed to the curious pronged implement on several occasions found in hoards with a Christian component.

A pronged-terminal strainer has been found in the Kaiseraugst Treasure accompanying a smaller strainer and two pronged implements, one inscribed with *chi-rho* (Cahn and Kaufmann-Heinemann 1984: nos 36–9); another incomplete pronged object has been found at Dorchester, Dorset, together with spoons with fish and *vivas* inscriptions (Dalton 1922: 90). Two other pronged-terminal implements with spatulate ends have been found in Roman Britain, one at Canterbury inscribed with a *chi-rho* (Painter 1965: 8–9), and another at Richborough, about 50 metres from the Christian church site (Bushe-Fox 1949: pl. XCIX, 127). The post-Roman example from St Ninian's Isle was found with other silver plate on the site of a pre-Norse church, and McRoberts (1965) argues strongly for an ecclesiastical purpose for the whole treasure. It would seem that the presence of strainers and a pronged-terminal on one signifies both a ritual purpose for this part of the Thetford Treasure and, it is proposed, a Christian origin.

In the report there is no discussion on wear on the strainers. It must be assumed that any wear on such utensils would have been slight, if detectable at all. They could have been originally either from a set of church plate, or made specifically for the cult of Faunus, copying strainers used in the Mass. The first seems more likely since there is no dedicatory inscription to the god.

Spoons, too, were used in the Mass, though their purpose is disputed. It is extremely unlikely that in the early Western church they were used generally to administer the sacrament, as was later done in the East (cf. Frend 1984–5: 149).[22] In Roman times they were probably used to administer the wine to infants.[23] In the early Middle Ages spoons were also used to transfer the bread to the paten (Cabrol and Leclerq 1920–53: vol. 3.2, col. 3175 s.v. 'cuiller').

The presence of spoons in a pagan hoard suggests a ritual use also. An examination of the manufacture, age and condition of the Thetford spoons may shed further light on the proposed Christian origin of some of these. Johns and Potter have enunciated in some detail a theory that the silver component in the hoard was made to a specific weight of metal. There is, nevertheless, a degree of doubt about the weight of a Roman pound of silver, and the argument is not conclusive. Further, there is little to suggest that all the spoons were made at the one time. Some were obviously made 'to order': these were engraved before being finished[24] and include, as would be expected, spoons dedicated to Faunus.[25] However, it has not been clearly demonstrated that all spoons were manufactured in this way. Some were pairs, or near pairs, but it would be rash to manipulate the evidence here. Indeed, there is some evidence that the spoons were not all made at the same time: the fish-and-plant spoon is stylistically of an earlier date; and the fact that some spoons (61, 62 and 63 – all of which could easily fit into a Christian context) show signs of wear, while others do not may be as easily explained by an earlier manufacture and longer use as by their having had a specific purpose in a pagan ritual (Johns and Potter 1983: 35).[26]

A study of the sizes of the spoons shows that no. 51 is well beyond the average weight (25–30 g) of the others. It is so large, in fact (weight 45.5 g, bowl 93 mm × 50 mm), that to eat from it would be quite a feat. Johns and Potter suggest that its extraordinary size is due to its being one of the last spoons to be made to a specific total weight of silver, thus using up all the remaining metal. Since, however, it is not certain that all the spoons were made for a particular order, it may be that spoon 51 had a special purpose in the pagan ritual, similar to that of ladles in the early Mass,[27] and that it was not intended to be used as an eating implement. Such explanation would suit the interpretation of the Treasure as proposed in this study.

The accumulation of evidence for a Christian component in the Thetford Treasure has resulted in a clear indication that the hoard was not entirely pagan in its origins. To deny this conclusion is to deny the long-accepted identification of a number of Christian symbols and inscriptions. Toynbee (1953: 13) once commented that while Christians borrowed widely from pagan art motifs, pagans themselves did not have any 'inducement' to use Christian symbols; elsewhere she wrote that she knew of no instance where a Christian symbol (she was referring to the *chi-rho* at Frampton) had been accorded a position of prominence in a pagan context (Toynbee 1968: 181). Pagan cults did not need to borrow from Christian symbolism; the reverse was usually the practice. In the Thetford Treasure, the situation we have is not that a pagan cult absorbed such symbols (Johns and Potter 1983: 40); rather that a group of Christians, renouncing their faith, 'paganised' their property and added it to the treasure of a small and exclusive cult they formed as part of the pagan revival in the latter half of the fourth century.

2: CIRCULAR LEAD TANKS AND THEIR SIGNIFICANCE[1]

With the discovery of three more whole or partial circular lead tanks in Britain,[2] it is timely to review all such finds, their decoration, provenance, dating and likely use, and to attempt to set them into the context not only of Romano-British Christianity, but of late Roman Christianity as a whole. A close examination of the evidence, both literary and archaeological, suggests that all the tanks were Christian, and had a use in the baptismal ritual in fourth-century Britain.

The most recent publication on lead tanks is that by Guy (1981) who discusses their construction, summarises the motifs used in their decoration and suggests possible uses for these containers. Thomas (1981: 202–27) has a chapter[3] on baptism and baptisteries in which he gives a persuasive reconstruction of the scene on the Walesby tank and also proposes a use for the vessels. The conclusions of these and other scholars are discussed below.

The decoration on the tanks is by means of either a single motif or a combination of motifs, usually divided into panels by vertical bands of cable, herringbone or cross-hatching. Of at least eighteen known examples of whole or partial vessels, six bear the *chi-rho*; one has *alpha* and *omega*; another, now lost, was reported as having been decorated with ornamental work 'imitating hoops of iron' and marked on one side with 'A' (Page 1911: 309); the find from Oxborough carries a symbol interpreted as a 'cross pattée' enclosed within a circle (Frere 1986: 403; Guy 1989), while six, possibly seven others bear circles or discs of varying diameters; seven have a decoration which includes a pattern of crossed diagonal lines, and a further four have a zigzag motif. Thus, there are several recurring motifs in their decoration, and these, it is proposed here, indicate a Christian identity for most, if not all of the tanks.

For two of the tanks from Icklingham (Kraay 1942: West 1976) (Figures 23a, 23b), one from Ashton (Guy, 1977) (Figure 23c), and those from Pulborough (Curwen 1943) (Figure 23d), Walesby (Petch 1961) (Figure 23e) and Caversham (Hassall and Tomlin 1989) (Figure 23f), a Christian identity is assured by the presence of the *chi-rho* and/or *alpha* and *omega*. As Guy (1981: 273–4) points out, the *chi-rho* was a Christian symbol even before its adoption by Constantine at the Battle of Milvian Bridge in 312, and it must therefore be accepted as unequivocally Christian by the mid-fourth century.[4] The *alpha-omega* symbol, based on Revelation 1.8 and 21.6, was a known Christian device before the fourth century, and its presence in late Roman Britain is well attested.[5]

A Christian identity for the other decorative devices used on the tanks is not so readily apparent; an investigation of the archaeological and literary evidence does, however, lead to the belief that these are also Christian symbols, despite the fact that it is sometimes very difficult to find fourth-century or even datable parallels.

Of those mentioned above, the most likely candidate for a Christian identification is the figure that has been variously described as a 'saltire' (Guy 1981: 271), '"X" motif' (Thomas 1981: 221) or 'cruciform design' (Donovan 1933: 378). It occurs in association with the *chi-rho* on the Pulborough and Caversham tanks, and thus can reasonably be interpreted as the *crux decussata*, or St Andrew's cross, a known Christian symbol found in the catacombs of Rome[6] and elsewhere. There is some debate as to when this form of the cross was first known,[7] but literary evidence

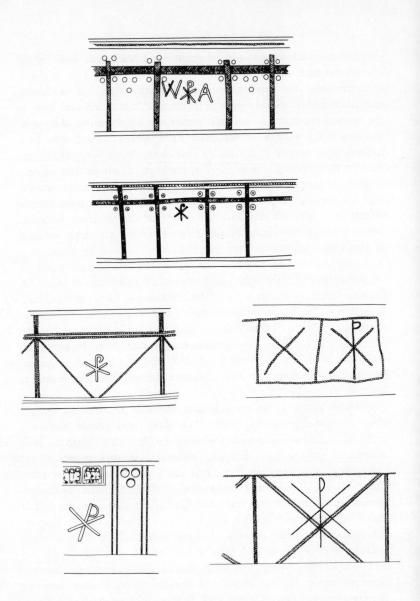

Figure 23 Decoration on lead tanks from Roman Britain (not to scale)
(a) Icklingham 1 (after West)
(b) Icklingham 2 (after West)
(c) Ashton 1 (after Taylor, in Guy 1977)
(d) Pulborough
(e) Walesby (after Thomas)
(f) Caversham

supports the view that it was recognised as Christian at least by the fourth and fifth centuries.[8]

In Britain, this cross is found along with an *iota-chi*, a *chi-rho*, and palm leaves, on the pewter plate from Stamford and now in the British Museum, mentioned earlier; on a stone from Maryport, also inscribed with a *chi-rho* (*RIB* 856); and on what may be a christianised pagan altar from Chedworth (Goodburn 1979: pl. 12.8; see also below, ch. V.3). The presence of this decoration on a number of circular lead tanks has prompted Thomas to observe that the often-repeated 'X' motif does not seem to be numeration. While it is allowed that the 'X' is one of the simplest forms of decoration and one found in undoubtedly pagan contexts, when it is found in combination with other known Christian symbols, it is very difficult to believe that it was not intended as a representation of the cross. By extension, such a symbol standing by itself on similar artefacts (that is, on the containers from Willingham (Phillips 1970: 208) (Figure 24a)[9] and Bourton-on-the-Water (Donovan, 1933) (Figures 24b, 24c)), or in combination with other devices (such as with circles, on the tank from Huntingdon (Donovan 1934: 116–17) (Figure 24d) and the Ashton fragment (Figure 24e)[10]) may point to a Christian identity for these vessels as well.

Another form of the cross is also probably represented on the tank from Oxborough (Figure 25a). The cross pattée within a circle, or cross alisée pattée (Webber 1971: 110), is up to now unattested in Roman Britain, although examples are found throughout the Empire. The cross itself resembles various early Celtic crosses (Child and Colles 1971: fig. 9),[11] the 'Lombard' crosses found in northern Italy and Gaul dating to after the fall of the Western Empire (Cabrol and Leclerq 1920–53: vol. 3.2, cols. 3097–102, s.v. *'croix et crucifix'*),[12] and others of the fifth or sixth century from Ephesus and Sinai (Child and Colles 1971: figs 11 and 13). In fact, crosses similar to that on the Oxborough tank are quite common in the East, and appear to have been popular throughout the Late Roman and Byzantine periods. Since tanks like the one from Oxborough have been found in Britain decorated with undoubted Christian symbols such as the *chi-rho* and *alpha-omega*, the Oxborough vessel itself is likely to be a Christian object; and this would add weight to the view that the motif on this tank is a Christian symbol, although one not previously recorded from Roman Britain.[13]

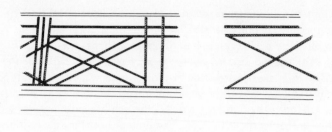

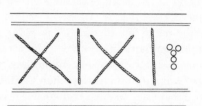

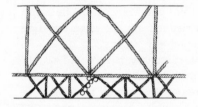

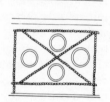

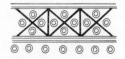

Figure 24 Decoration on lead tanks from Roman Britain (not to scale)
(a) Willingham (two pieces)
(b) Bourton-on-the-Water 1
(c) Bourton-on-the-Water 2
(d) Huntington (after Donovan)
(e) Ashton 2

The Oxborough cross is enclosed within a circle, and circles or discs form the whole, or part, of the decoration on the tanks from Burwell (Guy 1978) (Figure 25b), Ireby (Richmond 1945) (Figure 25c), Cambridge (Donovan 1934: 116–17) (Figure 25d), Huntingdon (Figure 24d) and the fragments from Ashton (Figure 24e) and Wilbraham (Figure 25e). If these objects are Christian and do have a liturgical purpose, as will be argued below, then it seems highly probable that the circle itself had a religious significance. Writers on religious symbolism see the circle as the symbol of God, of eternity and never-ending existence (Ferguson 1961: 153), of completeness and perfection (Webber 1971: 363), of the cosmos, time or the world (Child and Colles 1971: 27),[14] a symbol which epitomises an everlasting God who 'was in the beginning, is now and ever shall be, world without end'. (This concept of deity was not new: the early Greek philosopher, Thales, saw God as having neither beginning nor end: Diogenes Laertius, *Thales* 1.36).[15] Even more significant for this study is the equation of the circle with the triumphal wreath, the symbol indicating God's rule over the earth and the triumph of Christ over evil (Cabrol and Leclerq 1920–53: vol. 3.1, col. 1501 s.v. '*chrisme*'). The circle surrounding the cross was a development from the cross standing alone, and can be seen as reinforcing the religious significance of both symbols (Child and Colles 1971: 27).[16]

The Huntingdon tank and Ashton fragment combine a *crux decussata* with circles in the four triangles. A search for fourth- or fifth-century parallels to this motif in a Christian context has produced a sarcophagus from Rouen which may have been as early as Victricius (bishop *c.*380) or as late as the Merovingian (Christian) period: one end of the sarcophagus is decorated with the *chi-rho* and *alpha-omega* symbols, the other with this cross and half-circles in the triangles formed by the diagonals (Cabrol and Leclerq 1920–53: vol. 15.1, col. 128 s.v. '*Rouen*'). Also from a cemetery at Ugium in Roman Gaul comes a series of fifth-century vases and plates decorated with Christian symbols including palm-like motifs, one of which also carries a *crux decussata* with full circles in the quarters (Cabrol and Leclerq 1920–53: vol. 15.2, cols. 2854–8 and fig. 11201.17 s.v. '*Ugium*'). Confirmation of the Christian usage of the symbol is found on *terra sigillata* from Argonne dating to the fourth century, on which known Christian devices such as the monogrammatic cross, the dove and the cantharus are interspersed with the cross and circle (Chenet 1941: 109–22, pls

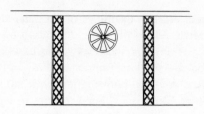

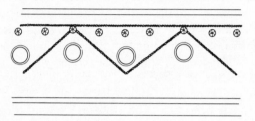

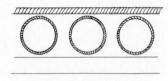

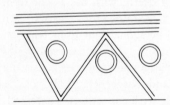

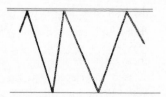

Figure 25 Decoration on lead tanks from Roman Britain (not to scale)
(a) Oxborough
(b) Burwell (after Hall, in Guy 1978)
(c) Ireby (after Richmond)
(d) Cambridge (after Donovan)
(e) Wilbraham
(f) Kenilworth

164

xxv, xxxv–xxxviii etc.).[17] Examples of the later use of this motif are more abundant, especially from Merovingian Gaul (Donovan 1934: 114–15); it appears, however, that it was employed as a Christian symbol by the late Roman empire, and its presence on the Ashton piece and the Huntingdon tank suggests that these vessels may also be Christian.[18] Furthermore, it is pointed out that the Ashton fragment was found with another complete tank decorated with a *chi-rho*.

It is now necessary to consider the circles themselves as possible Christian symbols, and it is here that the identification of the circle with the wreath of triumph seems particularly apposite. The circle occurs on tombs, perhaps signifying the triumph of the risen Lord: an early fourth-century use of the circle with a cross and a cruciform anchor is found on a tombstone fragment from the catacomb of Domitilla (Gough 1973: pl. 17); later examples include a circle beneath a Latin cross on a seventh-century tomb[19] from Gaul (Cabrol and Leclerq 1920–53: vol. 12.1, fig. 8668 s.v. '*Nantes*') and a circle together with known Christian symbols of *chi-rho* and peacocks on another sarcophagus from Gaul, probably of the same period (Cabrol and Leclerq 1920–53: vol. 15.1, fig. 10800 s.v. '*sarcophage*'). One of the earliest Byzantine inscriptions on Crete is a funerary inscription, the symbols in the first line of which are: *chi-rho*, circle, *chi-rho*, circle, *chi-rho*, *sigma* (Janthoudidis 1903: 95).[20] The circles here cannot be interpreted other than in association with the *chi-rho*. The circle or wreath also occurs in a baptismal setting, however, in line with the teachings of Ambrose that baptism is a form of death, with the ascent from the font after baptism a resurrection (*De sacramentis* 3.2). A wreath appears on one side of a late Roman octagonal font from Khŭrbet Tekûå in Palestine, on three other sides of which are two crosses enclosed within circles (one a cross pattée) and a device consisting of two interlaced squares (Conder and Kitchener 1883: vol. 3, 368). If the identification of the circle with the wreath is accepted, then it does seem that the circle itself may be considered a Christian symbol.

In addition to those from Oxborough, Huntingdon and Ashton[21] already discussed, there are four, possibly five, other tanks bearing circles or discs as a main decoration. The Ireby vessel has five circles on one panel and four and three-quarters on the other,[22] topped by a wide cable at the rim; the one from Burwell and the Wilbraham fragment have a decoration of circles and zigzags; the lost Icklingham tank was also reportedly decorated with 'hoops', but identification of these with circles is not certain. The circles on the extant containers are about 100 mm in diameter. In a slightly different category are the circles on the tank from Cambridge. They are more properly described as small discs, around 25 mm in diameter. From two to five of these are arranged in rows on the panels, and on two panels the circles are linked with two raised straight lines. The interpretation of this decoration can only be speculated, yet it is perhaps significant that the tank is very similar in other respects to the Icklingham vessels with *chi-rho* and *alpha* and *omega*. A Christian identity for the tanks from Ireby, Burwell and Wilbraham and perhaps Icklingham and Cambridge is at least a real possibility.

The other major motif employed in the decoration of the Romano-British lead tanks is the zigzag: with circles on the Burwell tank (Figure 25b) and Wilbraham fragment (Figure 25e), with a *chi-rho* on one of the vessels from Ashton (Figure 23c), and as the sole decoration on the Kenilworth fragment (Figure 25f). While one might hesitate to propose that such a common and simply applied device could have had any religious significance, it is perhaps worth mentioning that a stone font from Galatia of the Byzantine period has as its sole decoration a zigzag motif (Ramsay and Bell 1909: 132, Fig. 95).

This analysis of the motifs on the lead tanks shows that, although the vessels themselves are unique to Roman Britain, their decoration may be seen as reflecting Christian symbolism of the Late Empire as a whole. This accords with the view expressed more than three decades ago by Toynbee (1953: 23) that the archaeological evidence for Christianity in Roman Britain was not insular in character, but part of the cosmopolitan tradition of a far-flung empire.[23]

Conversely, the find-spots for the tanks (Figure 26) are not distributed over all the known Christian centres of Britain, but are concentrated in the East Midlands and East Anglia, with a single find in the south at Pulborough, one from Oxfordshire, one from Warwickshire, two tanks from Bourton-on-the-Water in Gloucestershire, and one from the north-west, at Ireby. If these objects are to be accepted as Christian, it is to be expected that there will be other evidence for Christianity in the vicinity of where they were discovered.

Figure 26 Distribution map of lead tanks in Roman Britain

Such evidence generally does exist. The vessels found in East Anglia are, in fact, from an area with the highest concentration of evidence for Christianity in Roman Britain (see below, Figure 28). Away from the east, the two tanks from Bourton-on-the-Water were found in a district in which a number of Christian finds have been made, the closest being at Chedworth Roman villa. The Caversham find was within 15 kilometres of Silchester, with its apsidal church and baptistery. The tank from Ireby seems remote from the other finds,[24] yet Ireby is but a few kilometres from Maryport and Carlisle, both of which have produced evidence for Romano-British Christianity (*RIB* 856, and Charlesworth 1978: 125). Moreover, this tank was found a short distance from where other Roman antiquities had been discovered, and, significantly, in the vicinity of a later twelfth-century church.[25] Two tanks only cannot, as yet, be placed near other known Christian finds: those from Pulborough and Kenilworth. As far as the Pulborough vessel is concerned, its decoration includes a *chi-rho*, so a Christian identity cannot be doubted. The new find from Kenilworth presents some problems but, if it is accepted as a Christian object, a provenance in Warwickshire does serve to expand the distribution map of Christian evidence in Roman Britain, extending it from an area of considerable intensity (see below, Figure 28).

For the tanks to be accepted as Christian objects from Roman Britain, not only must they fit the distribution pattern for Romano-British Christianity, but they should also be able to be dated to the fourth or fifth century. Unfortunately, this evidence is not so readily available, although such evidence as exists suggests a fourth-century date: the tanks from Bourton-on-the-Water were found with coins of Valentinian I (364–75), but the excavator deduced that by then the vessels were not being used for their original purpose (Donovan 1934: 100); those from Ashton and Caversham were found in wells with late fourth-century pottery (Hadman and Upex 1977: 8; D. Miles, pers. comm.); the one from Burwell in a field with fourth-century pottery (Guy 1978: 3); and the Willingham tank in the vicinity of sherds dating from the second to the fourth-century (Phillips 1970). Less conclusive is the evidence from Icklingham, where, although fourth-century coins were found, they were not closely associated with the tanks (Kraay 1942: 219; West 1976: 79–81). However, the presence of the *chi-rho* on these tanks, as well as those from Ashton, Pulborough, Caversham and Walesby, indicates a fourth-century date as most likely (see n. 4).

This leaves the vessels from Cambridge, Ireby, Huntingdon, Kenilworth, Oxborough, Wilbraham and the lost Icklingham tank as undatable, except on stylistic grounds. Guy (1981: 273) has drawn attention to the similarity in decoration of the Icklingham and Cambridge tanks. Richmond (1945: 167) points out that for the eight tanks then known to him, the method of manufacture was basically the same – a base, and two sides curved to fit; this seems to apply to the later tanks as well, while the method of applying the decoration also seems to be the same, with the exception of the Oxborough vessel (Guy 1989). Despite the fact that the evidence is not conclusive, it is sufficient to indicate that the tanks are probably datable to the fourth century, perhaps from early to mid-fourth. This would accord with the purpose proposed for them below.

The function of these lead tanks has been much discussed. Richmond (1945: 169) suggests water-troughs, or vats for dyeing, fulling or brewing. Donovan (1933: 379) merely suggests a 'bath or basin'. Curwen (1943: 156–7) proposes water storage, the measurement of liquids in bulk, or a religious use, such as font or baptistery. Guy (1981: 274–5) also favours water storage, but feels that there would have been the danger of lead poisoning had the tanks been regularly used. He suggests that those at Icklingham and Ashton were connected with the cemeteries there, and contained water to be added to the wine at a *refrigerium* held to honour the dead. Toynbee (1953: 15–16) believed the vessels with undoubted Christian symbols probably fulfilled a religious function, and even those without such symbols may also have had the same purpose; she appears to favour baptism by affusion as the most likely function. Frend (1979: 136) also accepts that the tanks were used in the baptismal rite, but does not enter into the debate as to their specific purpose. Thomas, in his discussion on baptism and baptisteries, concludes that Romano-British churches would have had fixed or portable fonts, and that the lead containers were, therefore, alternatives to fixed fonts. West (1976: 78–9) proposes they were not fonts, but were intended to be used in 'ritual ablutions' in connection with baptism.

It is impossible for some of these proposals to be a satisfactory explanation for all the tanks. An industrial purpose is highly unlikely on the site of church, baptistery and cemetery, such as at Icklingham. A lead water-storage container would have been an unusual and extravagant domestic accessory, while the presence of three similar containers for use at a *refrigerium* is difficult to justify for the cemetery at Icklingham; it was, after all, the burial place of only about forty persons. A device for the measurement of liquid in bulk must be dismissed as the tanks have no common denominator, and no known relationship to Roman measurement of capacity.

This leaves a baptismal function as the most likely purpose for these objects. Thomas argues, on the evidence of the fourth-century tombstone of Innocens at Aquileia, that baptism was by affusion and that, therefore, the lead tanks were fonts. He adduces further evidence with the fragment of the tank from Walesby, which, he believes, depicts a female *competens*, supported by her sponsors, about to step into a *lavacrum* to be baptised.

There are three objections to this interpretation. The first was mooted by Thomas himself. At Icklingham there is an apsidal structure of coursed tiles with a step taking up part of the interior. This has been generally accepted as a font, in accordance with fourth-century Church teaching: Ambrose refers to the baptismal candidate as going *down* into the water[26] as Christ did (*De sacramentis* 2.16, 1.19). In his study of the architectural setting of baptism, Davies (1962: 102) says that the font was 'habitually sunk below the level of the floor, and the steps down symbolized the descent of Christ into the Jordan',[27] and this could also have been the practice in house or estate churches: Rogers (1903: 314), in his work on the baptismal rite, suggests that the ceremony conducted in a private house (such as a house at Bourton?) would have taken place in a bath room; Thomas has proposed that the nymphaeum at Chedworth may have been christianised to be used as a font. In both cases the candidate would have stepped down into the water. If the permanent structure at Icklingham is indeed a font, complete with step, then it is hard to believe that the two, possibly three, lead tanks found there are also fonts; and the dimensions of the two extant tanks are such that they could not be placed inside the apsidal structure.

This leads to the second objection to such identification, that more than one font should be found at a rural Christian site.[28] There are two tanks from Bourton; two, possibly more, from Ashton; and three from Icklingham. Given that it was the bishop who normally performed baptisms (Tertullian, *De baptismo* 17), although priests and deacons were also present (Ambrose, *De sacramentis* 2.16), then it would seem necessary to have only one font. That the bishop still performed the actual baptism into the fourth and fifth centuries[29] is confirmed by John Chrysostom (*Baptismal Instructions* 2.25 (Wenger)) and Theodore of Mopsuestia (*Baptismal Homilies* 3.14–15), both of whom died in the fifth century. It was only later that it became the usual practice for a priest to carry out baptisms.

Finally, it does seem that not all the lead tanks would have been of an appropriate dimension to have performed the function of a font. The sizes should be closely examined: there is considerable variance in both depth and diameter. The deepest vessel would have been the (incomplete) one from Walesby (0.55 m), the shallowest, that from Ireby (0.17 m). The maximum depth would have presented little problem for conducting baptism by affusion for adult candidates, but might have proved more difficult for children. However, the vessels were probably not buried in the ground to a more convenient level since the decoration of *chi-rho* or other religious symbol would thus have been covered. The tank with the greatest diameter is one of the pair from Bourton (0.97 m), the smallest, the one from Ireby (0.46 m), with the Oxborough find slightly larger (0.49 m), and the Kenilworth tank 0.50 m. It does seem highly improbable that the containers from Ireby, Oxborough and Kenilworth would have been wide enough to allow affusion to have been performed without thoroughly wetting the officiant standing beside the vessel. Moreover, the water had been consecrated, not merely blessed (Ambrose, *De sacramentis* 1.15; Cyril of Jerusalem, *Mystagogic catechesis* 3.3),[30] and it is unlikely that it would have been allowed to spill all over the ground, especially when there were a number of candidates to be baptised.[31] Another interpretation for the tanks should be sought.

There remains the proposal by West that the tanks were for 'ritual ablutions' in association with the ceremony of baptism. Thomas did look at this possibility, but rejected it: 'Are they for the obscure rite of *pedilavium*, and is it really credible that this was a feature of worship in fourth-century Icklingham?' Nonetheless, West's interpretation is, on balance, the most likely one.

The evidence is substantial. Although Thomas describes the footwashing rite as 'obscure', there is no doubt that, while it was not carried out in Rome itself (Ambrose, *De sacramentis* 3.5), it was practised in Christian churches both east and west of Rome. From the proceedings of the Council of Elvira of *c*.305, canon 48 enacts that the footwashing was (henceforth?) to be done not by the bishops but by the priests.[32] Ambrose (*De sacramentis* 3.4), from his see in Celtic Milan in about 390, describes the baptism ceremony in which, following the ascent from the font, the candidate's feet were washed; and in Gaul, Caesarius of Arles (*c*.470–542) mentioned the same ritual (*Sermones* 204.3). In the African Church, evidence for the *pedilavium* at baptism is found in the writings of Augustine (*Ad Ianuarium* 2.33) and, for Syria, Aphraates (*Homilies* 12) possibly implies the rite (Yarnold 1970: 460). Clearly, since this was part of the baptism ceremony in many parts of the Empire, it would be wholly reasonable to believe it was also practised in Roman Britain.[33]

Archaeological evidence also suggests that the rite was carried out in both East and West. Davies (1962: 26) cites examples from Fréjus and Albegna, where a much smaller basin was found at the side of the font. Akeley (1967: 54) gives another in Spain at Vega del Mar. At the eastern end of the Empire, similar devices have been found at S'baita and Emmaus (Davies 1962: 26). At Emmaus, in Palestine, there is a fourth-century baptistery: on each side of the font is a small shallow basin with a drain which connects it to the font itself (Cabrol and Leclerq 1920–53: vol. 2.1, col. 455 and fig. 1371 s.v. '*baptistère*'). An identification of these devices for use in the *pedilavium* rite does seem reasonable.[34]

The problem of multiple tanks at a site must now be addressed. There is some help from *De sacramentis* 3.4. According to Ambrose, the footwashing was done by both bishop and priests, although the evidence of the Council of Elvira suggests that it may have been performed only by the priests in the Church in Spain. This would explain the presence of more than one tank for footwashing: since not every parish or house church[35] would have had a baptistery,[36] presumably baptisms would have been arranged on a regional basis for the occasion; and as only one person, normally the bishop, performed the baptism, there would thus be more than one priest available to carry out the *pedilavium*. This would speed up the overall baptism ceremony – a point not without merit at a chilly Eastertide, even more so if baptisms were also carried out at Epiphany (see above, n. 31).

The use of the lead tanks for footwashing would account for the apparent decline in their use about the middle of the fourth century. It could be that, following the first flush of enthusiasm, the large numbers of converts after 314 slowed down to a trickle, and the vessels were no longer necessary.[37] Perhaps, too, as Guy (1981: 275) suggests, the pagan resurgence of the second half of the fourth century was responsible for the deliberate damage to some tanks, and for the fact that the tanks from Ashton, one bearing a *chi-rho*, ended up in a backyard well.[38] If these tanks were put into store in, say, a sympathiser's workshop, they were then more accessible to pagan zealots than if they had been in use in places of Christian worship at the time.

The evidence of the scene on the Walesby tank might now be interpreted in the light of the above. Ambrose puts the footwashing immediately after the ascent from the font (*De sacramentis* 3.4). The scene portrayed on the Walesby tank could as easily be that immediately before the footwashing, as one preceding the actual baptism (so Thomas 1981: 221–5). In either case the candidate would be naked.

One further feature of two of the tanks should be considered, and linked to their identification as vessels for footwashing. It is noted that the Pulborough tank and one of the pair from Bourton have holes punched around the rim. Thomas goes to considerable lengths to show that some sort of temporary structures would have been built around baptisteries used infrequently during the Church year, and that such evidence is not always detectable archaeologically. As shown above, the need for privacy would have been as great for the footwashing part of the ceremony as for the baptism itself, and it may be that the irregular holes around two of the lead tanks are the evidence for temporary and partial screens such as would afford privacy for this ritual and some protection from the elements.

The published evidence for the lead tanks of Roman Britain is not always specific or well illustrated. Only in recent years have these objects been reported in any kind of detail. This reappraisal of the available evidence has shown that they may all be regarded as Christian, and that, although the tanks themselves are unique to Britain, their decoration and purpose do allow them to be seen as reflecting Christian symbolism and ritual throughout the Empire in the fourth century.

3: PROBABLE CHRISTIAN SYMBOLS FROM CHEDWORTH AND POUNDBURY

In a provocative Presidential Address delivered to the Bristol and Gloucestershire Archaeological Society in 1983, Dr Graham Webster proposed that the building complex at Chedworth was not a villa but, rather, part of a *Tempelbezirk* such as was found at Lydney and Nettleton (Webster 1984). Webster's thesis can, at this stage, be neither proved nor disproved, since large-scale excavation would be necessary; it does, however, provide a stimulus to re-examine the archaeological finds from Chedworth, particularly those with possible religious associations. This has led to the conclusion that there are Christian symbols employed here which have not been recognised as such, but which furnish further evidence for a Christian presence at Chedworth. It also seems an appropriate time to appraise another artefact from Roman Britain, from Poundbury in Dorset. It is hoped, as a result, to add these finds to the *corpus* of evidence for Christianity in Roman Britain and to the list of Christian symbols found there.

Despite the large number of publications referring to Chedworth,[1] there is still confusion about which objects bear likely Christian symbols, and indeed about what symbols are actually depicted. The confusion arises as much from the fact that the original drawings by Grover (1867 and 1868) and Fox (reproduced in Goodburn 1979: pls 11, 12) are incomplete and poorly labelled, as from what may have been a conscious effort to enhance those inscriptions which could be identified as positively Christian,[2] while ignoring others which appeared at the time not to fit any preconceived ideas on what constituted a Christian symbol. Any attempt to clarify the situation more than a century after the site was first found is made more difficult because the local oolite limestone is very soft: inscriptions which may have been sharp to Grover or Fox are not now so well defined; alternatively, additional marks may have been added accidentally or purposefully since the original excavations.[3]

However, if study is restricted to those inscriptions which are generally accepted as recognisable symbols, the problems of identification are not insurmountable. For the purposes of this chapter, the one definite *chi-rho* (Goodburn 1979: pl. 11.C) and two further possible examples of this symbol (pl. 11.D, F) will not be discussed.[4] Instead, it is suggested that a closer examination be made of the symbols on one of the small shaped stones (Goodburn 1979: pl. 12.8, 9) which Webster has identified as portable altars (Webster 1984: 16, no. 8), and to which scant attention has so far been paid.

There were four such stones found at Chedworth. Two have a crudely carved figure, probably of the god Mars–Lenus, on a side panel (Goodburn 1979: pls 10.1, 10.3, 13). There is a small depression on the top, presumably for equally small or symbolic offerings, or perhaps blood from a sacrificial animal. The second pair are similar in shape, though somewhat more tapered (or worn) towards the top.[5] As Webster points out, these stones resemble the two found at Nettleton (Wedlake 1982: figs 68, 71), although the Chedworth stones, about 100 mm high, are only half the size of those from Nettleton; and the identification by Wedlake and Webster of these objects as portable altars is more acceptable than as 'candlesticks' (Grover 1868: 132).[6] The provenance of none of the four stones is published, although it is probable the carved examples were found near a Romano-Celtic temple excavated earlier this century some little distance from the main buildings (Baddeley 1930; Goodburn 1979: 18). The absence of a representation of a specific god on the other two suggests that they may have come from near the octagonal structure usually interpreted as a nymphaeum; a larger uninscribed altar was found buried (perhaps on purpose?) close by (Fox 1887: 335).

In a consideration of the lineal inscriptions on one of this second pair of stones, it must be kept in mind that there appears to have been a deliberate christianising of the nymphaeum with the carving of at least one *chi-rho* on the stones from that structure.[7] The altar itself bears four symbols: two + , one X, and one ‡, all of which may be shown to have been employed as Christian of which may be shown to have been employed as Christian symbols. Therefore, it is proposed here that these inscriptions are further evidence for the christianising of what may have been a pagan household or, if Webster is correct, a pagan religious site.

The first two symbols, the one known variously as the *crux quadrata*, Greek cross or cross of St George, the other the *crux decussata*, saltire or St Andrew's cross, have been discussed elsewhere.[8] It is necessary here only to reiterate that they were both known Christian symbols prior to the fourth century. The third symbol, which may be described, as it appears on the altar, as a vertical bar cut by three shorter horizontals,[9] should in fact be viewed with the stone turned ninety degrees, that is, as a horizontal bar cut by three shorter verticals. When viewed thus, the symbol becomes a ligatured IH, or *iota-eta*, the first two letters of the Greek IHΣΟΥΣ, and the earliest Christian monogram.[10] This monogram was known at least from the second century: Barnabas, writing in the early part of that century (*Epistle* 9.7–8), and drawing on Genesis 14.14, found a Christian allegory in the number 318, observing that it was made up of:

> ten [which in Greek is] I, and eight [which is] H. There you have IHΣΟΥΣ [abbreviated to IH]. But since the Cross, prefigured by a T, was to be the source of grace, it adds the three hundred [which is written T]. It therefore points to Jesus in two letters, and to the Cross in the one.[11]

The monogram is found possibly as early as the second century in the catacomb of Priscilla, and is more frequently encountered in the third and fourth centuries (Sulzberger 1925: 383, figs 22, 23).

It may be alone or in combination with other symbols. Indeed, the use of two or three Christian symbols on the one object is quite common throughout the late Roman period, and the appearance of this lineal device with the Greek cross and the *crux decussata* supports the interpretation of this symbol as the IH monogram.

It could be objected that the placing of the symbol sideways on the altar is irregular, if not sacrilegious; but it is likely that the significance of the Greek would have been lost on Romano-Celtic Britons, since a number of examples of confusion with the more common Greek symbols of *alpha* and *omega* also exist in Roman Britain.[12] This does not, therefore, seem to be an issue.

The presence of what may be taken as Christian symbols on a pagan altar can best be explained as the deliberate christianising of the object, an action paralleled by the inscribing of the *chi-rho* on the stones of the nymphaeum; and this gives further weight to the belief that Chedworth was, for part of its history at least, in the hands of Christians.[13] This also conforms with the evidence presented in the previous chapter (IV), on the christianising of pagan sites.

There is no doubt that some Christian symbols are much rarer than others, but it must be realised that, in the early centuries of Christianity, its iconography was still developing, with much of the symbolism adopted either from the Jewish or the pagan religions. This would have been the case in the use of the letter Y as a Christian symbol, an example of which has been found in Roman Britain: a non-functional metal object, shaped in the form of a Y, was recovered from a grave in the cemetery at Poundbury, Dorchester, a cemetery which is almost certainly Christian (Green 1981; 1982; see above, ch. III).

The Y is still found in the Church today in the form of the pallium and on chasubles, these varying little from vestments of the early middle ages; it may be seen as symbolic of the crucifixion (Webber 1971: 375). On chasubles, the vertical of the Y is sometimes extended upward about the same height as the diagonals to give a symbol resembling the prayerful *orans* attitude with arms extended upward, frequently found in paintings in the catacombs of Rome or at Lullingstone in Britain. There is evidence to suggest that early Christians saw the *orans* stance as a form of the cross (Minucius Felix, *Octavius* 29.6).[14] It also represented Christ's suffering on the cross: in the eucharistic prayer of the *Apostolic Tradition*, dating to the early third century, Christ is said to have stretched out his hands when he suffered.[15] It seems then that the Y became a 'cryptogram of the Cross of Christ' (Child and Colles 1971: 44).[16] But most commonly in the ancient world the symbol was seen as depicting moral choice in life, or, as an extension of this, as representing a life hereafter where the 'good' were rewarded, the 'bad' punished.

Although it was Pythagoras who called the Y the symbol of human life, the base representing childhood, the arms the later choice of man for good or evil,[17] the idea of a choice in life was also voiced in Greek literature: Hesiod, in his *Works and Days* (287–92), writes of the two roads which people might travel in life, and Xenophon (*Memorabilia* 2.1.21–34) also refers to the paths of virtue and vice, quoting the sophist Prodicus. This concept was evidently transferred by neo-Pythagoreans to the fate of the deceased in a life hereafter: a pagan tombstone of the first century AD from Philadelphia in Lydia is decorated with a Y (Cumont 1922: 151). Neo-Pythagoreanism had spread to Rome and Alexandria from about the first century BC, and the philosophy is reflected in the literature of the period: Cicero (*Tusculanae disputationes* 1.30.70) refers to the two roads for souls to travel,[18] and Vergil (*Aeneid* 6.540–3) appears to have much the same view of the afterlife. It seems to have spread to the extremities of the Empire: by the first half of the third century of the Christian era, at Holborough in distant Britain, a small child was buried in a lead coffin ornamented with a large Y, pecten shells and the figures of a maenad and a satyr (Jessup 1954: pl. XIII). This suggests that by now the Y had also become an Orphic emblem (Henig 1984b: 201).

Meanwhile, Christians had not been averse to adopting this useful didactic device:[19] even before the Peace of the Church, Lactantius (*Divinae institutiones* 6.3–4) was writing both of the philosophers' concepts of the Y symbol, and the 'need of the letter Y' as a guide for Christians. Here he incorporates the idea of moral choice in life with that of reward or punishment after death, to the extent of quoting *Aeneid* 6.540. Archaeological evidence of the use of the symbol by Christians comes from the catacombs of Rome where the Y has been found amongst other Christian symbols such as the *iota-chi* and X on vases associated with the burials there (Garrucci 1872: vol. I, 167).

From this background, it is a simple matter to set the curious metal object found in the Poundbury grave[20] into a Christian context. That the cemetery there is Christian is virtually certain (above, ch. III), and the final report on the site will create a great deal of interest when it is published. Even without that evidence, however, it does seem that religious practices in Roman Britain varied little from those closer to the centre of the Empire, and that the religious thought and iconography there generally reflected that current in the Empire, though there would probably have been some local idiosyncrasies. An intriguing question with regard to the Poundbury Y is whether the woman buried there (or her relatives) was Christian with neo-Pythagorean leanings, or neo-Pythagorean with Christian inclinations. That she was merely a simple Christian Briton with no disposition towards philosophy is less likely, since the grave was evidently of a person of some distinction (Green 1981: 134; 1982: 67), and this could suggest some degree of philosophical erudition in fourth-century Roman Britain.

All this is, of course, within the realms of speculation only. The facts are that, in a cemetery which has many features that suggest a Christian identity, a grave has been found containing a Y-shaped device, and that this symbol was a known Christian emblem at the time the burial took place. It is therefore proposed that this is further evidence for the Christianity of the Poundbury cemetery, and that the Y should be added to the *iota-eta* from Chedworth to give two more Christian symbols from Roman Britain.

VI

LINKS WITH PAGAN
RELIGIONS AND PRACTICES

1: THE EVIDENCE

The evidence for Christianity was reconsidered in Chapters III–V of
this study: probable Christian cemeteries and churches were
analysed and criteria for their identification developed, and some
symbols and objects with a likely Christian association, beyond
those treated by Thomas (1981), were identified. It has been
apparent as research has progressed that, in Romano-British
Christianity, there was evidence, not only of an expected and
understandable Jewish influence, but also of pagan Roman and
Celtic elements. While links between the Jewish and Christian
religions are beyond the scope of the present work, the Roman and
Celtic elements in the Christianity of Roman Britain are relevant,
and may be identified; they are classified and analysed here and, in
Part 2, an assessment of these features and their possible impact on
Romano-British Christianity is made.

It would seem appropriate to begin with the most obvious feature
of Christian religion, its churches. Undoubtedly the early Church
took time to establish traditions in building as well as in ritual and
dogma, and the more romanised areas would reflect more
accurately current trends in the development of Christian religious
tradition. As noted in Chapter IV, in the period after Constantine's
conversion and the emergence of Christianity from house churches,
the basilical or simple apsidal shape, with variations, came to be
the preferred plan for Romano-British churches. Its origins are
debated: Davies (1962: 26–31) and Ward-Perkins (1954) trace the
origins of the basilical plan by way of the Roman secular building
to the Greek temple, rather than to Roman domestic architecture,

a theory favoured by earlier writers and restated by Dix (1954: 22–7). For Christians the basilica achieved a three-fold purpose: it gave space for adherents of the faith inside the building, a provision not required in Roman temples, since the *cella* of a temple was reserved for the cult statue, the priest and perhaps a select few attendants; it gave privacy to satisfy the exclusiveness of Christianity, which, following the tradition of the closed or upper room (John 20.19, 26; Acts 22.7–8), rigidly excluded non-believers; and it was a visible departure from the classical Roman or the indigenous Romano-Celtic temple form. The fact that, in several ways, it resembled a Mithraeum may have contributed to the intense animosity felt by Christians towards that equally exclusive cult, which appears to have manifested itself in the destruction of various Mithraea in Britain in the fourth century.

While the apsidal or basilical building was found mainly in the towns, the simple rectangular shape was employed in churches in the rural areas and was also later used in the small Early Celtic (post-Roman) churches or oratories. But even before the arrival of the Romans, rectangular buildings had been constructed for pagan religious purposes, such as the shrines at Chelmsford, Danebury, Heathrow, Maiden Castle, South Cadbury, Uley (Drury 1980: 45–55 and fig. 3.2) and Stanstead (Brooks 1989). In the following centuries, despite the evolution of the *cella*-and-ambulatory type temple, religious structures of rectangular plan were still found in Britain in the Roman period; Lewis (1966: 75–8) lists Colchester 6, Nettleton 1, Springhead 4 and Wycomb 1. Similar temples were found in Gaul and Germany.[1] Of the four examples Lewis gives from Britain, only one, Colchester 6, might be considered urban, but, since it was built outside the *colonia* and on a site which had likely pre-Roman origins (Crummy 1980: 258), it is best considered as rural also. It may be that the simple rectangular church, found in Britain and common in Northern Italy around Aquileia until the sixth century (Radford 1968: 27), was a successor to the pagan rectangular shrine or temple; the failure of the plan to be maintained in the urban, and presumably more romanised areas, either in Britain or in other parts of the Empire, suggests that, for urban Christians, its architecture was neither sufficiently distinctive for their tastes nor adequate for their larger congregations. The adoption of the plan by the rural Early Celtic church is perhaps not coincidental.

Christian churches, while having a different appearance from that of temples, borrowed features from them.[2] From an early period, churches had altars, as did pagan temples: the pagan outside the building, the Christian inside. The Book of Revelation, written about AD 100, has three references to Christian altars (6.9, 8.3, 9.13), but it was not the pagan *arae* which were installed in churches: Minucius Felix (*Octavius* 32) could say firmly that Christians had neither shrines nor [pagan-style] altars.[3] In Britain, the dedicatory inscription on a vessel (no. 9) in the Water Newton Treasure honours a *sanctum altare* (Painter 1977b), the term *altare* apparently having been consciously adopted by Christians to distinguish it from the pagan *ara*.[4]

From the little evidence as yet available, it seems that Romano-British Christians also decorated the interiors of their buildings in much the same way as the pagans. Lewis (1966: 33–4) says that most temple sites have produced wall plaster, and floors were most commonly of plain red terracotta *tesserae*, less commonly of stone, either as *tesserae* or slabs, with the *cella* occasionally covered with a mosaic. Where such evidence is available, it would seem that Christians tended to follow the same practice, and, on occasion, provided a more elaborate covering for the most important part of their religious structures. Of the putative churches, the Silchester building had a red tessellated floor, with a feature geometric mosaic 1.5 metres square on the chord of the apse, and its internal plastered walls were painted in an imitation marble design (Fox and Hope 1893: 563–8). The Nettleton cruciform conversion was marked by a repainting of the plastered walls, and the laying of a new floor of stone flags in the central shrine, replacing the *opus signinum* of the previous eight-chambered structure (Wedlake 1982: 104–5). St Paul-in-the-Bail, Lincoln, a timber-built structure, appears to have used for flooring the paving stones of the forum in which it was built (M. Jones, pers. comm.). The Butt Road building had plastered stone walls, painted red on white at the apsidal end; its floor was possibly only soil or sand (C. Crossan, pers. comm.; Crummy 1989: 13).

When a Christian building replaced a pagan one, it seems, at least where comparisons can be made, to have been on a more modest scale. The pit F32 at Icklingham contained a stone pillar and fragments of an elaborate type of roofing tile, and these plus *tesserae* found nearby are thought to have been from some previous pagan building. This points to a more opulent structure than the apsidal fourth-century church which replaced it. With the exception of the pit, nowhere else on this site have similar building materials been found above the chalk layer which sealed the presumably pre-Christian phase; but building A, aligned with the church, and believed to be contemporaneous, may give an indication of the decoration of the church; it had plastered internal (timber?) walls and an *opus signinum* floor (West 1976). Similarly, the successor to the Romano-Celtic temple at Uley was less elaborate. The temple had been a large building (12 m × 14 m) with stone foundations, though probably with at least partial timber superstructure; its tiled roof, plastered interior and portico suggest some architectural pretension; and it would have been adorned with the well-executed statue of Mercury found at the site. The temple was partly replaced by a masonry building of much smaller dimensions (6 m × 4.2 m), and then by a timber structure of about the same size. In the interim report (Ellison 1980) there was no mention of decorative features for either of the later buildings. Another example is from Lamyatt Beacon, where a temple of stone base and part timber construction, with slab floor, plastered interior and a roof of lias limestone slates was followed by a much smaller masonry building with dirt floor (Leech 1986: 264, 268). The Witham rectangular building may also be considered here, although final details are not yet published: this small structure, on stone foundation and possibly with plastered timber walls, was built on a site where previously there had been a building of some substance, with box tiles, window glass and material which suggests perhaps a bath-house or guest-house associated with an earlier pagan temple (R. Turner, pers. comm.). At these four locations, at least, it is clear that, while Christians occupied earlier pagan sites, and built with the same kinds of material, their structures were of a less pretentious, less wealthy kind. The implications of this will be discussed below.

With the notable exception of cemetery churches, pagan and Christian religious buildings tended to occupy much the same kinds of sites. This is not surprising, if it is accepted that Christians often built on sites or even used structures previously occupied by pagans. Gregory the Great (*Dialogues* 2.8) describes how, at Cassino, near Rome, St Benedict (*c*.480–550) destroyed the idol, overturned the altar, cut down the sacred grove, and turned the temple of Apollo into a chapel dedicated to St Martin of Tours. A similar situation seems to have occurred at Athens, where the earlier religious structures were adapted and the local religious tradition was exploited by Christians (Dyggve 1951: 8–9).

This type of action apparently had official endorsement by the Church, even in the fourth century: Socrates (*Historia ecclesiastica* 4.24) writes of pagan statues being pulled down and of the conversion of temples into churches in Egypt.[5] In Roman Britain, Christians also destroyed pagan buildings, reusing the sites for churches, or adapted them for churches; in Chapter IV, probable examples were discussed. Such action must be seen as a means of christianising a pagan site, and preserving the tradition of sanctity. But in order to determine if Christians could have had further reasons for their adoption of pagan sites, it would be useful to look at other likely factors determining the original location of a pagan temple.

Lewis (1966: 129–31), dividing his sites into rural and urban, concluded that, in or near towns, temples were 'built to serve specific groups of people', that is, that the choice of site was not based primarily on religious considerations. In the country, however, other factors could be involved as well: temples might be built on earlier sacred sites, near roads and favoured hunting grounds, on tribal boundaries, associated with fairgrounds, marketplaces or theatres, or on hillsides (not necessarily on the highest point). Presumably such sites would have had some religious association, but most were also places where people would have passed or congregated. While there have been more recent studies of Romano-Celtic religion, no great changes have been suggested to Lewis's list, and it may be taken as fairly comprehensive.

If such considerations are applied to the locating of hypothetical Christian churches, and if we exclude the attraction of earlier sacred sites, it could be argued that, because numbers of people would pass or gather at these locations, probably fairly regularly, a Christian building at such a site would be fulfilling the mission of the Church. With regard to locating on tribal boundaries, presumably these would have lost much of their significance during the Occupation; the process, however, may have been romanised: Frontinus (*De limitibus* in *Corpus Agrimensorum Romanorum* (Thurin edn, p. 13)) writes of a temple in Umbria located where maritime and mountain *properties* adjoined. Perhaps this then was transferred to a Christian context in the late Empire. Such may have been reasons for locating Christian churches.

But what actually happened in rural Roman Britain does not appear to fit those models. Of nine possible churches, two may be regarded as cemetery churches; all the others had pagan predecessors. No other obvious factor would seem to have been involved in their siting.

The situation is very different in the towns, however, and accords with the needs of specific groups of people proposed by Lewis for Romano-Celtic temples. No presumed church is so far known to have been built on the site of a previous sacred place or building. But some were built in prominent places, where people would gather: St Paul-in-the-Bail, Silchester 9 and probably Canterbury Cathedral are good examples. The cemetery churches, sited as they were along the roads leading into the towns, would generally have been well placed to attract the attention of travellers, for example, St Pancras at Canterbury, Verulamium 7 and Colchester 9 (Butt Road). Christians' benevolence to strangers, dispensing charity to Christian and pagan alike, their care for the graves of the dead and the holiness of their lives, as disparagingly described by Julian (*Ad Arsacium* 429D, Loeb edn), would have been readily observable in locations such as these and help to increase the popularity of the religion.

It would seem that, while there were differences in rural areas, Christians in Roman Britain in locating their churches generally followed much the same pattern as had their pagan forebears. This is obviously because the needs still remained. The coming of Christianity was not to mean a major shift in the locating of religious structures.

Moreover, it was not to mean a major change in orientation of the structures. Wait (1986: 172, 180) notes that, of known Celtic shrines, 95 per cent were built with entrance between north-east and south-east, and he believes that this cannot be by chance. In his analysis of Romano-Celtic temples, he finds that all known circular or polygonal temples and 93 per cent of the rectilinear temples were orientated within this same quadrant. When Christian churches were built in Britain, on available evidence it appears that they, too, favoured a west–east or east–west alignment; of those buildings analysed in this study which are possible churches, only one was positively north–south. It was pointed out in Chapter III that the east held special significance for Christians, and this was translated at least by the early third century into Christians turning to the east to pray and by their being buried so as to face east in the event of a physical resurrection. But the Constantinian structures, while favouring west–east or east–west, were not rigid in their orientation; it cannot, therefore, be seen as a 'rule' for construction of churches even into the fifth century, although Paulinus of Nola (*Epistulae* 32.13) indicates that it was the usual fashion to build churches with entrance to the east (that is, with apse to the west) in his day. The fact that west–east or east–west was the preferred orientation may reflect the universal and age-old association among primitive peoples of religion and the sun.

Formal churches have been analysed for features in common with the pagan, but house churches or chapels should also be considered. They were the earliest form of Christian building, and, although the very first churches were probably merely Roman *triclinia*, religious activities expanded and the house church came to be a suite of rooms. Likely examples from Britain have been discussed previously. They may be seen to be paralleled by the Roman household shrine, and these *aediculae* or *lararia*[6] were often as hard to identify as house churches because there was no fixed model. They could be as simple and unpretentious as a recess in a wall, as was possibly the case at Colliton Park, Dorchester, where a small niche had been formed between two piers in the cold room of the bath suite (Drew and Selby 1937: 11 and pl. ix); a room set apart, and more elaborately decorated, as perhaps house XIV.2 at Silchester, which had, in addition, a platform at one end of the room (Boon 1974: 161; 1983: 36); an outdoor feature, such as the purported nymphaeum at Chedworth (Goodburn 1979); or even a 'secret' room, such as the deep rooms at Lullingstone (Meates 1955: ch. VII) and Rivenhall (Morris and Roxan 1980: 188–9; Rodwell and Rodwell 1985: 28 and fig. 21), parallels for which have been found on the continent (Boon 1983: 40–3). The ultimate would have been the villa temple or shrine, as perhaps at Fring (Edwards 1977: 234–6), Stroud (Smith 1978: 125, fig. 38) or Walton on Hill (Anon. 1940: 181). There is very little evidence that these are, in fact, household or villa shrines. The least doubtful would be the deep room at Lullingstone and, less certainly, at Rivenhall; the former because sculptures, presumably *imagines* of ancestors, were found *in situ*, and the almost certain Christian house church was established directly above it, the latter because it became part of the foundations of a seventh-century mausoleum or chapel, and later church. With regard to household shrines and, by extension, house churches, there is always the temptation to interpret any unusual feature in an ancient structure as being 'of probable religious significance'.[7] Identification is often not secure. Even so, the tradition of household shrines would seem to have been reflected in the Christian house church, and perhaps the site at Icklingham represented a villa church, serving the entire household, including slaves.

One further feature which may be interpreted as a pagan–Christian link in Romano-British churches should be mentioned: the existence of votive objects either overtly or covertly associated with a church. The best-known are the gold votive leaves found with the undoubted church plate at Water Newton, belonging either to a house church or to a purpose-built structure and possibly nailed into position there. Objects such as these have been the subject of a study by Toynbee (1978); although further votive leaves have been found since the time of her writing, her findings remain valid. The objects were found in association with pagan temples and shrines throughout the Western Empire, often in military areas, dedicated to both Roman and native gods, and on occasion affixed to the cultic building. Some of the Water Newton leaves had been christianised with the addition of the *chi-rho* symbol, but, given the inscription on fragment no. 12 (*Anicilla votum quo(d) promisit conplevit*), there is little doubt that they were identical in intent to pagan ones (Henig 1980: 101). Thomas (1981: 113–21) in a full discussion of the Treasure, wonders if the leaves may earlier have been the property of a temple and, in the event of the conversion of some wealthy residents of the district, the leaves then became church property. Alternatively, it could be that they were always intended for a Christian church, and that, as was proposed for the continuation of the coin in the mouth in Christian burials (above, ch. III), the practice of affixing the leaves somewhere in a religious structure was one to which the Church was prepared to turn a blind eye, particularly as there were no images on the leaves. Had they caused offence, they could easily have been converted to ingots. That bullion could be part of Church property was shown by the hoard from Canterbury (Johns and Potter 1985).

One probable votive object which, if known to them, would most certainly have incurred the wrath of church authorities was the stone head of Mercury in the foundations of building 8, a presumed church, at Uley. The deposition, although carefully carried out, must have been done covertly. Ellison (1980: 314) describes how pieces of the fragmented statue were incorporated in the foundations of building 8, but the head had been 'carefully placed in a small pit . . . beneath the earliest platform'. The interpretation of this would seem to be that, while the newly converted Christians at Uley were prepared to break up their pagan images, raze their temple and remove votive offerings from the site, one, at least, still retained the Celtic reverence for the head; perhaps seeking the best of both worlds, he carefully placed the sculpture under this manifestation of the new religion.

A similar deposit seems to have been made at Witham. Here, beneath the foundation of the first phase of the rectangular building, believed to be an oratory or church, a small pit contained a complete colour-coated beaker in which a coin of the second century had been placed. The stratigraphy is such that it can be interpreted as a foundation deposit of the fourth century (R. Turner, pers. comm.). Foundation deposits were a feature of both secular and religious structures in the pagan period, and a similar deposit to this is found at Lamyatt Beacon temple (Leech 1986: 271).

The pieces of deer antler also found beneath Romano-Celtic temples at Lamyatt Beacon and Brean Down and the possible association of deposits of this kind with the later west–east buildings have been noted above (ch. IV). It was observed that, in his final report on Lamyatt, Leech (1986) did not postulate a relationship between the antler pieces and the later buildings. But the archaeological evidence is not definite here. The antler pieces amongst the west–east burials may have been votives honouring the Celtic horned god, Cernunnos, for which there are 'oblique traces' of the cult in the Severn area generally (Ross 1967: 140), perhaps because Cernunnos was one of the few Celtic deities thought to preside over the dead (Black 1986b: 224). Equally, the presence of the antler pieces could be merely the discarded remnants of a pagan cult practised at the site, and abandoned with the advent of Christianity, since Cernunnos came to be regarded as the anti-Christ or Satan (Bober 1951; Ross 1967: 165).

There were, nonetheless, a number of other identifiable pagan features in Christian burial rites. Although the early Christians of the Middle East had inherited from the Jews their burial practices and inhumation (Rowell 1977: 1), with the spread of Christianity westward Roman influences would have become stronger. Romans practised three methods of disposing of the dead – cremation, inhumation, and embalmment – cremation being the most common at the time of the death of Christ, but it is not clear when Christians adopted either inhumation or west–east burial. At the end of the second century, apparently, Christians were being cremated (Minucius Felix, *Octavius* 11.2), but even then the preference was for inhumation (*Octavius* 34.8–12). By the fourth century, inhumation had come to be the method of disposal of the dead in the Roman world generally, and the evidence from Lankhills (Clarke 1979) and the late fourth-century Gallo-Roman cemetery at Merteville (Loizel 1977) shows that, along with Christians, even pagans were now adopting west–east orientation.

In the Christian cemeteries of Roman Britain, distinguished by west–east, supine, extended and undisturbed burials, the occasional pagan practice may be detected; some will be seen to be intrusive, others were absorbed into Romano-British Christian burial practices. Morris (1983: 25) observes, 'The physical characteristics of Christian burial were in the main acquired through a sieving out of pagan mortuary practices.' But pagan practices and influences were, in some cases, slow to die out in Christian burials. It is difficult to reconstruct from early writers how Christians were actually buried. The burial of Christ, the most detailed account of which is in John 19.39–40, gives a description not only of a Jewish burial, but of an expensive one.[8] Green (1977a) considers that this continued to be the preferred method of burial for Christians, quoting Tertullian (*De resurrectione carnis* 27).[9] But as Jewish burials had involved great expense and often reduced the family of the deceased to penury (Josephus, *Bellum Judaicum* 2.1.1), at the end of the first century Rabbi Gamaliel introduced reforms which made funerals simpler and less expensive (Rowell 1977: 4–5). A century later, at the same time as Tertullian was writing of the Christian tradition in Africa, or, more likely, describing the burials of the wealthy members of his flock there, Hippolytus was describing the poor Christian's burial, which clearly followed the Roman tradition: the simple grave covered with tiles (*Apostolic Tradition* 40). By the early fifth century, Augustine was still to write that there was no advantage in an expensive burial (*De cura pro mortuis gerenda* 4); and this precept, it is proposed here, was followed in Roman Britain.[10]

Evidence from Romano-British cemeteries supports this. There are innumerable places where a body could have been 'anointed with myrrh and aloes, and bound up in linen cloths before deposition in a tomb which had never previously been used' (Green 1977b: 46), most of which could not be proved archaeologically; but there are two cemeteries, the large Butt Road, Colchester phase II site and the small Verulam Hills Field period III, both putative Christian burial grounds, where undoubtedly the area had been used for previous burials: in both cases west–east inhumations were made over north–south ones. The evidence from Dorchester shows that some of the Poundbury 3 burials overlay Iron Age inhumations (S. Davies, pers. comm.). Furthermore, monuments or mausolea, which Tertullian saw as the hallmark of the Christian grave, were few in Britain, and still fewer in the Christian fourth century, Poundbury being the notable exception; and incense and spices would have been far beyond the resources of the poorer Romano-British Christian, even had these exotic imports been available in distant Dorchester, Colchester or St Albans.

There is, however, ample evidence for the simple grave, stone-covered, at Nettleton A (Wedlake 1982: 90), tile-covered, at Poundbury 3 (Green 1982: 64) and stone-lined, at Ancaster (D. Wilson, pers. comm.); and sometimes the grave with neither coffin nor cover, as at Ashton (B. Dix, pers. comm.), the body being interred on a bier of planks. All these were in presumed Christian cemeteries, and all illustrate burial practices which are completely indistinguishable from those in the undoubtedly pagan cemeteries of Roman Britain. On the other hand, the burials of wealthy pagans, in lead-lined stone sarcophagi, were paralleled by the burials of wealthy Christians in the cemeteries of Poundbury and Colchester. As Rowell (1977: 19) has pointed out, the fact that information on early Christian burial rites is so hard to find in the sources indicates that these burial rites were not controversial, and, therefore, were not offensive to either pagan or Christian writers. This would seem to confirm that the burial practices of Romano-British pagans were generally replicated in cemeteries of Romano-British Christians.

Of those pagan practices absorbed into Christian burials, one of the most widely remarked was the 'plaster' burial. It has often been taken as a strong indicator of Christian rites, but, as was shown in Chapter III, this is not necessarily the case. In his study of the origins of the practice, Green (1977b) has traced it to Africa in the last three pre-Christian centuries. It spread to Europe and finally to Britain, and occurred in burials in almost all parts of Roman

Britain. It may be compared with the embalmment practised by Jews and Romans, and more particularly the mummification of bodies by Egyptians. The aim seemed to be to prevent or delay the decomposition of the body. In the case of Jews, Egyptians and Christians at least, such practices were associated with a belief in the afterlife; for Christians they seemed also to have been closely tied to the prevailing belief in a physical resurrection at the Second Coming. As for pagan Romans, belief in life after death was at best only loosely held with, over the centuries, a fairly vague and changing picture of what an afterlife would be like;[11] nevertheless, a belief in the survival of the soul was probably sufficiently deep-seated (Toynbee 1971: 311) for those in Britain to accept and, for some, to adopt the practice of plaster burial.

It is likely that the Celts also believed in a physical afterlife. They may even have believed in the transmigration of souls (Caesar, *De bello Gallico* 6.14; Diodorus Siculus 5.25), although Ross (1967: 55) says there is no convincing evidence of this. The burning of a dead man's possessions with him on the funeral pyre (Caesar, *De bello Gallico* 6.19) would seem to suggest a belief in a material afterlife.[12] Indeed, the Roman geographer, Pomponius Mela (*De chronographia* 3.2.19), writing in the first century of the Christian era, said it was the Celts' belief in an afterlife which led them to burn or bury the deceased's possessions with the body, and that on occasion they flung themselves onto the funeral pyres of their relatives in order to share the afterlife. Like the Romans, they probably had only a vague or confused belief but sufficient for some of them also to adopt plaster burials in the hope of ensuring immortality.[13] The presence of plaster burials in the Christian cemeteries would, therefore, not have been seen as intrusive, but could easily be rationalised as indicating a belief in the resurrection. Augustine, however, warns Christians, in their treatment of the dead, not to heed the pagan notions found in Vergil of the inability of the unburied to cross the River Styx: Jesus had said (Luke 21.18) that not a hair of the head of a Christian would perish, even when in the hands of the enemy; destruction of the physical remains of a Christian was no cause for concern, as re-formation of the body itself was promised to Christians when the time came for their resurrection (*De cura pro mortuis gerenda* 3–4). There is a very thin line between this and a belief in a physical resurrection, which most early Christians would not have appreciated.

In a discussion in Chapter III, it was concluded that absence of grave goods did not necessarily indicate a Christian burial; rather, certain types of grave furniture would be found less offensive to Christians, and their presence in a Christian cemetery would not be extraordinary, although it could be expected that their incidence would be much less. The practice of including objects in a cremation or inhumation had a long history. For the immediate pre-Roman period, Collis (1977b: 2–4, 8–11) found that, in burials representative of the 'North Gallic culture', almost all of the burials would have had some pottery vessels; other, richer ones contained jewellery (beads, bracelets, brooches etc.) and weapons as well; and the richest contained these plus a variety of luxury items and, in some cases, wagons and horse trappings. In the south of Britain and away from the continental influence, however, at sites such as Maiden Castle,[14] Whitcombe and Christon, graves usually contained only one or two pots, while brooches were almost unknown in this context. There were exceptions, such as the 'warrior burials' at St Lawrence on the Isle of Wight, at Whitcombe and Ham Hill, and the 'totally exceptional' burial at Birdlip in Gloucestershire. It was not until a generation or two after the advent of the Romans that there was any discernible difference in the grave goods of Britons.

Roman grave deposits were varied, but even here the most common objects were vessels for holding food and drink, as nourishment for the departed. Yet such vessels are also found very occasionally in putative Christian burials of the fourth century: they occur in small numbers in the two large cemeteries, Poundbury 3 and Butt Road, Colchester II, in one grave in Lankhills feature 6,[15] and one grave at Ancaster, although this last is somewhat irregular, as the pot is dated to the second or third century (Wilson 1968). Its insertion would seem to indicate a votive purpose, rather than to contain food. The practice by Christians of holding commemorative meals at graves has been discussed earlier; the insertion of vessels in a Christian's grave would not have been approved by the Church. It may have been, however, that these vessels, at time of insertion, were empty. There appears to be evidence that pots were placed even in pagan graves in such a position that they could not have held anything (Rook 1973: 3), and it is noted that, in grave 250 of feature 6, the probable Christian enclosure at Lankhills cemetery, the vessel with the burial was inverted (Clarke 1979: 149). The fact that no animal or fowl bones, the inclusion of which would presumably have indicated token sacrificial offerings, were found in the cemeteries which have been proposed as Christian, may support the view that no actual food or drink was placed in the few vessels which occur in presumed Christian burials; their presence was likely to be a vestige of a long-established pagan (more likely Celtic, than Roman) practice which survived into the Christian period.

A similar interpretation may be proposed for the placing of a coin in the mouth before burial. The examples in presumed Christian cemeteries are from Icklingham and Poundbury 3. Charon's fee had a long history, and reached Rome from Greece in the first and second century of the Christian era (Grinsell 1957: 266). The practice may even have assumed a pseudo-Christian identity by the fourth century: canon 4 of the Council of Hippo of 393, later incorporated into canon 18 of the *Codex canonum ecclesiae Africanae* at Carthage in 419, prohibited the administering of the *viaticum* (the sacrament normally administered to the dying) to the bodies of the dead; church law also forbade burial with the Host in the mouths of the dead, since it was believed by some Christians to be the equivalent of Charon's fee (Rowell 1977: 15), guaranteeing a safe passage to eternal life. That later Councils in 525 (Carthage), 578 (Auxerre) and 692 (Trullo) also condemned the practice suggests that it was still widespread and, although such a practice is archaeologically undetectable, no doubt it took place in fourth-century Roman Britain, alongside the few recorded cases of the placement of a coin in the mouth. This proposal could possibly be supported by the evidence from Poundbury. It is remarkable that there were twelve coins in the mouth in the putative Christian section (i.e., 1.2 per cent),[16] but none found in the contemporaneous pagan burials (D. Farwell, pers. comm.).

The presence of a small collection of coins in a grave at Ancaster, and the coin in the hand and others in graves at Poundbury, Icklingham and Butt Road II, may also be seen as the remains of pagan ritual, and quite probably deposition was carried out covertly.

Charon's fee would have come to Britain by way of Rome, but the presence of hobnails in Romano-British burials, and in Christian graves of the fourth century, does not seem to have had Roman origins. At least, no hobnail burials have, as far as is known, been recorded from there or further eastward, though they are found in Gaul and Germany. The occurrence of hobnails in cremations and inhumations in Britain began in the first century, and, in the absence of evidence to the contrary, one can only assume that it followed a native tradition which was archaeologically undetectable before the introduction of shoes or boots with hobnails, that is, with the coming of Rome. In Chapter III, it was suggested that the inclusion of footwear in a grave may have related to the belief in a journey to reach the River Styx, yet this is a Roman concept. Tertullian (*De anima* 5.65) says that pagans believed that those souls that meet a premature death wander about until they have completed their allotted span. But archaeological evidence does not support this as a reason for the hobnails: they are found with young and old. To confuse the issue still further, in the thirteenth century, Durandus of Mende (*Rationale* 7.35.43) claimed that some people said (*quidam dicunt*) Christians should be buried with their boots or shoes on, in order to be ready for the Last Judgement. That hobnail burials were pagan, and probably a Celtic, rather than a Roman custom, is all that can be concluded. The presence of very small numbers in the two large cemeteries at Poundbury 3 and Butt Road II is an indication that such practices, though presumably disapproved of by the Church, continued into the Christian period.

A further curious burial practice, so far found only in a handful of Christian cemeteries, is the insertion of stones in various parts of the grave. The examples of Ancaster and Ashton are treated first. At Ancaster, where most of the burials were in coffins, a large stone was often placed at the top and bottom of the grave, and, on occasion, one or two stones along the length of the coffin; some graves were completely stone-lined. The soil is stony at Ancaster, and such evidence might be interpreted as fill of the grave; yet the presence of these stones, particularly at the head and feet, is too common for it to be accidental (D. Wilson, pers. comm.). A little further to the south, at Ashton, numbers of graves contained one or more stones, placed apparently at random. The graves in the west–east and presumably Christian cemetery were uncoffined; in the adjacent 'backyard' pagan burials, most of the burials were in coffins, but here, too, the same feature occurred, and it was noted that the stones were actually placed in the coffins with the body (B. Dix, pers. comm.). Whatever the significance of the stones, it is clear that it was a regional pagan (Celtic) practice which continued into the Christian period. As a postscript to this, it has been recorded that, at Girton College, Cambridge, not far distant from Ashton, excavation of a late Roman to early Anglo-Saxon cemetery revealed burials accompanied by large stones. The Roman burials were from the late first or early second century to the fourth or early fifth, the Anglo-Saxon considered early; stones were found in burials from both eras (Liversidge 1977: 19).

A similar type of feature occurred in one of the graves of the triple tomb at Verulam Hills Field west–east cemetery. The middle burial was of a woman whose head rested on a pottery dish (Wells 1968: 41). Davies (1977: 13–14) has observed that it was a Samnite custom to prop up the head in burial, and, since Verulamium would have been exposed to Roman customs from a very early date, it is possible that this was a burial practice to come from Italy. Pillow stones, however, seem to have been a Celtic practice: Whimster (1981: 230) records an Iron Age example from the Isle of Wight; they were also found in the presumed Christian cemetery at Cannington (P. A. Rahtz, pers. comm) and in the fourth-century Romano-British cemetery at Frilford (Buxton 1921: 91). The widespread practice of inserting pillow stones cannot rule out a Celtic influence in the 'pie-dish' burial.

The small quantity of jewellery in probable Christian cemeteries should also be examined for pagan influences. The objects, worn or merely deposited in the grave, include bracelets, beads and pins; they were found at Ancaster, Butt Road II, Cannington, Icklingham and Poundbury 3. The age and sex of these burials have not yet been published; if the Lankhills cemetery (Clarke 1979: 152) may be taken as a guide, however, it is likely they were female and/or young. The limited occurrence of jewellery in Christian burials would suggest that it was seen as a practice indicating belief in a physical afterlife to which the Church did not officially subscribe but a practice which, if a body were enshrouded, would be difficult to detect. Jewellery similar to that listed here has been found in many Iron Age graves in Britain and Ireland. It would seem to be a custom which had Celtic origins, or, if imported, to indicate Belgic rather than Roman influence, although Alcock (1980: 62) cites examples from the classical world of the burning of clothing with cremations.[17]

The presence of combs in seven graves of Poundbury 3 cemetery (D. Farwell, pers. comm.), in seven at Butt Road II (C. Crossan, pers. comm.) and one each at Lankhills feature 6 (Clarke 1979: 56–7) and Ancaster (D. Wilson, pers. comm.) is also worthy of comment, since these are the only cemeteries where such objects occur in a presumably Christian context. In his discussion on the combs found in twenty-one graves at Lankhills cemetery, Macdonald (1979: 412–13) suggests that they may reflect Celtic influence. However, unless the Celts made their combs solely from wood, traces of which have now disappeared, this would not appear to be the case. There appears to be no evidence for combs from the Iron Age burials in Britain or Ireland, but, since the inclusion of toilet articles,[18] mirrors and so forth was quite common in Roman graves, it is more likely that combs represent a Roman element. In almost every case in the presumed Christian cemeteries the combs were found near the head, most likely worn in the hair at burial rather than intended as grave goods. One further point is of interest: the combs were found in the graves of both males and females.

Finally, there were the fourteen knives in burials at Cannington, one at Butt Road II, Colchester (C. Crossan, pers. comm.) and one at Poundbury 3 (D. Farwell, pers. comm.). This constitutes a type of grave deposit which appears to have been neither Celtic nor Roman. In his discussion of 'foreign elements' in the Lankhills cemetery, Clarke (1979: 377–404) proposes that the presence of weapons in graves indicates Anglo-Saxon burials. This could be the case at Cannington. On the limited evidence as yet available, at least two of these burials are at the eastern and less-populated section of the cemetery, and are among a group of about seven graves on a slightly different alignment from others in the vicinity. It is not possible, however, to come to any definite conclusion about the Cannington 'knife' burials until it is known in what part of the cemetery the others occurred. If the burial sequence can be determined and the knives identified, this may shed further light on the spread of foreign influence before or after the departure of Roman military forces from Britain. The Colchester example is also curious. It occurred in burial 171, that of a 12–15 year old of indeterminate sex. There were hobnails at the feet and, near the head, a knife and items of jewellery, apparently originally wrapped in a cloth. While there is no indication that any of these items other than the knife was abnormal in a Romano-British burial, the grave was later than the one adjoining it; but such evidence is inconclusive. Nor is there anything to suggest that Poundbury burial 960, that of a young woman found with a knife under the right forearm, is late in the burial sequence of the cemetery. All that can be concluded at this stage is that knives are most unusual in a Romano-Celtic cemetery, and do seem to indicate an intrusive pagan element in what are presumed Christian cemeteries.

Following an examination of the grave furniture in Christian burials, it is useful to look at the position and condition of the body to find possible pagan influences. In the putative Christian cemeteries there are exceptionally few irregular burials, virtually all being west–east, supine, extended and undisturbed. The only burials not west–east occur in Bradley Hill group III and Ancaster cemeteries, and are mostly north–south. In his study of Iron Age burials, Whimster (1981: *passim*) found a predominance of north–south orientation; in pagan cemeteries of the fourth century, it is found that they could have no fixed orientation,[19] be orientated north–south,[20] show a change from north–south to west–east,[21] or follow a west–east orientation.[22] Thus the trend seemed to be a move from the traditional Celtic orientation to the west–east position introduced from either Gaul or Africa. The Bradley Hill north–south burial seems to have been the earliest in that particular cemetery, and thus may have been made before the inhabitants of the homestead presumably converted to Christianity and west–east burial. Of the sixteen graves at Ancaster that were not west–east, thirteen were north–south and three east–west, but all except two infant burials were in the less-organised part of the cemetery; this suggests either earlier or later burials than the west–east graves. In view of the fact that the only known prone burials in putative Romano-British Christian cemeteries also occur in this part of the cemetery, it could be that these irregular burials indicate a breakdown of the Christian character of the cemetery and of the community it served, and even a reversion to Celtic pagan rites.

This leads to a consideration of the incidence of crouched and prone burials in west–east, undisturbed and presumably Christian cemeteries. Crouched burials are very few: the only examples are three from Cannington cemetery and one from Ancaster, although four other burials from Ancaster were on their sides with legs slightly flexed, a position found in Anglo-Saxon cemeteries.[23] Prone burials are even fewer: two only have been found, at Ancaster. Although there were exceptions, the crouched position is usually taken to indicate pre-Roman burial customs, for it does seem that the supine and extended position was adopted by the native population not long after the advent of Rome. In areas where, perhaps, the impact of *Romanitas* was more diffused, crouched burials continued for some time: the burials at Jordan Hill are a good example, yet they were buried with hobnailed footwear. Moreover, there are instances where, even as late as the fourth century, crouched burials occurred in a pagan context: at the Old Vicarage, Fordington, Dorchester, in a cemetery of cremations and inhumations, a crouched burial appears to post-date the second- to third-century cremations (Startin 1982); of the twenty-one bodies on their sides at Lankhills (Clarke 1979: fig. 49), some may be sufficiently flexed to be considered 'crouched', yet the cemetery is regarded as wholly fourth- to early-fifth-century. The crouched burials at Cannington and Ancaster perhaps reflect the return to the old burial rite, or could indicate a late intrusive culture. This would be, especially for Cannington, a reasonable proposal, as there were also burials with knives at the site. With regard to prone burial, the two instances at Ancaster were likely to have been from a late phase of the cemetery, and to have represented, as with the crouched burials, a Celtic burial practice, or a rite belonging to a later culture. The position was probably not accidental, since one case was that of a woman buried with a baby: both were prone.

One further pagan burial practice may be detected in a presumed Christian cemetery: there was one decapitated body in cemetery 3 at Poundbury. Decapitation was practised in pre-Roman Britain, and is found in native graves in Gaul (Whimster 1981: 188); it was also known in Iron Age Ireland (Raftery 1981: 192) and can thus be seen as a Celtic practice, generally taken to reflect the Celtic cult of the head. The presence of the one decapitated burial at Poundbury, in what was probably a Christian cemetery, is quite remarkable, and the excavator has suggested that the grave may have become especially important to Dorchester Christians (Green 1982: 74).

Decapitation has been discussed at some length in Chapter III, and it has been thought to be some form of punishment or indignity imposed on the body. The examples from Dunstable, however, where one was also a 'plaster' burial, and from Ashton, where the two decapitated bodies seem to have been given more elaborate burial (B. Dix, pers. comm.), do seem to indicate that punishment may not have been the purpose of such a rite. Even so, and whatever the reason for it, the practice was clearly pagan, and its occurrence in the almost certainly Christian cemetery at Poundbury does give that burial special significance.

The contents of the graves of Christian cemeteries have revealed several pagan practices. The cemeteries themselves reveal a further feature which was taken from Roman burial practice, the mausoleum. The Roman mausoleum was a fusion of Greek, Samnite and Etruscan traditions, and came to be built at a time when Rome's prosperity was increasing (Davies 1977: 13–18). It may thus be seen as a symbol of wealth. Because of the law forbidding intra-mural burials, the cemeteries lined the roads into Rome, where the passerby would be impressed by the size and splendour of the monuments (cf. Petronius, *Satyricon* 15.71). In Roman Britain, types of mausolea and structures for more than one burial are found in cemeteries in the earlier period, but there seems to be much less evidence for them in the cemeteries of the fourth century. Rather, they are found on villa sites, and not in association with contemporaneous burials. This could be due merely to the lack of excavation in Roman extra-mural areas; or it could indicate that the kind of wealth that existed in Rome did not exist in Romano-British towns in the fourth century.

In his study of Roman-British burial customs in the south-east of England, Black (1986b: 201–39) lists a number of examples of burial enclosures or mausolea, all of which are dated to the second or third century, and almost all of which contained cremated remains. None seems to be in a general burial area with other cremations and inhumations. Others are described in some detail by Jessup (1954), although he concentrates on the architectural and burial features, rather than the date of the structures. The examples he discusses are likely to be family groups, some over a period of, perhaps, generations (such as at Keston, associated with a villa), or are single burials. From elsewhere in Britain further examples are recorded; dating is not clear in every case, however, and it is not always possible to determine if the buildings were intended for the rich, or for the poor, as members of a burial club. Some are in association with other burials, such as those at Colchester, dating from the second to the fourth century (Hall 1946), Caistor (Boileau 1847: 72–3) and Lincoln (Richmond 1946: 52),[24] although the building at Lincoln was probably for the poorer, rather than for the richer, members of society. At York, a subterranean stone tomb was found in the same location as several cremation burials, one at least dating from the second century (RCHM 1962: 95–6). At Radley, a second-century cremation seemed to be have been given its own small enclosure in a cemetery which began in the first century and continued to the fourth, with a total of forty-seven cremations and inhumations (Chambers 1984). In the north, the second-century mausoleum at Shorden Brae was still standing when a few burials up to the fourth century were made around it (Gillam and Daniels 1961). Another tomb chamber has been recorded some 30 metres from a first- to fourth-century cemetery of cremations and inhumations at Litlington, but no dating evidence for the tomb survives (Liversidge 1977: 31). Other examples, apparently not associated with cemeteries, include a possible third-century buttressed tomb at White Notley and an underground tomb at Pleshey, containing cremations (Richmond 1963: 19); a building at Lincoln which may have been a mausoleum or even the place (*ustrina*) where the bodies were cremated (Pownall 1792); and a mausoleum of unusual shape found at the villa at Roman Farm, Pitney, dating to the second century (Leech 1980: 341).

Fourth-century structures are also known: a subterranean tomb with four inhumations, one with gold and silver jewellery, at Water Newton (Wilson 1969: 219), apparently associated with a substantial house in a suburban settlement; in association with villas, at Lullingstone (Richmond 1959a: 132–3) and Bancroft (Frere 1984a: 302–4), the structure at the latter being later dismantled to provide stone for a series of eight west–east graves nearby (Williams 1984); and the well-known structure at Stone-by-Faversham (Fletcher and Meates 1969: 1977), situated about 750 metres from the Ospringe cemetery. At Arbury, near Cambridge, a small stone structure had been built over five previous burials to house a lead-lined stone coffin. Liversidge (1977: 14) suggests it was a family burial plot, but the treatment of the earlier burials does seem rather cavalier for that interpretation.

There are, therefore, burial structures – either enclosed graves, subterranean tombs or mausolea – in cemeteries and on private property in Roman Britain. But there is little evidence for the construction of mausolea in cemeteries in the fourth century: of over thirty cemeteries examined for this study, only three, Lankhills, Poundbury 3 and Butt Road phase II, have definite evidence for mausolea or burial enclosures (four, if the triple grave at Verulam Hills Field is included) and all of these have a presumed Christian presence; in addition, Nettleton A, another likely Christian cemetery, has buildings in its west–east cemetery, although no graves were found.[25] Information on the Colchester enclosure is not yet available; the Lankhills and Poundbury examples, however, are particularly interesting: of the four enclosures at Lankhills, only one, feature 6, that of presumed Christians, was made large enough for more than one burial. All the Poundbury 3 structures contained more than one burial, although the three enclosures (not, apparently, buildings) beyond what seems to be the boundary for the Christian section have only one burial each. The best-preserved of the enclosures with multiple burials, structure R8 at Poundbury, continued the Roman tradition of family portraits in mausolea, but as wall paintings, not as the sculptures found in pagan tombs such as at York (RCHM 1962: 69) and Colchester (Toynbee 1964b: 419); it may be that the Church opposed three-dimensional portraits in a religious context as image-worship, since they are extremely rare in the period from about AD 200 to 500 (Toynbee 1968: 179). There is evidence for family connections between the groups of burials in mausolea at Poundbury (S. Davies, pers. comm.), which suggests that three members of a dominant and wealthy family built mausolea for their own particular branch of that family and perhaps even the (Christian) family retainers.

Thus, it seem that, although the construction of mausolea or enclosed burials in an organised cemetery was not common in the fourth century, Christians adopted the practice from Roman pagans and, to some extent, adapted it to their own purpose. Late mausolea containing a number of burials are rare, and the ones that are known are likely to be Christian. It appears to have been a practice which pagans themselves did not carry on, the wealthy being content instead to build mausolea on their own properties.

The single burial in a mausoleum found in a pagan context might also be seen to be the origin of the focal graves found at Cannington and perhaps at Poundbury. But the singling out of one particular grave had been a practice not only of the Romans, and Romano-Britons did not have to look beyond their own shores for models. Richmond (1946: 170) sees the mausoleum as descendent from pre-Roman *tumuli*, as at Lexden or Welwyn. Thomas (1971: 58–64), in a detailed discussion of circular focal or special graves from the Iron Age to the seventh century of the Christian era, shows that at least one of the two focal burials at Cannington, that of a grave in a shallow circular ditch, followed the tradition of Iron

Age special burials. The second grave was apparently distinguished by some sort of marker or even, Thomas postulates, a rough wooden cross. A well-worn path to the grave suggests it was the focus of pilgrimage for some considerable time. At Poundbury, two or three graves may have been given special attention, but a close examination of the cemetery plan does not prove this. Two were mentioned in Chapter III: the woman buried with the Y-shaped metal object, and the decapitated woman; a third, a man with his hands on the heads of two children, was in a dense part of the cemetery, but the layout is such that this cannot be taken to have any special significance (S. Davies, pers. comm.). Of the three, the first-mentioned burial would seem to have been the most isolated, and thus a possible focal grave. While the Poundbury evidence is insecure, Cannington is less so. The grave within a circle at the latter site would seem to indicate the continuation by Christians of a tradition for singling out special graves which stretched back to pre-Roman pagans.

Christians also took their symbolism from the pagan cults, and occasionally from the Jewish religion; but, apart from their cult instruments, the Jews themselves had no iconography and had taken their symbolism from the pagan as well (Goodenough 1953–68: vol. 12, 43): the Jewish catacomb at the Villa Torlonia shows the extent of the borrowing from pagan art. Despite the undoubted connection between Jewish and early Christian art, however, it would seem more appropriate to look to the pagan world to seek the origins of Christian symbolism found in Roman Britain. In doing so, reference will be made to those texts which may have provided inspiration, or possibly justification, for the adoption of such symbols by Christians.

Virtually all Romano-British Christian symbolism had been borrowed from the Graeco-Roman secular or pagan and given another identity. The only truly Christian symbols found were the *alpha-omega* combination, based on Revelation 1.8, 21.6, the IH monogram, representing the first two letters of IHΣΟΥΣ (Barnabas, *Epistle* 9.7–8), and the Greek and monogrammatic crosses. The *alpha-omega* is one of the most common of Christian symbols; in Britain it was inscribed with varying degrees of sophistication, from the elegant version on the Water Newton silver bowl to a graffito on the vessel from Welney (Thomas 1981: figs. 6.2, 5.8); it was added to the *chi-rho* before the end of the first half of the fourth century (Allen 1887: 92). The second symbol, the IH, is among the rarest: to date the only example from Roman Britain is the small christianised stone altar from Chedworth. It has been discussed in detail above (ch. V.3). The Greek cross, or *crux quadrata*, was used as a Christian symbol by the beginning of the third century, or even as early as mid-second century; it is as yet rare in Britain, probable examples being inscribed on spoon 69 of the Thetford treasure, examined in Chapter V.1, and the same small stone altar from Chedworth mentioned in connection with the IH. The monogrammatic cross was a late addition to Christian symbolism, and may been seen either as a simplification of the *chi-rho*, or a variation of the *crux quadrata*. It is found on several objects from Britain, some of which have been mentioned by Thomas (1981: *passim*); further examples include a silver brooch of the crossbar type, probably from Sussex (Frend 1955), and two spoons from the Canterbury treasure (Painter 1965; Johns and Potter 1985).

Other symbols, particularly forms of the Christian monogram and the cross, were also pagan or secular signs, or a combination of both: the *iota-chi* is found as a decorative motif, and also possibly as a pagan religious symbol (Sulzberger 1925: 394–6): in Roman Britain, it was found on a foundation stone of a temple to Serapis in York, dating to the second century (Henig, 1984: 114 and fig. 46). If the *iota-chi* is turned ninety degrees, it becomes a symbol frequently found on pagan funerary inscriptions. But the symbol was also one of the earliest Christian monograms, representing the initial letters of ΙΗΣΟΥΣ ΧΡΙΣΤΟΣ, and Sulzberger suggests it was adopted by Christians because it was unlikely to attract attention, and could be taken for the sign for *denarius* or for the pagan funerary symbol (Sulzberger 1925: 396). As a Christian symbol, it is known from about the middle of the third century; it is found in Britain on several objects, noted above (ch. V.1, n. 9).

The most widespread Christian symbol of the fourth century, however, was the *chi-rho*. It had also been used as a ligature on Eastern, Greek and Roman coins prior to Constantine's conversion and his promotion of the symbol (Lactantius, *De mortibus persecutorum* 44; Eusebius, *Vita Constantini* 1.31). It is one of the ironies of history that the *chi-rho* appears on the coins of one of Christianity's greatest persecutors, Decius (Cabrol and Leclerq 1920–53: vol. 3.1, cols. 1482–3, s.v. '*chrisme*'). The symbol must have been adopted by Christians not long after the issue of that coinage in 249–51, and certainly before the end of the third century. On available evidence, it was the most popular Christian symbol in fourth-century Roman Britain, and only towards the end of that century did the monogrammatic cross come to replace it. Thomas (1981: fig. 4–7) gives most of the examples of the *chi-rho* in Roman Britain; some others discovered since Thomas's study, or not reported by him, include a lead tank from Reading (Frere 1989), and a pewter dish from Stamford, mentioned above (ch. V.1), a pronged implement from the Canterbury hoard (Painter 1965), a graffito from Colchester (Drury 1984: 48), and a ring from Carlisle, found with another engraved with a palm branch and *ama me* (Charlesworth 1978: 123).

Two other forms of the Christian cross, the *crux decussata* and the *crux gammata*, were known in a secular or pagan context. The *crux decussata*, or St Andrew's cross, was also a punctuation sign in Greek inscriptions, a fact which has caused dispute as to when it was first used as a Christian symbol.[26] It has also been said to be an old symbol of good fortune (Schiller 1972: vol. 2, 103). The Christian symbol was used in the catacomb of Lucina in Rome about the middle of the second century. In Britain, it is found on several of the lead tanks which appear to have been used for the *pedilavium* in baptism (above, ch. V.2), on the pewter plate from Stamford, and on the small christianised stone altar from Chedworth (above, ch. V.3). The second cross, the *crux gammata*, or swastika, had a long history as a pagan symbol and is found throughout the world, perhaps as a representation of the sun. Schliemann found an example at Troy (Hulme 1899: 219), and others, now in the Museum of Anatolian Civilisations in Ankara, were found at the Bronze Age site of Alaca Hüyük. The swastika was a late addition to Christian symbolism, and is not found in the catacombs until the third century (Hawkes 1973: 153). In Britain, there is, as yet, only one positive example, that of a Roman buckle from Tripontium, with two peacocks and crosses of the *crux gammata* type flanking what may be a tree of life (Hawkes 1973). A similar symbol has been found in Roman Britain, on a mosaic from Westbourne Park villa (RCHM (England) 1983: 147 and pl. Va). This villa has, on other grounds, been suggested as a possible Christian site. The presence of the swastika, a mosaic design which the excavators say is 'without known parallel', may support this identification. On the other hand, it could merely reflect the fashion for geometric mosaics popular in fourth-century Britain.

One further symbol which has been taken to represent, among

other things, a form of the cross, is the Y symbol and it, too, may be traced back to pagan origins. The symbol, found at Poundbury cemetery, has been treated in detail above (ch. V.3); suffice in this discussion to note that the Y was first said by Pythagoras to represent moral choice in life and it was adopted by Christians who gave it much the same interpretation – one of the very few examples where the pagan and Christian interpretations of a symbol corresponded. Another likely interpretation was that it depicted the *orans* attitude, which some early Christian writers saw as representing the cross.

Several symbols used by Christians in Britain were more obviously borrowed from pagan art and iconography, but their meanings were changed considerably. There is diversity of opinion as to why Christians borrowed their symbols from the pagans. Some would argue for a didactic purpose (Toynbee 1968: 180; Johnson 1969: 14); another sees the pagan motifs as an indication of the transition to a new faith which had neither evolved nor standardised (Richmond 1950: 46); yet another notes that, in one church built immediately after the Peace of the Church, while its decoration was rich in Christian associations, it contained little to offend pagans (Radford 1968: 25–7), the implication being that pagan iconography was consciously adopted to make Christianity as inconspicuous as possible.

In some cases there appeared to be some kind of official Church approval, if not sponsorship; in others, particularly those in the mosaics of the putative Christian villas, the motifs could have originally been intended as crypto-Christian, offending neither believer nor non-believer. But it is equally possible that symbols not overtly Christian reflected what was fashionable in mosaic design at the time, rather than a deep-held religious conviction (Branigan 1977b: 61–2). Before considering such mosaics as Christian, there would have to be other evidence for Christianity at the site.

A Christian symbol of long standing is the fish, and it is represented both by the actual depiction of a fish, or by the word ΙΧΘΥΣ. Examples from Roman Britain were given earlier in a discussion of the Thetford Treasure. The fish could also be a secular or pagan religious symbol: a topical theme on the walls of baths buildings (Toynbee 1953: 17), a talisman, a sign of the zodiac (Cabrol and Leclerq 1920–53: vol. 7.1, cols. 1991–3 s.v. 'ΙΧΘΥΣ'), or a symbol of the journey to the Blessed Isles after death (Henig 1977: 352). The symbol was adopted from the pagans, or more likely the Jews (Henderson 1935: 51), very early in the history of Christianity. It is mentioned by Clement of Alexandria (*Paedagogus* 3.11.59.1), while two centuries later Augustine (*In Iohannis evangelium tractatus cxxiii* 2) specifically equates the symbol with Christ.

Other aquatic symbols adopted by Christians were the dolphin, the pecten shell and nereids. The dolphin is found on the mosaics from Frampton and Fifehead Neville, and in three-dimensional form as handles for ladles or spoons in the Mildenhall (Painter 1971) and Traprain (Curle 1923) Treasures. The fish in the catacombs' paintings often take the form of a dolphin, and it here that the connection with the Roman pagan is clear: the dolphin as friend of man, saviour of the shipwrecked, guide for souls to the Blessed Isles – all these meanings then applied in a Christian context to death and to baptism. Dolphins were also associated with music, the New Song (Psalm 96) which brought Christianity to the world (Clement of Alexandria, *Protreptikos* 1 (pp. 9–17, Loeb edn)). The shell was quite obviously borrowed from the pagan, occurring in pagan funerary art on tombstones in Britain[27] and on lead coffins[28] as a symbol of the journey to the Blessed Isles. As a Christian motif, it was the symbol for a pilgrim, for baptism and also the symbol of St James the Greater (Webber 1971: 367). It seems, from canon 48 of the Council of Elvira, that a shell was used in the baptism ceremony, presumably as a patera. The occurrence of the symbol in a Christian context in Britain is as yet rare: an almost-certain Christian example is the decoration on the lid of the lead coffin from Butt Road phase II cemetery at Colchester (Richmond 1963: 19), and its use in this funerary context is a good example of the syncretic nature of Romano-British Christian symbolism.[29] The motif of the nereid is, to date, found in Britain only on the Isle of Ely bowl (Clarke 1931), and, according to Toynbee (1953: 22), represented baptismal regeneration. In pagan art, nereids were part of that watery host accompanying the dead to the afterlife.

Birds, too, were Christian symbols taken from pagan iconography. Those found in Romano-British Christianity with pagan parallels were the peacock and the owl. Thomas (1981: 129 and fig. 8) describes or illustrates peacocks from Rivenhall, Orton Longueville, Tripontium and the Isle of Ely. Further examples of the peacock motif, without any other certain Christian symbol but accompanied by what may be interpreted as a tree-of-life symbol (similar to the Tripontium and Rivenhall tags), have recently been recorded: one from the temple site at Harlow on a tag found in a fourth-century context (France and Gobel 1985: fig. 46 no. 19; Bartlett 1987), and the second from Wortley, in Gloucestershire (Wilson 1986: 44). The decoration on the latter closely resembles that on a strap-end from Stanwick, Yorkshire, possibly dating to the fifth century (Hawkes and Dunning 1961: fig. 15m), not referred to by Thomas (1981). The peacock also occurs on several fourth-century mosaics which have been suggested as Christian. In Roman religion, it was the bird of Juno and, since its plumage was renewed each spring, it was also seen as a symbol of immortality (Hawkes 1973). Coins of Faustina depicted the bird's head encircled with a nimbus, symbol of the glorified soul (Hulme 1899: 57). The peacock was adopted by Christians as a symbol of immortality, along with the belief that its flesh was incorruptible (Augustine, *De civitate Dei* 21.4).

On the Isle of Ely bowl, the peacock appears with the less spectacular owl; according to Toynbee (1953: 22), in a Christian context this bird signifies divine wisdom, which is an echo of pagan symbolism, since the owl was the bird of Athene, goddess of wisdom. It also had a far more sinister meaning for pagans, being associated with evil and witchcraft (Hawkes 1973: 152). It may have had some association with death as well, since a comb with a stylised owl was found in a grave at Bath Gate, Cirencester (McWhirr *et al.* 1982: 129) and there were two other examples from Lankhills (Clarke 1979: fig. 31, nos 323, 479).

Various trees and fruit were Christian symbols, found in a pagan context as well. Trees appear on a silver patera handle from Capheaton, in association with a relief of a classical temple, and Henig (1980) says these 'sacred trees' were probably illustrative of Romano-Celtic symbolism. Despite the general lack of evidence for Celtic iconography, the tree-of-life motif has been found on many Iron Age Celtic objects, particularly coins and wine jugs (Kruta and Forman 1985: 102 *et passim*). It does not seem a part of the iconography of the Roman pagan world, but is understandable for the Celts, given their predilection for ascribing a sanctity to works of nature. The Christian motif of the tree of life, found in Britain on strap ends in association with the peacock, and on the Hinton St Mary mosaic, is found in literary allusions from the first century: Paul (1 *Timothy* 3.6) refers to the newly baptised as 'neophytes', that is, newly planted, and Clement of Alexandria (*Stromata* 3.17,103,4 and 5.11,72,2) calls Christ the tree of life. The Christian symbol would certainly have had its origins in the Old Testament: Genesis 2.9 has the tree of life in the midst of the Garden of Eden; in Revelation 2.9, it is in the paradise of God. The use of the tree in Christian symbolism, paralleled by that of the Celts, would have been understandable to Romano-British Christians.

The palm had a place in both secular and religious symbolism, before it was adopted by Christians (Origen, *Commentary on John* 21; Psalm 92.12; Revelation 7.9–17). Although the Christian use of the palm as a symbol, noted earlier in Chapter V.1, was probably adopted from the Jewish faith (Daniélou 1964: 1–24), the symbol was in fact an emblem of victory of great antiquity, found in various ancient civilizations. In Roman Britain, a pagan epitaph is surrounded by palm branches and solar wheels which, combined with the sentiments of the inscription (*RIB* 758), indicates an optimistic belief in an afterlife (Henig 1977: 351).

The pomegranate, found on the Hinton St Mary mosaic, is said to be the emblem of Church unity (Webber 1971: 78). In the Old Testament, the pomegranate adorned the robes of Aaron (Exodus 28.33–4), and it symbolised royalty, hope, future life and fertility (Webber 1971: 78). It was probably borrowed from pagan iconography, where it was a long-standing symbol for immortality (Toynbee 1968: 183) and fertility (Arthur 1977: 371). The head of a silver pin in the British Museum, dated to the first or second century, is in the form of a hand holding a pomegranate.

Other symbols found in a Christian setting, but taken from pagan mythology, are present only on mosaics; as has been observed earlier, identification as Christian depends on supporting evidence. Only two will be dealt with here, the Orpheus motif, and Bellerophon and the Chimaera. That Christians represented Orpheus as Christ is undoubted: Eusebius (*De laudibus Constantini* 14.5) compares Christ with Orpheus, and it has been suggested that the Orpheus mosaics with tame animals represent a Christian version, as compared with a pagan version portraying wild animals (Huskinson 1974). Even so, there would have to be further evidence to identify these mosaics and sites as Christian. In his study of the villas of south-west Roman Britain, Branigan (1977b: 66–7) proposes two which may have this evidence: Withington and Woodchester. At the former, two peacocks flank a cantharus (a motif found in the catacomb in the Via Latina: Mancinelli, 1981: pl. 74); at the latter, among the tame creatures are peacocks and doves, known Christian symbols in the fourth century. The second pagan myth to be translated into a Christian setting, Bellerophon and the Chimaera, is best seen as the victory of good over evil and life over death (Toynbee 1968: 182–3). Its use as a Christian allegory in the mosaics at Frampton, Hinton St Mary and Lullingstone is supported by the addition of the undoubted Christian symbol of the *chi-rho*.

There are several minor motifs, such as the vine, cantharus, four seasons and hunt scenes, found in Romano-British mosaics, which need concern us only briefly here. All were found in both pagan and Christian mosaics, and in many which cannot with certainty be identified as Christian. The cantharus and the vine are very common motifs in ancient art; undoubtedly Christians adopted them from the Roman, and gave them their own special meaning. The vine had particular significance in Christian iconography, representing Christ and the whole Church (John 15.1, 5). The hunt scene on the Frampton mosaic has been seen as a Christian allegory of the struggle with the forces of evil (Toynbee 1968: 182), the four seasons the 'endless cycle of eternity', or of celestial blessings awaiting Christians (Toynbee 1971: 163). In pagan art, the cantharus and vine were Bacchic symbols, the hunting scenes represented the pleasures in store for the deceased in the afterlife (Toynbee 1968: 182), and the seasons may simply have been popular motifs because they were four, ideal for the corners of rectilinear mosaics, and later given a Christian meaning.

One further area where the pagan influence is seen in Romano-British Christianity is in the various inscriptions which appear on objects such as spoons and rings in the fourth century. The inscriptions on the Thetford spoons have been examined at length (above, ch. V.1), and it is necessary here only to reaffirm that *vivas, utere felix* and *vir bone vivas* can be paralleled in a Christian context in the fourth century, although such inscriptions had their origins in the pagan and secular world. The borrowing of such pagan formulae is a further instance of the syncretism which is found in Romano-British Christianity.

This survey has demonstrated that in its buildings, burials, symbols and inscriptions, Christianity had much in common with the pagan and secular. Features were adopted or adapted both from the Roman world, and from the native Celtic cults. It is now possible to assess the impact of the links with pagan religions and practices and the place of Christianity in Romano-British history.

2: ASSESSMENT

As has been shown, in Romano-British Christianity there were similarities to the pagan religions, or actual pagan elements in churches, cemeteries, inscriptions and symbols. It is likely that this had the effect of making Christianity fairly inconspicuous in the context of fourth-century Romano-British religion, and, therefore, more acceptable to relatively unsophisticated Romano-British. Nevertheless, the incidence of Celtic, rather than Roman, pagan practices, particularly in burial rites, suggests that native traditions were still retained, despite more than two centuries of romanisation; this probably contributed to the decline of Christianity after the departure of the Romans. It does seem that where Celtic practices were more commonly observed, that is, in rural areas, these were generally the locations that were unable to resist the pagan revival of the late fourth century; in the more romanised towns, however, Christianity was able to carry on at least until the end of the fourth century and some decades beyond and, indeed, in certain areas to survive into the Saxon era. Few sites, rural or urban, were able to withstand the twin disasters of Roman withdrawal and Saxon incursions, but, even here, with a few notable exceptions,[1] it was where Roman influence was stronger that there is more evidence for continuity.

It is noted, at the outset, that there is greater evidence for pagan characteristics in burials than in buildings. This is, of course, likely to be an accident of archaeology, since, by its very nature, a well-preserved cemetery is direct and undisturbed evidence, while an above-ground Roman building can be analysed only by its foundations and fragments of its structure, and those, on occasion, only poorly preserved. But this very accident of archaeology probably works in our favour, because cemeteries involved presumably the whole Christian population of a town or *vicus* over a period of fifty years or so, whereas the construction of a building would have reflected the whim of, perhaps, the local bishop or priest, the preferences of those who were financing its construction and the fashion for building at a particular time or place. Even so, since death and burial are such a fundamental part of any culture, it is likely that, in a newly christianised community, old superstitions and long-established practices were slow to be discarded. While a neophyte may have embraced the new faith unequivocally, his or her relatives may not have shared the same beliefs; thus the Christian's burial included practices from the old religion as well as the new. The grave cannot, therefore, be said with certainty to reflect the Christianity of its occupant; furthermore, the incidence of pagan practices in Christian burial could depend much on the training of the local priest and the supervision by his bishop.

The value of inscriptions and symbols in such a discussion might also be questioned, since these usually appear on objects which either had been on the surface or were buried, as hoards, only deep enough to keep them safe, and to allow a good hope of recovery at a later period. They are thus chance discoveries. Because of their often highly portable nature, they are not necessarily representative of an area, or indicative of the influences on Christianity there, although they can be used as an indicator for Roman Britain as a whole.

While the cemetery is possibly the best guide to the pagan influences in a Christian community, therefore, all three kinds of Christian evidence have their shortcomings.

There is no doubt that Christianity would have been seen as a different religion from those prevailing in the first part of the fourth century and earlier, but the adoption of architectural styles which were familiar would have lessened the novelty. Moreover, there was such a diversity of architecture for Romano-Celtic temples that a new form of religious structure, the basilical or apsidal building, would probably have caused little comment; as noted previously, the apsidal form had also been used for some earlier religious or quasi-religious buildings in Britain. It could be that the choice of this shape by Constantine or his architects was not accidental, and the fact that it had been the plan for the building from which Roman justice was dispensed may have lent a certain authority to those churches which adopted the basilical or apsidal plan. (It would be interesting to know, for instance, why the apse seems to have been a later addition to the fourth-century Butt Road building in Colchester, and why the first small church at Uley, built after about 380, had a squared, apse-like projection, while the second building, built in the fifth century, discarded this feature.)

The rectangular plan, however, was a common one for both

Celtic and Romano-Celtic religious structures, and its adoption for a Christian church would have been quite unremarkable; and if, as will be proposed below, Christianity was not generally the religion of the wealthy, the simple rectangular structure, such as the putative churches at Brean Down, Lamyatt Beacon, Nettleton 23, Uley and Witham, would have required less expertise and probably less money to build.

The choice of site for churches has been shown to have reflected the earlier pagan tradition, and the locating of churches on previous pagan sites, particularly in the rural areas, was obviously a conscious and deliberate act intended to reinforce the position of the Christian religion as the one approved by the imperial government. An additional motive would have been to give the appearance of religious continuity, and this undoubtedly made acceptance of the new religion much easier. It is of interest that the building of presumed churches on these pagan sites took place, in every case where dating is reasonably secure, before the decree of Theodosius of 391 which closed all the temples. This suggests that the Christians' takeover of the various sites generally had not been opposed. The evidence from Nettleton is that the shrine of Apollo had lost its importance before it was converted into a probable cruciform church about 330. At Lamyatt Beacon, votive objects were apparently thrown out of the temple prior to the construction of the rectangular building nearby. But at Witham, there may have been pagan resistance: first, because the presumed church is very small, implying a small following, and secondly, because, when pagan rites were resumed at the site, the building material from this structure was heaped into and over the font with which it had been associated (R. Turner, pers. comm.). At Brean Down and Uley, material from the pagan structures was re-used in the (presumed) Christian successors.

If the putative churches are divided into urban and rural, it is seen that the simple, rectangular structure is found only in the country, while the apsidal belongs mainly to the towns. This suggests a lesser degree of sophistication and romanisation in the rural areas and, perhaps, a lesser degree of commitment to the new religion, although this last can in no way be proved from evidence available. It is supported by the fact that the examples of votive deposits at Christian sites were from the rural areas. Moreover, there is evidence for only a short span of Christian activity at Nettleton, Icklingham, Witham and possibly Brean Down and

Lamyatt Beacon buildings. This can be narrowed down even further to a period ending about 360 in the case of Nettleton and Witham, a date which coincided with the reign of Julian the Apostate. On the other hand, continuity of Christianity is known from literary sources or is found at urban sites such as the Cathedral at St Albans, St Pancras and the Cathedral at Canterbury, and St Paul-in-the-Bail, Lincoln.

The pagan evidence in presumed Christian cemeteries is of great interest. As was remarked earlier, Christian burials must have been seen to differ very little from the pagan, yet, as the study of Romano-British burials has demonstrated, there were certain characteristics which marked the Christian from the pagan. Those pagan practices detected in Christian burials could have occurred with the connivance of the Church authorities, or without their knowledge, or because such practices were not seen to have been counter to the Church's teaching.

An attempt has been made to differentiate between Celtic and Roman origins in Christian burial practices. The style and orientation of graves reflected burials of the Roman world, but this is to be expected, and the same kinds of burials are found in undoubtedly pagan cemeteries. Most other practices were more likely Celtic: the insertion of stones in grave cuttings or under the head was the continuation of a pagan tradition – and, judging by its frequency, one not questioned by Christian authorities. Hobnailed and decapitated burials were Celtic in origin, but few were found in Christian graves, and then in only two cemeteries. Grave goods were very few: the insertion of pots might be paralleled in both pre-conquest Celtic and Roman burials, but, since they are the most common of the grave goods, can probably be taken as representative of the native cult; jewellery most likely reflects a Celtic influence, and its incidence was more common than that of combs, the inclusion of which was likely to have been a Roman practice. The placing of coins in the graves and in the mouth (and one instance, at Poundbury, in the hand), was a practice to come from Rome, but it was suggested that this may have taken on a quasi-Christian character.

The pattern is not altogether clear, but it would seem that, while Christians were given west–east, supine, extended and undisturbed burial, the occasional native Celtic, and, to a lesser extent, Roman practice intruded. It appears that, while Romano-British Christians adopted the Roman style of burial, any pagan practices which continued either overtly or covertly were more likely to have been Celtic. That pagan elements were found at all suggests that, for some, at least, the commitment to Christianity was not total; that these elements were predominantly Celtic may indicate, as in the case of churches, above, that these Celtic pagan influences were stronger than the Christian. It has been remarked,

> From the pre-Roman Iron Age to the high Middle Ages there is a continuous substratum of . . . superstitious practice which scarcely seems to have been affected by the comings and goings of Imperial deities or by ecclesiastical opposition
> (Morris and Roxan 1980: 176)

and it would appear that, in some parts of Roman Britain, the hold of Christianity was at best tenuous – a point to be taken up in the concluding chapter of this study.

With regard to symbols and inscriptions, since the religion of the Celts had little iconography and no writing or literature, most that has been found in a presumed Christian context has been Roman in origin.[2] This would have facilitated the acceptance of Christianity and contributed to its relatively inconspicuous place in Romano-British religion of the fourth century. But it also means that now, as perhaps then, identification of symbols and inscriptions as Christian is often problematical, and dependent on other evidence. Clement of Alexandria (*Paedagogus* 3.11,59,1) had urged Christians to adorn their rings with the dove, fish, ship, lyre or anchor. Presumably other Christians recognised such symbols. There must have been many cases when, even in the fourth century, the Christian significance of a symbol, mosaic motif or inscription was in the eye of the beholder. Apart from those symbols which were originally Christian, or the *chi-rho*, which came to be so in the late third century, identification relies on other evidence, on a combination of motifs or symbols, or the physical context in which the object so inscribed or decorated was found. That has been the basis for the identification of symbols and inscriptions in this study (above, ch. V). It has been found that the distribution of objects with inscriptions or symbols that may be Christian is in keeping with the evidence for Christian churches and cemeteries in Roman Britain, but, beyond noting the syncretic nature of inscriptions and most symbols, there does not seem to be any other conclusion that can be drawn for the present.

There is no doubt that, while it had absorbed many pagan

influences or had features in common with the pagan religions, Christianity was different from the other religions of Roman Britain. Its imperial patronage and hierarchical organisation, and, more especially, its monotheism, rituals, exclusiveness and the lifestyle it espoused all set Christianity apart from the pagan, even from the Mithraic cult. But these were not physical differences. To ordinary uncommitted Roman Britons, Christianity would probably not have appeared vastly different from other esoteric cults which had come to their shores from the East or the horde of Celtic or Romano-Celtic cults that had sprung up in Britain itself over the centuries. That Christians borrowed from the pagans is evident in the sites and the buildings they put there, in their style of graves, and in their symbolism and inscriptions; that some pagan practices continued within the Christian religion is clear from the evidence of the cemeteries and from such presumably covert acts as the deposition of votive objects. Undoubtedly this syncretism assisted the acceptance and spread of Christianity. But the Celtic influence seems to have been stronger than the Roman. This was an inherent weakness of Christianity in Britain, and one which made it unable to retain its hold, particularly in the rural areas, with the withdrawal of Rome and the advent of the Saxons.

VII

CONCLUSIONS

From the material presented in this study, it is clear that not all the evidence for Christianity in Roman Britain has as yet been recognised. By close examination of archaeological finds already reported, it has been shown that various objects or symbols, additional to those recorded by scholars such as Toynbee, Frend and Thomas, had a Christian association; a reinterpretation of the evidence at archaeological sites has made it possible to classify structures more confidently as 'almost certain', 'probable' or 'possible' churches; and a detailed analysis of major cemeteries published and as yet unpublished has led to the development of a set of criteria which will identify Romano-British sites as Christian or pagan with a reasonable degree of certainty. A further study has identified possible pagan origins or elements in churches, cemeteries, symbols and inscriptions. In the light of this research, it now remains to assess the distribution and, a more difficult task, the commitment of Christians in fourth- and early fifth-century Britain and the place of Christianity in the history of Roman Britain as a whole, and to indicate areas of possible future research.

The additional evidence adduced not only reinforces the identification of many sites as Christian, but suggests, in addition, that the religion was more widespread than has hitherto been proposed and its appeal broader. The commitment of the converted, assessed on archaeological evidence only, would seem to have been stronger in urban than in rural areas, especially in the face of a pagan revival in the 360s and beyond. In Chapter I, it was shown that Christianity in Roman Britain came to Britain as a Roman religion, and this may be the reason that it was, it seems, stronger in the more romanised (that is, urban) areas. The failure of Christianity in some areas (particularly rural ones) before the

Roman withdrawal may have been the result of its dilution by the conscious or unconscious admission of pagan elements; and, while it is likely that these same pagan elements made the assimilation of Christianity into Romano-British religion as a whole so unremarkable, their coincidence with the early Saxon incursions and the resurgence of paganism resulted in the overall decline of Christianity probably even before the end of the fourth century. But the final withdrawal of Rome at the end of the first decade of the fifth century did not mean the extinction of Christianity. The evidence of the Pelagian controversy[1] indicates that there were still numbers of influential Christians, probably in the larger towns; and it is likely that, in these centres, commitment to the religion only gradually dissipated by the middle of the fifth century. Christianity lived on in the sub-Roman period, however, not only in those areas where the British influence was maintained away from Anglo-Saxon elements (Thomas 1981: fig. 49), but also in towns such as Lincoln and Canterbury, where the archaeological evidence for a continuity of religious tradition is complemented by the literary evidence of Gildas and, to a lesser extent, Bede.

The extent of fourth-century Christianity has been charted by various scholars over the years, the most up-to-date maps being those by Thomas (1981: figs 14–16). When the evidence of the present study is added to Thomas's fig. 16, it will be seen that there is an intensification of the density of Christian evidence in the east, from Lincoln southward, and that the blank area west of The Wash now shows some evidence for Christianity with the inclusion of Ancaster cemetery and the pewter plate from Stamford. The Stonham Aspal ring with *zeses* and palm inscription allows some progress in filling the gap east from an area with strong evidence for Christianity stretching from Colchester to Icklingham. In the west, there is an increase in density in the area around the Severn and an extension further westward with the addition of Cannington cemetery in Somerset and the *chi-rho* graffito at Exeter mentioned by Thomas (1981: 108), but not included in his fig. 16. The lead tank from Kenilworth in Warwickshire closes another gap, and thus the evidence tapers off northward from the area around the Severn. One puzzling aspect of the distribution map is the absence as yet of any evidence for Christianity in a large area stretching from the Cotswolds to the Chilterns; the late or possibly sub-Roman cemeteries at Church Piece and Queensford Mill (above, ch. III) do not appear to be

Christian,[2] no possible churches have been published, and there is nothing to suggest that the Dorchester-on-Thames silver hoard (Johns and Potter 1985: 345–50) was Christian. Yet it seems most improbable that this region did not have a Christian element in its population. The very recent discovery of a lead tank with *chi-rho* near Reading now confirms a Christian presence in Oxfordshire. Future reports of archaeological excavations in this region will be awaited with great interest.

Thomas's density map and the revised version appear as Figures 27 and 28. It would seem that, on present knowledge, Christianity was strongest in Britain in those civilian areas which were most highly romanised,[3] and not just in the south-eastern third of Roman Britain.[4] With further evidence available, it is more than likely that future studies will refine the map to show a gradual lessening of density away from the regions of greatest influence, particularly into Powys, Hereford and Worcester and the more northerly parts of Gloucestershire, now shown as blanks. Of the other gaps, east of Oxford and Swindon, and in Kent, Hampshire and the eastern parts of Norfolk and Suffolk, given the density of the evidence in the adjoining regions, evidence for Christianity undoubtedly exists and remains to be uncovered, especially since these areas were among the earliest to be romanised.

The widely accepted view that Romano-British Christianity was essentially an urban and aristocratic religion[5] or, at least, that it was the religion of the upper classes[6] must now be seriously questioned. No doubt such an opinion was justified in the light of knowledge of Romano-British Christianity at the time. The present study shows, however, that the religion was somewhat more widely distributed than was previously believed, and that it was a religion of the poor as well as of the owners of villas and silver plate; this brings it into line with other parts of the Roman Empire and with the literary evidence.[7]

The evidence of probable Christian churches and cemeteries confirms that of the meaner small finds, those sherds with almost unrecognisable *chi-rho*s, rings with confused inscriptions and other objects whose rudimentary symbols proclaimed the Christianity of a poorer and probably uneducated class. Moreover, the churches, by their construction alone, do not imply wealthy congregations. In cases where a church was built on an earlier temple site, the later structure was often neither as large nor as elaborate as its pagan predecessor. This would seem to indicate a religion of no great wealth. It is true that masonry was not usually employed in

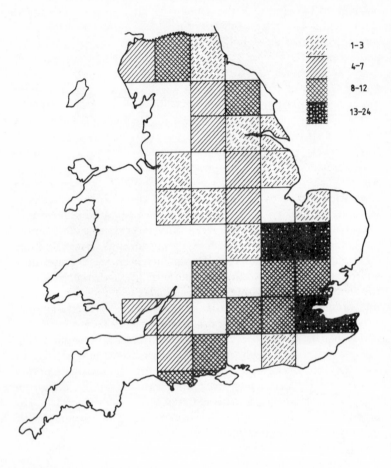

////	1-3
—	4-7
▒	8-12
▓	13-24

Figure 27 Earlier density map of Christianity in late Roman Britain (after Thomas)

buildings of the second half of the fourth century in Britain, quite possibly because, by then, the art of the stonemason was already being lost. But even in such a prominent position as the forum in Lincoln, the church erected there had timber walls, while, for flooring, the builders thriftily made use of the existing flags. Other examples, cited earlier, such as Icklingham, Lamyatt, Uley and Witham, follow the same pattern, while the church at Butt Road,

218

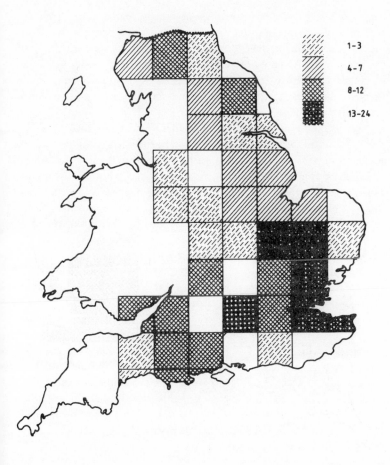

Legend:
- 1-3
- 4-7
- 8-12
- 13-24

Figure 28 Revised density map of Christianity in late Roman Britain

Colchester, according to preliminary reports, was of such poor construction that major repairs were required during its lifetime (C. Crossan, pers. comm.). Clearly, if the church buildings are any guide, there were not great numbers of wealthy Christians in Roman Britain.

An examination of the putative Christian cemeteries reveals the same situation, although, while Christians were encouraged to eschew the elaborate burial, wealth could still be advertised by the

219

extravagantly heavy timber coffin, the lead-lined stone sarcophagus, and, on rare occasions, the family mausoleum. Even so,
such burials were not usual for Romano-British Christians. Most
graves were simple: the general impression is one of modest
circumstances, if not of outright poverty. Indeed, in some
instances, poverty of burials was obvious. Christianity in Roman
Britain was not, it would now seem, the preserve only, or even
primarily, of the wealthy.

Nor was it necessarily a predominantly urban religion. Many of
the small finds are from the rural areas, but this could be merely an
accident of archaeology, since such objects are generally surface
finds; in a highly urbanised centre such as London, Lincoln or
York, the likelihood of the survival to the present day of even
small Christian objects is fairly remote. The evidence from
cemeteries and churches is perhaps a more reliable indicator of a
Christian presence.

Of the thirteen cemeteries presumed to be Christian, seven are
from rural sites, and most of these are not of any appreciable size.
The largest, Cannington, does not appear to have been associated
with any town, merely with a hillfort nearby; the size of the
cemetery was due to length of use. Ashton cemetery was a burial
ground for a small, unwalled town, the limits of which have not
yet been ascertained. The complex at Icklingham of church,
baptistery and cemetery may have served a villa; the graveyard at
Bradley Hill belonged to a farmstead. The Nettleton cemetery was
associated with a religious complex, and was presumably the burial
ground for local believers during the Christian phase of the site.
The cemeteries at Brean Down and Lamyatt Beacon were probably
sub-Roman, and connected in some way with earlier small,
oratory-style churches which served rural communities whose
locations have not yet been determined. In all these cases, there is
no indication that any large numbers of Christians were involved at
any one time, but the distribution, from Suffolk to Somerset,
shows that Christians did not live only in the large urban centres.

In the study of probable churches (ch. IV), of the seventeen
analysed, eight were urban and nine rural, but, if the two
buildings at Uley and Nettleton are taken as representing only one
site each, this last figure is reduced to seven. Even so, there is a
reasonable balance between urban and rural churches, although the
rural buildings were not the size of those in the large towns, a
situation which reflected that of the cemeteries.

It would appear, therefore, that Christianity was not restricted to the towns, and that, in the country as in the towns, there was no strong indication of wealthy congregations. This contrasts with the evidence of wealth in the probable house churches of Roman Britain, suites of rooms which were, presumably, used for worship by the villa owner, his family and household, but not necessarily by the wider community.[8]

Thomas (1981: 188–91) compared the congregational areas of putative churches of Britain with others of the Roman world, using Silchester 9, St Pancras phase I at Canterbury, Verulamium 6 and the buildings at Verulam Hills Field and Richborough for his analysis. He found that the mean for these structures was similar to that of twelve European churches of the fourth to fifth century;[9] he did not include the building at Icklingham, presumably because he believed that such a small building was atypical. But other small structures of much the same dimensions have now been shown to be likely churches. When we aggregate those buildings which, in the present study, have been proposed as almost certain churches (that is, those ranking 3 on a 3–0 scale) and delete Verulamium 6, which Thomas himself (1981: 169–70) lists as only a possible church (that is, a ranking of 1), the mean is considerably smaller than the European (Figures 29a, 29b). The implication is that congregations were also smaller than those elsewhere in the western empire, and, by extension, that Christianity did not have the same appeal. It would be a brave person who would venture to suggest what percentage of the Romano-British population was Christian in the late fourth century, but the archaeological evidence of churches and, to a lesser extent as yet, cemeteries, does suggest that Christianity in Britain attracted a smaller proportion of the population than in the western empire or Africa.[10] Undoubtedly, it remained a minority religion, even at its peak during the Roman period.

Romano-British Christianity should be assessed not only quantitatively but qualitatively; in the absence of literary sources, an objective assessment of the commitment of Romano-British Christians can be based only on archaeological evidence. In the previous chapter, it was seen that pagan elements were discernible in the churches and cemeteries of Christian communities and in the symbolism employed by individual members. Such syncretism was, no doubt, a factor which assisted in the absorption of

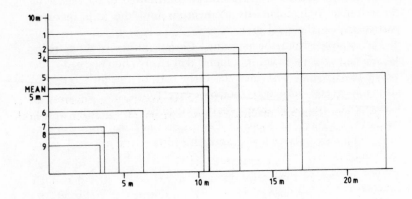

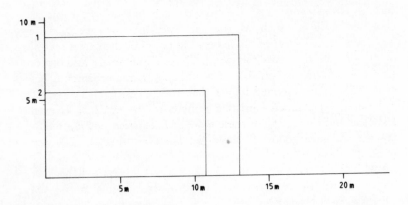

Figure 29(a) Congregational areas of nine almost-certain churches in Roman Britain, showing mean: (1) Richborough (2) St Pancras (3) St Paul-in-the-Bail (4) Silchester 9 (5) Colchester 9 (Butt Rd) (6) Icklingham (7) Uley 8 (8) Uley 7 (9) Witham

Figure 29(b) Comparison of congregational areas of (1) twelve fourth–fifth-century European churches and (2) nine Romano-British churches (from Figure 29a)

222

Christianity into the mainstream of Romano-British religion, but it was also a weakness which probably contributed to the failure of the religion to maintain its momentum into the fifth century, particularly in the rural areas.

The evidence from the presumed Christian sites confirms this. Where dating is possible, it is found that many churches had a life which extended at best into the early part of the fifth century, although there are some notable exceptions: Sts Pancras at Canterbury and Paul-in-the-Bail, Lincoln, and perhaps the mausoleum-church at Stone-by-Faversham, not far from Canterbury, probably survived well into the fifth century,[11] and there may have been little, if any, gap between the Roman and post-Roman or Saxon phases of these buildings. The evidence from Lincoln is the most conclusive: that a burial, carbon-dated to $c.450$,[12] was made outside a church which was, apparently, still standing, suggests that the church was still in use at that date. The buildings at Richborough and Butt Road in Colchester most likely continued in use into the early fifth century, and those at Icklingham, Silchester, Brean Down and Lamyatt Beacon possibly to the end of the fourth century, although the evidence for the last three is very scanty, and they could have had a briefer life as churches. Others, such as that at Witham and the two at Nettleton, could very well have been casualties of the pagan revival of 360–2 and the years following. Despite the small number of sites where dating is available, it would appear that urban churches as a general rule survived longer than rural ones.

From the presumed Christian cemeteries the evidence is even less clear and the dating of these more problematical, owing to the absence of grave goods. It could be, however, that the renewed interest in paganism was responsible for the deliberate abandonment of rural Christian cemeteries such as Icklingham, Ashton or Nettleton; in those cemeteries, there is no gradual decline of Christian burial practices.[13] Yet in at least two urban cemeteries, Poundbury 3 at Dorchester and Ancaster, there seems to have been a discernible deterioration in the management of the cemeteries,[14] suggesting not only the decline of church organisation but also the continuing use of the cemeteries by Christians or nominal Christians for some time after the Roman withdrawal. The Cannington cemetery in rural Somerset is clearly exceptional: its well-ordered, west–east, supine, extended and undisturbed burials date from the fourth to the seventh century.[15]

It was seen in Chapter VI.2 that features in common with Celtic cults were more evident in the presumed churches in the country than in the (romanised) towns, and that cemeteries were more likely to reveal a Celtic element than a Roman; that is, the pagan element in Romano-British Christianity seems generally to have represented the old native beliefs. While there is a danger in over-emphasising this factor, it would seem, particularly in the rural areas, that the hold of Christianity was at times slight and the depth of commitment not great. Had circumstances allowed the religion the backing of the Roman government for another couple of generations, very likely it would have come into its own. But the latent paganism of Romano-British Christians laid them open, first, to the pagan revival sponsored by Julian, and then to internal dissension, heresy and, for many, reversion to the old religions, when left to their own devices following the Roman withdrawal and, it is assumed, the break in the hierarchical control and organisation of the Church.

The effects of the pagan resurgence on Romano-British Christianity may be detected to some extent in the archaeological evidence from churches and cemeteries, but such evidence is not always unequivocal. A revival of paganism has already been suggested as the cause of the demise of some churches, and, in particular, a reversion to pagan rites at Nettleton and Witham. It may have been the reason why the house church at Lullingstone failed to grow into a fully-fledged church in the second half of the fourth century, as continental examples had been found to do. It has also been suggested as the reason for the abandonment of Christian cemeteries at Icklingham, Nettleton and Ashton. The absence of grave goods and, thus, dating evidence, in presumed Christian cemeteries, however, makes it virtually impossible to date any such influence there.

A more profitable source than archaeological sites for evidence of the strength of paganism may be that of the small finds of the period, particularly those with a Christian association. In particular, it is useful to look at the fate of the lead tanks which were probably used in the baptismal ceremony in Britain. Of the tanks or fragments of tanks whose provenance is known, at least four seem to have been no longer in use by about 370, while the tank and fragment from Ashton were found under late fourth-century pottery and the Caversham tank was also found with fourth-century pottery and tiles (D. Miles, pers. comm.). The apparently deliberate damage to a number of tanks and the discarding of others has been suggested as indicating a pagan resurgence in the late fourth century (Guy 1981: 275). This is quite possible, and the fact that six tanks or fragments were discovered at sites where there was also water, one near Oxborough by the River Wissey (C. Guy, pers. comm.), the Pulborough tank in the flood plain of the River Arun (Curwen 1943), the tank from Huntingdon in the River Ouse (Donovan 1934), the tank and fragment from Ashton vessel from Caversham in a well (Hadman and Upex 1977; Frere 1989: 319; Hassall and Tomlin 1989: 333–4) may indicate the desecration of these vessels and perhaps even a rededication of them to some Celtic water spirit[16] as part of a pagan resurgence.[17] Furthermore, the discontinuation of use of the tanks by Christians could indicate a fall in numbers of those being baptised (suggested in ch. V.2) – a result, presumably, of the revival of paganism.[18]

Even more conclusive is the evidence of the Thetford Treasure, which was associated with a late fourth-century cult of Faunus. The introduction of a cult honouring an ancient Latin deity was wholly in keeping with the policies of Julian the Apostate. The conflation of Faunus with Celtic deities and the attributing of Celtic epithets to the god, as indicated by the inscriptions on the spoons, implies that, even in wealthy communities, the old Celtic cults had not been abandoned; the probable Christian component in the treasure suggests that the cult included lapsed Christians. The treasure itself is clear evidence that, in certain areas, especially in the Romano-British countryside, paganism was alive and well in the last decades of the fourth century.[19]

Corroboration for this premiss comes from a study by Horne (1981). He shows that, in Britain, there was generally a dramatic decline in the use of Romano-Celtic temples from a peak in the middle of the fourth century to the end of that century, and a further drop in use from the late fourth to the early fifth; but when the sites are divided into urban and rural, the urban temples decline in use throughout the fourth century, while rural temples peak in the mid-fourth, then fall away to the early fifth. When compared with the European example, where the use of pagan temples declined steadily from a peak in the mid-second century, with an acceleration of this decline in the fourth, clearly Britain went against the trend (Horne 1981: figs. 3.1, 3.2). This was particularly so in the south-west, with the construction of temples such as the complexes at Lydney and Maiden Castle. Nonetheless, it would seem that, by the late fourth century, Romano-Celtic paganism was generally in decline, especially in the cities and in those areas where there was a military presence. In view of the higher level of romanisation in such areas, Christianity was also more likely to show a degree of continuity into the fifth century.

The question of religious continuity into the sub-Roman period has been thoroughly discussed, mainly on the basis of place names, by Thomas (1981: ch. 10). He argues very strongly and persuasively that the Christian Church in Britain did not die out in the mid-fifth century, to be resurrected by Augustine in 597. The archaeological evidence presented in this study, as yet rather limited, confirms Thomas's findings and expands on them; it reinforces the view that Christianity in Britain remained, although greatly reduced in numbers, its followers to some extent paganised and seemingly schismatic,[20] after the removal of direct Roman influence from British shores. There is the undoubted evidence of the Cannington cemetery, the almost certain continuity at sites such as Uley, St Paul-in-the-Bail, St Pancras and the cathedral sites at St Albans and Canterbury, and the probable continuation of religious tradition at Stone-by-Faversham, Brean Down and Lamyatt Beacon. The remnants of the religion, witness to the faithfulness of the few in a time of great adversity, were not restricted to the north, north-west and south-west, as proposed by Thomas (1981: fig. 49), but were also located within the area occupied by the Angles, Saxons and Jutes.

The place of Christianity in the religions of Roman Britain should now be assessed. It must be seen as more than just another cult from the East, since it had come to Britain from Rome, and had had the backing of the emperor for almost a century; yet, as Frend (1955: 16) says, it failed to gain the popular support of the people that it enjoyed elsewhere. This may not have been the fault of Christianity itself, but of attendant circumstances at the time. Had the Roman withdrawal not come so close on the heels of the pagan revival, the weakened Church would surely have recovered, and possibly even retained its hold despite the Saxon menace. That able Church leaders were still present in Britain in the fifth century is shown by the Pelagian affair. Another Martin of Tours may have emerged to root out paganism as violently as Martin himself had done in Gaul. But the withdrawal of Rome from Britain precluded any such missionary effort, for, without the patronage of the emperor and, implicitly, the protection of the Roman army, success would have been impossible.

Even so, although Christianity in Britain seems not to have been taken up initially with vast enthusiasm and by large numbers, the abandonment of pagan temples attests the overall decline in paganism in the fourth century; the destruction of pagan sites and objects suggests that Roman Britain produced some Christian zealots. While doctrinal differences between Christianity and the pagan religions were very great, many features of contemporary cemeteries and churches would have been familiar to the average Romano-Briton, and it can probably be assumed that most fourth-century Romano-British Christians felt comfortable in their conversion. The wide distribution of Christianity and its appeal to both rich and poor suggest that, had Rome not withdrawn from Britain and the Western Empire not fallen, Christianity would have become as strong as it had in Gaul in the fourth and fifth centuries,[21] and would have emerged as the predominant religion of Britain centuries before it finally did.

It is appropriate now to indicate areas of possible future research. It will have been noted that two of the most important centres in Roman Britain, London and York, have not featured in this present work. This is because much of the evidence of the Roman occupation here has long since disappeared. As was noted in the Preface, unpublished records and objects held by museums and local authorities have not been examined for this study, and it could be that a reappraisal of those from London and York might produce a little more than the glimpse of Christianity the occasional artefact affords. It would seem highly improbable that these cities did not have a large Christian presence, and museum storerooms may hold evidence until now not recognised as Christian. Moreover, the archaeological records, particularly of burials found at York in the nineteenth century, could usefully be re-examined in an attempt to establish which was the major burial ground for Christians in the Roman period. For London, the recent publication of a summary of Roman burials, with valuable bibliography, (Evans and Pierpoint 1986) is a step in the right direction in this respect and provides a convenient starting point for further research.

A similar reappraisal of material held in museums and elsewhere might profitably be carried out in other centres where the evidence for Christianity is based on one or two finds or sites. This is already being carried out at Colchester by the Colchester Archaeological Trust. Since there are regions in which little or no evidence has been found to date, suggested centres for research are Caerwent, Chester, Chichester, Cirencester, Eastbourne, Exeter, Gloucester, Lincoln, Oxford, Norwich and Worcester.

Complementary to an investigation of old material would be the reappraisal or, where possible, the excavation of sites where there has been shown to be a Christian cemetery, in an effort to locate a church. One of the most likely sites would be Ashton, where one lead tank with *chi-rho* and the fragment of another tank were found not far from an undoubted Christian cemetery. Another is Ancaster, and it is possible that a Romano-British church may lie in the vicinity of St Mary's, where pagan statuary has also been located (Hawkes 1946: 19–20). Other sites where there is, as yet, little hint of the location of an early church, although the cemeteries indicate a Christian element in the population, are Cannington and Poundbury Camp, Dorchester. The Cannington Hillfort excavation data may yet reveal a church, perhaps a rectangular one; the Dorchester site, in a built-up area, has not been fully excavated, and could still yield a cemetery church, although, in view of the mausolea in the Poundbury 3 cemetery, structures which may have doubled as small churches, it would seem more likely that an actual congregational church had never been built there. An intra-mural church is more likely at Roman Durnovaria.

If Christians existed in any numbers in an area, they would have expected not only to pray together, but also to be buried together. Where churches have been shown to stand, it is likely that the same district would have had a Christian cemetery. Locations (or records of archaeological investigations) which might profitably be examined for evidence of fourth-century Romano-British cemeteries along the main Roman roads are Canterbury, Lincoln, Richborough, St Albans and Silchester. Another town which has, to date, not recorded any evidence for Christianity, but which may have a Christian cemetery, is Gloucester. The Kingsholm Road site, reported only briefly (Frere 1984a: 314–15; Aitken 1987) has at least some of the characteristics of a Christian burial ground. Further excavation and detailed reports should give a clearer picture.

There has been considerable discussion in this study on the

question of continuity of religious tradition. It seems very likely that, in the late fourth century, changed use of a temple or the abandonment or dismantling of the structure could have indicated a Christian presence in the district. Several pagan sites which Lewis (1966: tables 7–9) lists as not having survived beyond the early fourth century might usefully be re-examined, along with their immediate environs. Others, reported since 1966, include Chelmsford 3 (octagonal) (Drury 1972), Harlow (France and Gobel 1985), Colchester 1 (the Temple of Claudius) (Drury 1984) and the complex at Bancroft (Frere 1984a: 302–4; Williams 1984). It is possible that the demise or changed use of these structures was due to a Christian presence, and further investigations might be undertaken with this in mind.

A number of later Christian sites were listed in Chapter IV as potential locations for earlier, Roman churches. As a general suggestion, any very early Saxon church might be examined for a Roman predecessor, particularly in a known Roman town, military centre or villa. Likewise, churchyards which yield sherds of Roman pottery could be more closely investigated for burials and buildings dating to the fourth century.

Any re-examination of Christian evidence should also include a reappraisal of the major silver hoards of the Roman and post-Roman periods. This could involve not just a consideration of the technical and stylistic features, but also the decoration, symbolism and possible use of the objects. The treasures in most urgent need of such a reappraisal are those from Traprain Law and St Ninian's Isle. A further examination of the Mildenhall silver would also be timely.

Finally, there are various avenues of research into the history of Romano-British Christianity which will open up as archaeological knowledge of fourth-century Britain expands. For example, with firmer dating, especially for churches and cemeteries, the chronological and geographical development of the religion and the effects of the policies of the Roman emperors, particularly Julian and his successors, on the Church may perhaps be traced; a reappraisal of the literary evidence and the inscriptions, in conjunction with new archaeological discoveries, may lead to fresh interpretations; the publication of the skeletal reports of Ashton, Ancaster, Butt Road II, Poundbury 3 and of Christian cemeteries yet to be identified will provide material for the social historian for years to come.

It will be many years before anything approaching a satisfactory interpretation of the history of Christianity in Roman Britain is achieved. The archaeology of the past two decades or so has more than doubled our knowledge, and there is no reason to believe that this process cannot be repeated several times over. In close collaboration with the archaeologist is the historian, who seeks to re-interpret the evidence taking into account new discoveries. There are many chapters where the story is still dimly perceived, but future scholarship will surely generate further light.

APPENDIX

Strainers and other instruments in early Church ritual

Eoin de Bhaldraithe

STRAINERS

Two strainers were used at the Papal Mass, according to the *Ordines Romani* (Andrieu 1948). The first text (1.21) refers to both strainers being carried in procession before Mass, the second (4.47) refers to the wine being strained as it is put into the main (or celebrant's) chalice; for this the large silver strainer was used. The third reference (4.47) is to the rite for consecrating the ministerial chalices. These were not consecrated by the eucharistic prayer as was the main chalice; they underwent a special process and then were used to give communion to the people.

A piece of the consecrated bread was broken off and dropped into the main chalice. (This much is still done in the Roman Catholic Mass where it is now an unintelligible piece of ritual debris.) Then the subdeacon took it out again with the small 'gold and silver' strainer and put it into the ministerial chalice. This was the main part of a rite called 'consecration by contact', well-known to liturgists. It was used also for communion at home on weekdays and, according to my own conclusions in a paper in *American Benedictine Review* (1990), for the rite of the *fermentum*, used for a ritual joining of the eucharist in the bishop's church with that of nearby presbyterial churches. (For a good description of the communion rite, see de Jong 1951.)

The subdeacon carried the strainer in his hand during most of the mass (*habens colatorio minore in manu sua*, 4.74), even while singing the epistle at the ambo, and so it became a kind of status symbol of his office (Braun 1932: 457).

LADLES

Another instrument carried in procession was the *cantatorium* (1.21) which I interpret as a 'ladle' from the late Latin *canto*. We are

231

fortunate to have a perfect sample of all three – ladle, large and small strainers – in the Canoscio Treasure. All three are in the Hama Treasure as well. The inscriptions show that this latter is certainly ecclesiastical. The fact that Canoscio has the same three instruments whose function is so clearly described in the *Ordines* puts it beyond doubt that it also is ecclesiastical. Engemann (1972: 160) had declared that, on the basis of the symbols (crosses, fish etc.) and inscriptions, Canoscio was not demonstrably (*erweisbar*) church treasure. Mango (1986: 277) in her magnificent catalogue goes even further and states that it is 'clearly domestic'. But those writers cannot be expected to be familiar with the ritual involved. More reliable is Milojčić (1968), even though he was unaware of de Jong (1951).

'PRONGS'

Cattaneo (1940: 182–205) describes the Canoscio strainers and has an intriguing footnote on page 186: in 1401, there was donated to the cathedral of Milan *forceleta una parva cum manica cristali*, with some eucharistic use similar to that of the strainers. He is at a loss to know what this use might be, especially as he is not sure of the meaning of the word *forceleta*. *Furca/forca* is a hayfork or pitchfork, never a table fork. So to designate something as small as an eating implement, it seems that three diminutives were necessary: *forc-el-eta parva*. Even then, the *una* is superfluous. Apparently it was used to indicate a single prong rather than two like a fork.

Soon after reading this, I saw an illustration of the St Ninian's 'prong'. It seemed to fit the description exactly. The instrument would serve almost as efficiently as a strainer for taking a piece of bread out of liquid. This then is also an obvious suggestion for the use of the well-known and mysterious 'ivy-leaf' instruments. It would explain why many of them are found on church sites (Canterbury, Richborough) or are decorated with the christogram (Canterbury, Kaiseraugst). It would also explain why some have a strainer at one end and an 'ivy leaf' at the other (Richborough, Kaiseraugst); one then had a choice of using whichever seemed more suitable. It is also possible that some were used at ordinary meals or for more exotic purposes (Martin, in Cahn and Kaufmann-Heinemann 1984: 97 ff.; good illustrations 123–8). But I suspect that, like all Christian liturgy, the rite and perhaps even the instruments have a Jewish origin – cf. the 'dipped morsel' in John

13.26. The rite could also be imitated or paralleled in pagan rituals where they ate *panem mero mixtum* (Cyprian in the story in the next paragraph).

SPOONS

In the Orthodox rite, spoons are still used to give communion from the chalice to infants carried in the arms. The present system of giving communion to adults also by the spoon is a late development deriving from the primitive method of infant communion. In the West, all baptised infants received communion till about the year 1200 (Martimort 1961: 565). The clearest evidence for the use of the spoon in the West is from Cyprian, *De lapsis* 25, where he tells a famous story: a child whose parents had fled persecution was given bread mixed with wine which had been offered to an idol. When persecution ceased and the mother returned, she took the child to Holy Communion. As the deacon was giving communion from the chalice, *faciem suam parvula instinctu divinae maiestatis avertere, os labiis obdurantibus premere, calicem recusare, perstitit tamen diaconus et reluctanti licet de sacramento calicis infundit.* Then the infant began to vomit as the eucharist could not remain in the defiled body. The Latin text can only be understood of a baby carried in the arms and the consecrated wine being poured into its mouth with a spoon.

Bolton Abbey
Moone
Co. Kildare

NOTES

I THE RELIGIOUS BACKGROUND

1 Considered below, ch. II.
2 Lucan (*Pharsalia* 3.412) writes of rough wooden images carved on tree trunks, but the evidence of Diodorus Siculus (22.9.4) suggests that anthropomorphic representations, or at least veristic ones, were rare.
3 Criticisms which Green rejects as 'irrelevant and inappropriate'.
4 Pomponius: *Unum ex his quae praecipiunt in vulgus effluxit, videlicet ut forent ad bella meliores, aeternas esse animas vitamque alteram ad manes.*
Caesar: *In primis hoc {Druides} volunt persuadere, non interire animas, sed ab aliis post mortem transire ad alios, atque hoc maxime ad virtutem excitari putant metu mortis neglecto.*
5 Both the dog and horse appear to have been linked by the Celts with deities associated with healing and death (Green 1986: 171–6). The bones of other domesticated animals were also found in Celtic graves.
6 e.g. *RIB* 144.
7 As at Uley in Gloucestershire (Ellison 1980).
8 e.g. Coventina at Carrawburgh (Lewis 1966: 62).
9 e.g. Lewis (1966: ch. 3); M. Green (1976: ch. 3); Macdonald (1977: 38); Thomas (1981: 88); Henig (1984b: ch. 5); Ireland (1986: ch. 14.3).
10 Widely accepted as Luke.
11 The evidence is not clear. Acts 2.46 and 5.42 say that believers met in the temple, while 5.12 says specifically that they met in 'Solomon's Portico' and 3.11 implies it.
12 Trans. R. Graves.
13 The differentiation is also made by Celsus (*c.*178–80) (Origen, *Contra Celsum* 3.1).
14 Because apostolic succession by the end of the second century had come to be regarded as the only form of orthodox government (Frend 1984: 243). Peter had been the beginning of that tradition, the authority being Matthew 16.18: 'You are Peter, and on this rock I will build my church . . .'
15 See below, ch. II n. 11 for a closer examination of Thomas's views.
16 Following Levison (1941: 349–50).

II SIGNIFICANT PRIOR RESEARCH

1 As this chapter deals exclusively with previous publications, it would become cumbersome to give page references for all the detail mentioned. For this chapter only, therefore, page references will be restricted to those which are considered to be essential.

2 This last, the *colonia Londinensium*, is obviously textually corrupt and Toynbee emends it to *colonia Camulodunensium* which, she says, as the senior *colonia* was most likely to have had a bishop, possibly the Primate of Britain. See also Thomas (1981: 133, 197 and references).

3 For a study of churches on the sites of Roman buildings, see Morris and Roxan (1980).

4 e.g. *RIB* 137, 955.

5 This paper was first presented at a conference on Christianity in Roman and sub-Roman Britain held in 1967; the papers, of varying relevance for the period to 410, were subsequently edited by Barley and Hanson (1968). In this summary, they will be referred to individually as necessary.

6 A moot point. See below for Thomas's argument for continuity of Christianity to Anglo-Saxon times.

7 e.g. his reference to the cult of martyrs and relics by the turn of the fourth century, citing Jerome, *Contra vigilantium* 5 and 9, and Bede, *Historia ecclesiastica* 1.18, is particularly relevant in view of the recently discovered apsidal building with burial on the chord of the apse found at St Paul-in-the-Bail, Lincoln (below, ch. IV).

8 To be dealt with in detail below, ch. III.

9 And, to some extent, on that of Radford (1971), particularly in regard to the continuity of Christianity into the post-Roman period.

10 This theme he carries further in a more recent publication (Thomas 1986).

11 Thomas argues that it is hardly likely that a localised incident at a date so early as 209 (so Morris 1968) would have survived to be recorded in such detail three centuries later; and, moreover, at the beginning of the third century Verulamium still contained a 'fair spread' of pagan temples. The date of 209 is accepted by authorities such as Cross and Livingstone (1984) s.v. 'Alban'; however, Frend (1984: 294) is more cautious.

12 Cf. Frend (1968: 44–5), who sees Pelagianism as 'a force in Britain for 30 years or more'.

13 These will noted as occasion arises throughout this study.

14 This criterion for identification of Christian burials will be discussed in detail in ch. III.

15 See also Henig (1987: 184).

16 Boon (1962: 343) suggests it could have been the property of a Christian community.

17 Thomas himself concedes that, in church buildings, as in other ways, Britannia 'could go its own peculiar way'.

18 The proposals so far: the *triclinium* of an owner of erudition or religious leanings (Ling 1982; Insley 1982); the cult room for an Orphic *collegium* (Walters 1981; 1984; Henig 1982; 1984b: 220); a fourth-century Christian estate church (Smith 1978: 134, fig. 43 and n. 31; Thomas 1981: 182). Toynbee (1981), however, believes the mosaic depicts Apollo, rather than Orpheus, and she does not enter into the debate as to the purpose of the structure.

19 For another interpretation of these tanks, see Watts (1988a) and below, ch. V.2.

20 Henig (1984b: 224). What proportion he envisages in unclear, since he says elsewhere 'the majority of the population remained pagan through most of the fourth century, if not longer' (Henig 1984b: 215).

21 Green's research is centred on iconographical evidence and she does not cover such areas as architecture and ritual except in passing. Much of the material in this volume is included in a later, more general, work on the gods of the Celts (Green 1986).

22 But he refers to this latter building as a fourth-century church, when, in fact, it is at least fifth-century, and possibly of the sixth (Ramsay and Bell 1909: 25, 80).

23 The last site has been effectively dismissed by Boon (1976: 175 n. 28) and Thomas (1981: 168); dating is very insecure and may be anything from the mid-fifth century to the sixth, or even mediaeval.

24 This accompanies a collection of papers on temples and churches presented at a 1979 conference on Romano-British temple archaeology and associated subjects (Rodwell 1980b), the individual contributions to which will be dealt with separately.

25 See most recently Wilson (1988) for further detail on the Richborough font.

26 The paper is one of a collection from a seminar on burial in the Roman world held in 1974 and edited by Reece (1977). Several are of considerable importance for a study of Romano-British cemeteries, and will be referred to individually.

27 Pagan customs found in Christian burials will be treated at length below, ch. VI.

28 This would be due, at least in part, to the deficiencies of the records from which he has extracted his evidence, much of which comes from nineteenth-century excavations.

29 To be discussed further in this chapter.

30 His work will be referred to in more detail in a study of symbols and inscriptions (below, ch. V).

31 See, however, Small et al. (1973), and especially pp. 144–8 for a different interpretation.

32 See also Volbach (1965) on Canoscio. A liturgical identity for this treasure has been challenged by Engemann (1972: 157–61) and, more recently, by Mango (1986: 277).

33 e.g. the identification by Martin of the pronged spatulate-ended objects as 'Zahnstocker-Ohrloeffelchen' (Cahn and Kaufmann-Heinemann, 1984: 122).

34 These last two papers are from a volume of papers presented at a conference on pagan religion in the Roman Empire held in 1984, and edited by Henig and King (1986). Papers will be referred to separately as necessary.

35 She includes Lancing Down. This site and the location of temples or churches near burial grounds will be discussed fully below, ch. IV.

36 M. Green (1976: 49); but see Harman et al. (1981) and below, ch. III.

37 Henig cites Tacitus, Agricola 21; the sons of chiefs were hardly representative of the whole of British society, however.

38 A view expressed by various scholars. See below, ch. IV, for a discussion on religious continuity.

39 e.g. his fig. 4.4.

40 See below, ch. IV.
41 Generally only pagan cemeteries of more than thirty burials will be analysed in this study.
42 A list of cemeteries from the Roman period appears in Clarke (1979: 348). Here only fourth-century Romano-Celtic sites will be considered for purposes of comparison.
43 e.g. seven burials listed in the report proper are not included on the microfiche.
44 Whimster does, in fact, include as Iron Age at least one site, Jordan Hill, (and thus the associated burial practices) which is almost certainly early Roman.
45 The occurrence of the name Senicianus on this ring and on a curse tablet from Lydney has caused comment: see Goodchild (1953). Note also Mawer (1989: 240 n. 65) for a possible pagan interpretation for this ring.
46 Neal (1981: 121) proposes ten, or possibly twelve.

III IDENTIFICATION OF CHRISTIAN CEMETERIES

1 Infant burials as a criterion

1 This is a slightly revised version of a paper appearing in *Archaeological J.* 146 (Watts forthcoming).
2 I am most grateful to the following for generously supplying plans and/or additional information on various cemeteries ahead of publication: Mr David Wilson and Nottingham University (Ancaster); Mr Brian Dix of Northamptonshire County Council Archaeology Unit (Ashton); Messrs Carl Crossan and Philip Crummy of Colchester Archaeological Trust (Butt Road, Colchester); Emeritus Professor Philip Rahtz (formerly York University) (Cannington); Ms Susan Davies, Messrs David Farwell and Christopher Sparey Green, and the Trust for Wessex Archaeology (Poundbury Camp, Dorchester, Dorset); and Messrs David Miles of Oxford Archaeological Unit (Radley II).
3 *Hominem mortuum in urbe ne sepelito neve urito* (Table X).
4 e.g. by Antoninus Pius (*S.H.A. Pius* 12.3).
5 *Aiunt mortuos infantes in subgrundariis condi solere.*
6 *Su(g)grundaria antiqui dicebant sepulchra infantium, qui necdum quadraginta dies implessent.*
7 *Melius suggrundarium miser quaereris quam sepulchrum.*
8 See Alcock (1980: 56–7) for a discussion of the significance of eggs with burials.
9 For the purposes of this study, it is felt that generally only cemeteries with thirty or more burials should be referred to.
10 Throughout this study, the alignment of the skeletal remains is given with the direction of the head stated first.
11 For published accounts see: Dix (1984), Hadman (1984), Frere (1984a: 300–1; 983: 305–6) on Ashton; Crossan (in Crummy 1980) on Butt Road; Green (1967–77a; 1981–2) and Kean (1968) on Poundbury.
12 It should be noted that the lines for division into the various phases at Poundbury are somewhat debatable; I have generally followed those of Green (1982) but with some modification for the northern part of the cemetery,

where there appears to be a pagan component, with north–south burials; the burials in the south-eastern part of the cemetery are treated separately as 'site C' (so D. Farwell, pers. comm.).

13 The fourth-century settlement may have been abandoned and then re-occupied at the end of the century for another fifty or sixty years (Matthews 1981: 62).

14 At the time of writing, the report on the skeletal remains at Ancaster was not yet available. Mr Wilson has supplied information from his excavation notes.

15 Those that were not were at one end of the cemetery. This is discussed in ch. III.2 below.

16 See Jones *et al.* (1978: 80–110), and especially p. 85 n. 1 for a discussion of the baptism rite in the third and fourth centuries.

17 That is, that no person born should be denied the mercy and grace of God, conferred by baptism (a decision of the Council of Carthage in 252: Cyprian, *Ad Fidum* 2).

18 Cyprian, *Ad Fidum* 3.

19 I am most grateful to Bro. Eoin de Bhaldraithe, Bolton Abbey, Moone, Co. Kildare, for his suggestion of the burial of catechumens, and for the following information on the catechumenate.

20 This would appear to be confirmed by canon 2 of the Council of Carthage of 418, which reaffirmed the need for infants to be baptised, since they have original sin inherited from Adam (Romans 5.12).

21 That is not to say, of course, that all Christians were buried with head to the west. See below, ch. III.2, for discussion on orientation.

22 Cannington and Ancaster are other very real possibilities. To these I would suggest as very likely the cemeteries at Bradley Hill (latest phase), Lamyatt Beacon, Lankhills feature 6, Nettleton cemetery A, and possibly Brean Down and the Crown Buildings site, Dorchester. These will be considered in ch. III.2.

2 Other suggested criteria

1 e.g. Tertullian, *De anima* 51.4. Minucius Felix, *Octavius* 11.4 has been taken to indicate Christian 'abhorrence for cremation' (Green 1977b: 46) but such interpretation takes the passage out of context; later in his *apologia* Minucius makes it clear that the reversion by Christians to inhumation was not based on fear that destruction of the body would prevent resurrection: *nec, ut creditis, ullam damnum sepulturae timemus, sed veterem et meliorem consuetudinem humandi frequentamus* (*Octavius* 34.8–12, cf. 11.4)).

2 e.g. Toynbee (1953); Frend (1979); Thomas (1981: 126).

3 Photographs kindly supplied by Mr Carl Crossan.

4 See Thomas (1981: 232–4 and references). To these may be added a study by Kendall (1982), who challenges the theory of Rahtz (1978) of seasonal variation in the west–east alignment of graves, and two discussions on orientation in more primitive societies: Næss (1970) and Ucko (1969–70: 271–3).

5 The alignment of burials in the catacombs was, of course, dictated by conditions of excavation, and there is little evidence that the larger Christian catacombs were planned (Toynbee 1971: 234–5) and no evidence of any attempt to place interments west–east. This would add weight to the

argument below that belief in a physical resurrection was not taught by the early Church.

6 Generally, only those of thirty or more burials, west–east or otherwise, will be referred to.

7 The cemeteries and buildings at Lamyatt Beacon and Brean Down are included in this study because, although the burials are not strictly datable to the fourth or fifth century, they display features which are also found in late Roman cemeteries. The buildings seem to be of Roman date, and I believe there is a close association of building and cemetery at both sites.

8 At Ancaster, where the occasional disturbance occurred, there appears to have been an attempt to replace the dislodged bones in their proper position (D. Wilson, pers. comm.).

9 *Qui ergo nihil fueras priusquam esses, idem nihil factus cum esse desieris.* The same sentiment is expressed by Paul (1 Corinthians 15.44).

10 It has been claimed that in the second and third centuries, Christian leaders such as Justin Martyr and Tertullian were teaching that, at the time of the Second Coming, there would be a literal resurrection of the dead (Green 1977b: 46). The text from Tertullian has been discussed and interpreted above. In the writings of Justin Martyr, two contradictory statements are made about the Second Coming: in *Dialogue* 80 he claims his is the 'orthodox' view that there will be a physical resurrection and a physical New Jerusalem, rebuilt for the millennium (Revelation 20.4); yet in *Dialogue* 113 he is of the opinion that the New Jerusalem will be a spiritual and eternal land, and in 1 *Apology* 18 he gives a view of the resurrection 'since we expect that our own bodies, even though they should be dead and buried in the earth, will be revived; for we claim that nothing is impossible with God' (trans. T.B. Falls), which conforms with New Testament teaching (e.g. 1 Corinthians 15.35–46). This, Barnard (1967: 165–6) says, 'is another example of how circumstances affected his eschatology . . . The language of Apocalyptic both mythical and quasi-physical are used according to the theme under discussion.' In view of such contradictions, it is not wise to use Justin Martyr's opinions on the resurrection as evidence for doctrine taught in the second century.

11 The belief seems to have persisted into the Middle Ages. Durandus (*Rationale* 7.25.39), writing in the thirteenth century, referred to the placement of a burial west–east with hands in a position of prayer, but as if ready to leap up at the Last Judgement.

12 It was reported in 1978 that, in the Oxford region, all the burials which had until then been excavated from the cemeteries at Queensford Mill (Queensford Farm) and Church Piece were prone (Harman *et al.* 1978: 16). This appears to have been an error, and a later report on the Queensford Farm cemetery (Chambers 1987) now describes all but two of the burials there as supine. Presumably this would also apply to Church Piece, but that cemetery is not studied in depth in the present analysis since the sample excavated at the site – five burials from a total estimated at from 500 to 1,000 – is much too small to be taken as representative of the whole cemetery.

13 e.g. M. Green (1976: 49); Macdonald (1979: 414–21); Harman *et al.* (1981: 167); Black (1986b: 226).

14 Chambers (1987: microfiche frame 20) indicates that, in the 1972 excavations at this site, burial 157, of an adult female, was found with 'skull back to front

and upside down'; this would seem to suggest a decapitated burial, or at least a disturbed one. This particular feature of the burial is not referred to in any of the reports on the Queensford Farm cemetery.

15 The decayed state of the skeletons at Ospringe would have made it impossible in many cases to recognise a decapitated burial. Often only a few fragments of the skull and the larger bones remained. In others, the skeleton had completely disappeared.

16 See Frend (1961 and pl. 1.3) (Timgad), and Gsell (1901: vol II, 403, n. 7) (Tipasa, Sidi Embarek, Tebessa and Zraia).

17 Unaccompanied, that is, except for a deep-flanged pie dish, upon which lay the head of burial B of the triple tomb; an object which, in view of the lady's poor dietary habits, Wells (1968: 41) humorously suggests may have contributed to her demise.

18 Information on Lamyatt Beacon, Leech (1986: 326), and Nettleton A, Wedlake (1982: 90–2). The criterion of the presence of neo-natal or very young infants need not be strictly applied to Brean Down and Lamyatt Beacon cemeteries, however; the cemeteries were both probably from the sub-Roman period. Nothing is known about the frequency of infant baptism in Britain after the departure of the Romans.

19 Augustine (*Enarrationes in psalmos 33* (2),14) warns against sumptuous funerals, and in *Confessiones* 9 gives an account of the simple burial of his mother, Monica.

20 Mausolea are not uncommon in Britain, but those of the late period appear to be found mainly on private property, rather than in public burial grounds. A recent paper by Black (1986b: 201–39) discusses structures, from the Iron Age and Roman periods, which might be classified as such. The subject of mausolea in Britain will be treated in a later chapter (below, ch. VI).

21 There are a number of problems in any consideration of enclosure F15 at Queensford Farm, a rectangular ditched area about 6 metres across, containing the remains of two adult females. It does appear, by their placement, that the enclosure was intended for these two burials, but there is no hint in the report (Chambers 1987) of any relationship, based on skeletal analysis. Furthermore, it was shown above, in reference to the Dunstable site, that a pair of family members could be buried in adjoining graves, even in a pagan cemetery. There are further difficulties in that the cemetery appears to have been in use for two centuries. Indeed, Chambers has proposed that the enclosure was very late in the sequence of the cemetery, well into the sixth century, and thus at least sub-Roman, or even post-Roman. Even though there has been only limited excavation at the site (164 graves out of a possible 2,000), Queensford Farm does have several features which would suggest a pagan identity.

22 This is expanded below, ch. VI.

23 e.g. *CIL* VIII.9585 from Africa.

24 There is evidence that, at least in some Christian cemeteries, burial plots were bought and sold (e.g. *IG* 14.83 and 96 from Syracuse).

25 See Grinsell (1961) for a study of this custom.

26 It has been suggested that the hillfort at Cannington had been re-occupied in the late Roman period (Rahtz 1969); this may have been a Christian community.

27 *Admoneri placuit fideles, ut in quantum possunt prohibeant ne idola in domibus suis habeant; si vero vim metuunt servorum, vel se ipsos puros conservent; si non fecerint, alieni ab ecclesia habeantur.*

28 This cemetery, from which only five graves have been excavated from an estimated total of 500–1,000, is not included in the analysis of figs 2 and 3.

29 Three-quarters, rather than higher, since absence of this type of grave furniture could also indicate the poverty of a community. The cemetery at Bath Gate, Cirencester, for instance, had only one chicken in a pottery vessel and very few other grave goods in a total of about 450 graves.

30 In all, about 2,300 nails were found in the cemetery, all except seven having 'large, round, flattish heads' (Wenham 1968: 39). Unfortunately, only the seven were illustrated. It does seem quite likely that hobnails were present in the cemetery at Trentholme Drive.

31 I am indebted to Dr Edward Yarnold, Campion Hall, Oxford, for this suggestion.

32 e.g. the Radley 1945 excavation (Atkinson 1952–3) and Lynch Farm (Jones 1975).

33 A policy admitted by Gregory the Great in his advice to Augustine (Bede, *Historia ecclesiastica* 1.27).

34 Indeed, many religious practices of fourth-century Christianity found their origins in the pagan religions. This will be the subject of a study later in this work (ch. VI).

35 In their site-catchment analysis of a prehistoric economy, Vita-Finzi and Higgs (1970) conclude that beyond a distance of 10 kilometres from his home base, 'the hunter-gatherer would find it uneconomic to exploit the available resources'. They add that, in their study, such area would be bounded by points within two hours' walking-time of home base. It would, I feel, be not unreasonable to find devout Christians travelling for a similar length of time, or longer, to meet with other Christians for worship; undoubtedly movement within Roman Britain would have been much easier than in prehistoric Palestine.

36 See Huskinson (1974: 77); Henig (1984a: 143–6).

37 Thomas's exclusion of the Mildenhall and Traprain Law Treasures is accepted with reluctance, and it is pointed out that Mildenhall is in area which has much evidence for Christianity, while, given the evidence for the northern area and the types of vessels in the hoard, the Traprain silver could very easily have come from an important Christian site in northern Britain.

38 For the finds at Caerwent and Fifehead Neville, cf. Thomas (1981: 123, 131).

39 Unpublished; see below, ch. V.1.

40 Another possible example from Gloucestershire recorded here, but not weighted, is the stone relief of a head set in an octagonal niche, perhaps a shrine, at the Portway, Upton St Leonards. The sculpture had been deliberately defaced so that only the features of the neck and hair are clear. Dating is only on stylistic grounds, the modelling said to be 'classical' (Rawes 1977; 1978).

41 One further, recently discovered, site might also be mentioned, but not ranked, since there is no evidence as yet that the destruction was deliberate: at a site opposite the Old Bailey in London, it appears that a large temple complex was destroyed by fire early in the fourth century (Milne 1988). It may be only coincidental that this occurred about the time that Christianity became an approved religion within the Empire.

42 The Thetford Treasure is a special case, and, while it has objects which have Christian associations, such as cross, fish-and-palm and *vivas* inscriptions, the

whole appears to be a pagan hoard. See Johns and Potter (1983); Watts (1988b); and below, ch. V.1, for various interpretations of this treasure.

43 Toynbee (1964b: 301–3, 338) has linked this find with the later one of 1962, which comprised fragments of what has now proved to be seven early Imperial silver drinking cups (Johns 1986b). Ms Johns does not mention the earlier find in her paper. The original report of the ritual headdresses says that 'a late Roman brooch, pottery and coins were also found' (Anon. 1957: 211).

44 It has been proposed that it may have been associated with a Romano-Celtic shrine at Upper Delphs, and that its deposition occurred in the late third or early fourth century, as a result of the incursions of Saxon raiders (Evans 1984).

3 Application of the criteria

1 Equally, in view of the small numbers of burials at Verulamium, it is recognised that the absence of decapitated burials, hobnails, animals and birds may also not be significant. The cemetery is too small to be significant in this analysis.

2 And, a corollary of this, that all other cemeteries analysed be ranked 0 on the 3–0 scale.

3 The plan for Brean Down cemetery, as far as I know, has not been published; at the Dorchester cemetery site much of the evidence was destroyed before excavation, and in the plan in Green *et al.* (1982: fig. 2) many of the burials are conjectural only.

IV IDENTIFICATION OF CHRISTIAN CHURCHES

1 Suggested criteria

1 He writes of a memorial church built as an octagon with chambers arranged 'as we see everywhere in the cruciform pattern' (trans. W. Moore and H.A. Wilson).

2 Cf. the suggestion that the normal position of Constantinian churches was with apse to the east, and that this was in line with the 'Emperor's enthusiasm for sun-worship' (Gough 1961: 134). More likely is the proposal that the alignment of the Constantinian church was dependent on regional custom and local topography (Krautheimer 1965: 69).

3 To clarify this, 'intra-mural' sites in this study are those found within the walls of a town, or, as in the case of Uley, Nettleton Octagonal and Witham, within a *temenos* or some sort of defining boundary.

4 Furthermore, it does not appear to have been as large as proposed by Thomas (C. Guy, pers. comm.).

5 See further detail above, ch. III, in a discussion of grave goods.

6 These deposits will be discussed further in ch. VI.

7 Similarities have been suggested between this site and that at Great Dunmow in Essex, but archaeological evidence is too scanty to determine if the second phase of site 273 at Great Dunmow was used for non-pagan religious purposes. The excavator also sees similarities between Great Dunmow and a

late Roman cemetery site at Verulamium, thought to be the burial site of Alban (Wickenden 1988: 91–2).

8 I am most grateful to Mr Robin Turner, of West Yorkshire Archaeology Service, formerly of Essex County Council Planning Department, for his assistance and for generously supplying information on the Witham site ahead of publication.

9 One further site might be re-examined. Boon (1974: 154), in commenting on the temple designated Silchester 3, says that the very fragmented remains of the statuary in the temple suggest this was due to deliberate destruction, and he postulates a connection between this presumed desecration and the presence nearby of a Christian church. In Frere's report on the Richmond excavations at Silchester, it is noted that the basilical building, a possible church, was found to be erected on the site of an earlier timber structure standing there until late in the third century; the purpose of the building is unknown, since its floors 'appear to have been kept swept fairly clean' (Frere 1975: 292). There was no evidence of domestic use, although Frere suggests a well nearby may have been associated with the structure. It may be that the earlier building had been a pagan shrine, and that the absence of evidence was due to Christians clearing the site, as at Icklingham, Uley and Witham.

10 e.g. Lewis (1966: 146), Morris and Roxan (1980: 175), Frend (1955; 1968; 1979; 1982), Thomas (1981: 240–74), Morris (1983: 19–48).

11 The absence of religious structures of pagan Anglo-Saxons does not allow this theory to be tested in the period between the decline of Romano-British Christianity and the conversion of the Saxons; however, the numbers of invaders were small in comparison with the British population (Thomas 1981: 244), and Christianity seemed to hold out in some intra-mural sites (below, ch. VII), and in areas not greatly affected by the invaders (Thomas 1981: fig. 49).

12 I am grateful to Dr Ann Woodward, formerly Ellison, Birmingham, for information on the Uley site ahead of publication. Since the time of writing Dr Woodward has indicated *in litt.* that her initial interpretation of the Uley site has changed considerably since the 1980 Interim Report; it was not possible to incorporate her findings here, but they will be published in her final report.

13 St Augustine's Chapel, according to a mediaeval tradition, contained a stone bearing the footprint made by the saint when he first stepped ashore in 597. The original church is almost certainly Saxon, and the legend of its origins gives a hint of a fairly early date in the Saxon period. The coins found 'in the vicinity' of the church, two *sceattas* and two pennies of the reign of Offa (757–96), suggest an early Saxon presence (Bushe-Fox 1928: 34–5, 37–40).

14 I am indebted to Professor Keith Branigan of Sheffield University for this suggestion.

15 I thank Mr W. J. Putnam of Dorset College of Higher Education for his examination of the Durotrigian pottery at Dorset Museum and his help in sorting out the dating of the cemetery at Jordan Hill. The most important references for this site are: Warne (1872), Oliver (1923), Drew (1931; 1932), O'Neill (1935). I believe Whimster (1981: 40, 52–3) errs in classifying the cemetery as Late Iron Age; he ignores the fact that there were hobnail burials, which do not occur before the Roman period, and that the Durotrigian pottery could have been in use as late as the end of the second century. The

crouched burials, which he sees as evidence of pre-Roman burial, could easily be a primitive anachronism in the early Roman period. Inhumations in this position were found even in the fourth century (see above, ch. III.2)

16 Bedwin (1981) reports that the Romano-Celtic temple had indeed been founded on an Iron Age shrine site, of immediate pre-conquest date.

17 A recent publication by Brunaux (1988: 13, 24) on the Celts of Gaul corroborates this; he states that, from his research on Belgic sanctuaries, 'there is at present no example of a sanctuary located within a cemetery or very close to graves'. Brunaux sees the Iron Age shrines at Gosbecks, Heathrow, Lancing Ring and Uley as related both geographically and culturally to the European examples.

18 However, his interpretation of the archaeological material at Lancing Down is unconvincing.

19 Ammianus Marcellinus (22.12) tells how the pagan emperor Julian had bodies which had been placed around the Castalian spring at Delphi removed, when he brought back the oracle into use; and Sozomen (*Ecclesiastical History* 5.19) relates that Julian had been told that Apollo was not producing oracles at Daphne because the sacred enclosure had been polluted by dead bodies – the remains of the Christian martyr, Babylas, had been moved to a church built in the temple of Apollo.

20 It is noted that, in his recently published study of the extra-mural areas of Romano-British towns, Esmond Cleary (1987) in his town plans shows only one 'temple' sited on a cemetery (fig. 24). This building is Colchester 9, the structure at Butt Road, which is undoubtedly a Christian church.

21 The Brean Down burials were situated some little distance from the temple and rectangular building site, but it has been suggested, quite reasonably, that this position was chosen to make excavation for graves much easier (Leech 1980: 346). This sandy soil is, of course, the reason why much of the cemetery has been lost to erosion.

22 No doubt, given either situation, identification of a Christian burial in perhaps mid-third-century Britain would be extremely difficult; Alban's remains, even if found, may never be identified. At such an early date, it would certainly be possible that cremation was still practised by Christians in Britain.

23 One wonders, too, if they were pagan graves, why they were placed around the building at all, rather than in the nearby and long-established cemetery.

24 I thank Dr John Drinkwater of Sheffield University for his great help in providing Gaulish analogies for this section of this work, and Mr Michael Jones of the Trust for Lincolnshire Archaeology for plans and information ahead of publication.

25 See especially Dyggve (1951: 115, 121 n. 48) on the origins of the martyr cult.

26 With regard to the decorations of the cathedral complex of Bishop Theodore at Aquileia, built about 308–19 with extensions over another century, Radford (1968: 27) points out that the decorations employed, 'though rich in Christian associations . . . contained little that need offend pagans'.

27 e.g. King (1983).

28 I thank Mr George Boon, National Museum of Wales, Cardiff, for providing me with information on this site, and in particular his suggestions concerning the layout of this possible house church.

29 Although the evidence of Caesarius of Arles (*Sermones* 204.3) suggests otherwise.
30 See above, n. 12.

3 Application of the criteria

1 These deposits, and the question of covert pagan features at presumed church sites are discussed in ch. VI on pagan influence and practices in Christianity.

V FURTHER CHRISTIAN SYMBOLS AND INSCRIPTIONS

1 A reappraisal of the Thetford Treasure

1 This is a slightly reworked version of an article published in *Ant. J.* 68 (Watts 1988b).
2 The site had been occupied sporadically from prehistoric times to the end of the fourth century, with a peak of coin evidence for AD 350–75. Two hoards of silver coins found in 1978 and 1981 range from 355–61 to 385. There is slight evidence for a substantial late-Roman wooden structure close to where the Treasure was found.
3 I am most grateful to Ms Catherine Johns for her help and additional comments in what has been a long and lively correspondence on the Treasure. Since almost all the material on the Treasure has been extrapolated from the Johns and Potter monograph, reference to page numbers from that text will be kept to a minimum in this chapter.
4 See below, n. 25.
5 For a discussion of conservatism as a characteristic of Roman religion, see North (1976).
6 Daniélou (1964: 42–57) has explored the Jewish origins of the symbol.
7 Information and photograph kindly supplied by Ms Catherine Johns. I thank Mr Brian Dix for drawing my attention to this find.
8 This ring, believed lost, has now been located in the Ashmolean Museum, Oxford. In her note on the ring, Ms Mawer discusses the typology of the ring and the Greek inscription, but does not comment on the palm leaf motifs.
9 According to Sulzberger (1925: 393), the *iota-chi* was the earliest Christian monogram, the letters I and X standing for ΙΗΣΟΥΣ ΧΡΙΣΤΟΣ. Examples of the *iota-chi* in Roman Britain include: a plate from feature 6 of Lankhills cemetery, with stylised fish on the reverse (Clarke 1979: 429–30); a shaped stone, possibly from a nymphaeum, at Chedworth (Goodburn 1979: pl. 11D); a compass from Dorset erroneously identified as a *chi-rho* (Henig 1983); a candlestick from Kelvedon (Eddy and Turner 1982: cover fig.) and a similar find from Colchester (Crummy 1983: fig. 207, cat. no. 4709); a locally made pot from Rockbourne villa (Hewitt 1971: pl. XXII A); and, most recently, a probable example from Verulamium, in the form of a graffito on a drinking cup of the late third century (Frere 1984b: fig. 84, no. 2026). (My thanks to Professor Keith Branigan for this reference.) The symbol had a long life; an early mediaeval example, possibly twelfth-century, was found on

a hone from an Irish monastery site at Church Island, Lough Currane (Anon. 1927).

10 See Appendix for a brief mention of the debate on the Canoscio Treasure.

11 The fragment from Caerleon (Alstone Cottage, 1970) is unpublished. I am grateful to Mr George Boon for photograph and information on this find. Thomas (1981: 130) suggests a Christian identification for similar unpublished finds from Springhead and Verulamium.

12 Kajanto cites no. 554 from De Rossi's 1857–61.

13 This interpretation is strengthened by a passage from Paul's letter to the Ephesians (6.18) in which he exhorts the faithful to perseverance in prayer. It is possible, of course, that the inscription is in the imperative; this would also suit a Christian identity for the spoon's owner, in view of the above.

14 See also Thomas (1981: 110–13, 125–6, 129–31) on these types of inscriptions.

15 The inscription reads *VTEREEELIX*; the second E is an error for F.

16 The ivy leaf also occurs on two spoons dedicated to Faunus, nos 52 and 74.

17 e.g. on rings from Brancaster (Toynbee 1953: 19), Richborough (Cunliffe 1968: 98–9 and pl. XLII), and Silchester (*CIL* II.1305), a spoon from Caistor St Edmund (Sherlock 1978–80) and an openwork bone mounting from a grave in York (RCHM 1962: 73, pl. 65.150).

18 Interpreted as *viri boni s(u)m*.

19 For a useful discussion on strainers, see Richardson (1980).

20 This Treasure, published in 1923, contains several Christian elements and should, I believe, be thoroughly reappraised in the light of more recent discoveries.

21 I am most grateful to Bro. Eoin de Bhaldraithe for making the fruits of his research on early Church ritual available ahead of publication. The material on the use of strainers, spoons and ladles in the early Mass has been specially prepared by him for this study. It is included as an Appendix: 'Strainers and other instruments in early Church ritual'.

22 Milojčić (1968: pls 19 (1, 2), 20 (2)) illustrates three representations from the eleventh and twelfth centuries of the administration of the wine with a spoon. However two sixth-century representations of the Communion of the Apostles – one on the Stuma paten from Syria, the other an illuminated manuscript, the *Codex Purpureus Rossanensus*, from Constantinople or Antioch – clearly show the distribution of both bread and wine: no spoon is used (Schiller 1972: pls 56, 57–8).

23 See Appendix.

24 In a more recent paper on the Treasure, Ms Johns says, 'The positioning and spacing of the inscriptions makes it quite certain that they were put on . . . at the time of manufacture' (Johns 1986a: 96); however she does not expand on this, and the evidence adduced in the monograph cannot support the conclusion that all spoons were engraved before being finished (Johns and Potter 1983: 42).

25 But the two *Restituti* spoons, 76 and 77, also fall into this category; and while a Christian identity for this pair is nowhere nearly as positive as for the other spoons with *vivas*, *uti felix* or Christian symbols, the association of Restitutus with them must carry some weight towards such identification. However, the pair are unique in several ways: they alone of the spoons with personal names have no *vivas* or cross; they alone of this group appear to have been made 'to

order'; if Professor Jackson's reading of *Ingenuae* is correct (Johns and Potter 1983: 46), they are the only 'secular' names in the genitive – all the others are gods' names; they comprise the only 'secular' inscriptions in a number dedicated to Faunus, said to be engraved by the one hand – Group A in the monograph. (It is felt that spoon 73, *DEIFAVASECI*, should also belong to Group A, or at least that it was engraved by the same hand as 55 – but this does not detract from the argument above). One wonders, too, if there is any significance in the name Restitutus. It was, after all, also the cognomen of a Bishop of London who had attended the Council of Arles in 314.

26 We are told in the report that a further fifteen spoons showed slight signs of wear, but such evidence has been too indeterminate to be of use in developing this line of research. (Ms Johns has made additional comments on this aspect of the Treasure *in litt.*)

27 See Appendix.

2 Circular lead tanks and their significance

1 This chapter is a later version of an article published in *Antiq. J.* 68 (Watts 1988a), incorporating the most recent tank, found in Warwickshire in the spring of 1989.

2 One from Oxborough (TF 7302), (Frere 1986: 403 and pl. XXIX; Guy 1989); one from Caversham, near Reading (SU 7374) (Frere 1989: 319; Hassall and Tomlin 1989: 333–4); and, most recently, a partial tank from near Kenilworth, Warwickshire (SP 2773). I am indebted to Professor Keith Branigan for informing me of the find from Caversham and to Messrs David Miles and John Moore of Oxford Archaeological Unit for supplying details ahead of publication; and to Mr Christopher Guy of City of Lincoln Archaeological Unit for supplying me with a copy of his article on the find from Kenilworth prior to publication.

3 As there are many references to Thomas's study of baptisms in this present chapter, page references to that work will be kept to a minimum here.

4 The *chi-rho* monogram was probably the most widely used Christian symbol in the fourth century, until it was replaced in popularity by the monogrammatic cross and the cross standing alone. This development could be attributed to the abolition by Constantine of crucifixion as a death penalty, and to the tradition of the discovery of the True Cross by Helena, the mother of Constantine (e.g. Paulinus of Nola, *Epistulae* 31.5–6). See Sulzberger (1925) and Cabrol and Leclerq (1920–53: vol. 3, s.v. '*croix et crucifix*' and '*chrisme*').

5 Thomas (1981: figs 4–7) gives a good coverage of these Christian symbols in Britain.

6 e.g. De Rossi (1864–77: vol. II, pls XXXIII–XXXIV.4).

7 See Justin Martyr, *1 Apology* 60 for a possible early reference. It has been claimed to be the oldest known form of the Christian cross (after the *tau* cross borrowed from the Old Testament) (Cabrol and Leclerq 1920–53: vol. 3.2, col. 3048 s.v. '*croix et crucifix*'); however, Sulzberger (1925: 367) believes the two **X**s on an inscription from Palmyra, and dating to AD 134 are merely punctuation signs. The Christian **X** is certainly found on early monuments at Chaqqa, in Syria, dating from the fourth century (Cabrol and Leclerq 1920–53: vol. 3.1, col. 515 s.v. '*Chaqqa*'). The *tau* in the Hebrew alphabet was

represented by + or X, so there would be no difficulty in believers' equating it with the cross of Christianity.

8 e.g. Isidore, *Origen* 1.3: X *quae in figura crucem, et in numero decem demonstrat*. It is possible that the X may also have been seen, in the fourth century, as a *chi*, and a monogram for Christ, although the evidence of Julian, *Misopogon* 357A (Loeb edn) is not clear; the reference here could equally have been to the *iota-chi* or to the *chi-rho*.

9 I am grateful to Dr David Phillipson, University Museum of Archaeology and Anthropology, Cambridge, for photographs of the tanks from Willingham and Wilbraham.

10 My thanks to Mr Brian Dix for providing a photograph of this fragment.

11 It has been pointed out that 'most of the types of crosses found in Ireland are universal to all Christendom at that time, and have been brought to Ireland from Gaul, Italy or the Near East' (Henry 1965: 54). This would also appear to be the case for Roman Britain.

12 See also Child and Colles (1971: figs 15, 16).

13 While it might be argued that the motif could as easily represent a pagan sun-wheel, it is important to note that each of the four symbols on the tank has been carefully placed so that it forms a cross pattée; there are no vertical or horizontal strokes. This gives further support to a Christian interpretation for the symbol. (Information on the tank kindly supplied by Mrs Elizabeth James, Curator of Lynn Museum, Kings Lynn.)

14 This concept is not new: see Isaiah 40.22.

15 My thanks to Mr Michael Dyson, University of Queensland, for this reference.

16 A similar intensification may be the interpretation of an inscription from Lyons, where the *alpha* and *omega* flanking a *chi-rho* are enclosed in equilateral triangles, the symbol of the Trinity (*CIL* XIII.2418).

17 I am indebted to Ms Brenda Dickinson of Leeds University for her help in this identification, and for the above reference.

18 One further point could be added here: among the pottery finds from the Romano-British building excavated at Bourton-on-the-Water in Gloucestershire is a piece of fourth-century grey ware. Its decoration, rare in Britain, consists of three rows of a stamped pattern of a saltire within a circle, with a round 'pellet' in each quadrant. An exact parallel to this decoration has been found on a small vessel from a seventh-century Merovingian cemetery (Donovan 1934: 113–14 and fig. 6). If the motif had been used by Christians in Britain as early as the fourth century, this could suggest a link between the pottery and the lead tanks found at Bourton, and add weight to a proposed Christian presence somewhere in the large settlement there (see Webster 1975: 59 and fig. 4), if not in the actual building where the tanks were found in an abandoned state.

19 As has been shown by the example above in respect of the motif on the Huntingdon tank, there is no reason to assume that, with the fall of the Empire, there was a break in the continuity of religious symbolism, although new motifs were introduced in the Byzantine period and some older ones of the Roman period declined in popularity.

20 This inscription is illustrated by Cabrol and Leclerq (1920–53: vol. 7.1, col. 653 fig. 5869 s.v. *'inscriptions grecques chrétiennes'*).

21 The Ashton fragment also has a band of circles below the cross and circle motif.

22 The circles were evidently applied to the panels before they were cut to fit the circular base, and the quarter circle was lost in the joining process (Richmond 1945: 166).

23 So, too, Painter (1971: 167).

24 Thomas refers to this tank as 'an atypical outlier'.

25 On the question of a tradition of sanctity and religious continuity, see above, ch. IV.

26 *Venisti ad fontem, descendisti in eum.*

27 And the descent symbolised to the candidate his sacramental union with Christ in his death upon the cross as he was 'buried therefore with him through baptism unto death' (Romans 6.4).

28 Dr Edward Yarnold, Campion Hall, Oxford, has drawn my attention to the fact that there were two fonts close together at Castel Seprio, near Milan. It may be that we are looking here at endowments from members of a wealthy congregation, in the same way that church plate was duplicated; this does not necessarily mean that both fonts were used at the one time. The evidence for Christianity in Roman Britain does not support a suggestion of great wealth amongst rural congregations generally: see below, ch. VII.

29 Ignatius, in the second century, says that it was not lawful for anyone but the bishop to baptise (*Ad Smyrnam* 8), but Tertullian indicates that his function could be delegated to presbyters, deacons and even laymen at the beginning of the third century (Tertullian, *De baptismo* 17). Even so, only the bishop could perform the imposition of hands, which was an integral part of the baptism ceremony. See Noakes (1978) for a discussion of the ritual before the fourth century.

30 That is, that this action brought the Holy Spirit down on it, giving it a supernatural effect (Yarnold 1971: 105 n. 28).

31 Baptism was normally performed only at Easter and Pentecost (Tertullian, *De baptismo* 19), though the sacrament was also administered at Epiphany in Cappadocia and perhaps elsewhere (Yarnold 1978: 97). In the fifth century, canon 19 of the Second Irish Synod under Patrick prescribes baptism at Epiphany, Easter and Pentecost.

32 *Placuit . . . neque pedes eorum {qui baptizantur} lavandi sunt a sacerdotibus, sed clericis*: this version from Rock (1869). Another, probably a later and amended version of this canon, forbids footwashing by either bishops or priests. It reads: *neque pedes eorum lavandi sunt a sacerdotibus vel clericis* (Hefele 1894: 157–8), which does make it appear that the Church in Spain no longer included this rite in its baptism ceremony. This does not, I feel, diminish the argument for footwashing in the Church of the West as a general practice in the fourth century.

33 The occurrence of footwashing in the baptismal ritual in the Church in Roman Britain could also explain the two rectangular structures associated with what is generally accepted as a fourth-century church at Silchester: the larger structure the font, the smaller a soakway for the *pedilavium*. There may also have been a similar arrangement at Witham (see above, ch. IV). These examples do not negate the proposed footwashing function for the lead tanks: it is suggested that the priest, having drawn water from a tank or other container with a patéra, would then have poured a small (symbolic) quantity over the feet of the newly baptised.

34 So Davies (1962: 26) for the Celtic examples. He does not accept this

explanation for the Eastern basins, however, since he believes 'there is no trace of the *pedilavium* in the East', and suggests they were 'probably for the baptism of children to allow economy in the use of water'. Yarnold (1971: 27 n. 145, 28), while demonstrating that footwashing probably was carried out in the East, believes that all these small basins were subsidiary fonts, perhaps used for the baptism of children who were 'too small to stand comfortably in the main font'. I would, nevertheless, question the need for permanent fonts for the baptism of children in the fourth century.

35 Private baptism lasted as late as the sixth century. It was forbidden, except in cases of necessity, in 527 at the Council of Dovin in Armenia (canon 16).

36 Davies (1962: 106–7) says separate baptisteries were generally found only in episcopal cities until the time of Augustine.

37 On the other hand, Ambrose believes it was because of the *large* numbers of candidates that the Church at Rome discontinued the *pedilavium* (*De sacramentis* 3.5). However, there is no evidence to suggest that Ambrose's influence went westwards; moreover, his episcopacy was several decades after Julian's reign and any pagan revival in Britain.

38 The tank from Caversham was also in a well. See below, ch. VII, for further discussion on the fate of the lead tanks.

3 Probable Christian symbols from Chedworth and Poundbury

1 Goodburn (1979) gives a comprehensive list.

2 I am much indebted to Mr Nigel Wilson, Administrator of Chedworth Roman Villa, for this suggestion, and for his patience and assistance as I have tried to sort out the confusion surrounding these inscriptions.

3 It is possible, of course, to read into these scratchings what signs one chooses.

4 These last are, I believe, more likely to be the *iota-chi*, which was an earlier Christian monogram than the *chi-rho*. See above, ch. V.1, n. 9, for a brief discussion of this symbol in Roman Britain.

5 Not 'pyramidal' as Grover (1868: 132 and pl. 12.1, 12.2) describes and illustrates them.

6 Grover offers that identification with some reluctance, he himself preferring some 'architectural duty' for them.

7 The stones were not *in situ* when found, but it is generally accepted that they came from this or another water shrine (e.g. Richmond 1959b: 22; Thomas 1981: 220; Goodburn 1979: 24).

8 e.g. Sulzberger (1925), Cabrol and Leclerq (1920–35: vol. 3.2, s.v. *'croix et crucifix'*). For examples in Roman Britain, see above, chs V.1, V.2.

9 This should not be confused with the papal cross, which does not appear to have been a symbol used in the Roman period.

10 The monogram is still found in churches today in the form IHS, the Latin S having taken the place of the sigma.

11 Trans. J. A. Kleist. The *tau* was perhaps the earliest representation of the cross, and was borrowed from the Jewish faith (Ezekiel 9.4).

12 e.g. Thomas (1981: fig. 7).

13 Mr Wilson has pointed out to me that there are markings, similar to those on the small stone altar, scratched on the undoubtedly pagan altars at

Chedworth; this seems to reinforce the view that someone set out deliberately to depaganise them. See below, ch. VII, n. 19, for further discussion on the fate of Chedworth.

14 *Crucis signum est . . . cum homo porrectis manibus deum pura mente veneratur.* Also possibly Barnabas, *Epistle* 12.2, although Sulzberger (1925: 352–3) interprets the passage from Exodus 17.8–13, to which Barnabas alludes, as indicating the *tau* cross.

15 *Extendit manus suas cum pateretur* (Hippolytus, *Apostolic Tradition* 4).

16 In the Middle Ages, the Y was an emblem of the Trinity (Child and Colles 1971: 44), found on stained-glass windows of churches.

17 e.g. Isidore, *Etymologiae* 1.3.7. For a list of references to the Pythagorean Y in ancient sources, see Harvey 1981: 93, n. 56–7. I am indebted to Mr Michael Dyson for this reference.

18 *Duae . . . viae duplicesque cursus animorum e corpore excedentium.*

19 Mention should be made here of the enigmatic graffito from the Palatine, of late-second- or early-third-century date, in which the figure of a man with the head of an ass is shown on a cross. Below him, another figure is portrayed in an attitude of worship. Above the crucified figure, a little to the right, is the letter Y, and below the whole is the legend, in Greek, 'Alexamenos worships God' (Cabrol and Leclerq 1920–53: vol. 3.2, fig. 3359 s.v. *'croix et crucifix'*). Scholars differ widely in their explanations of the graffito, and of its possible Christian application. It may be simply a blasphemous caricature of the death of Christ, or, at the other extreme, a genuine expression of piety, since the ass was the symbol of Seth or Typhon, and Seth had been identified with Christ by one of the gnostic sects. The Y is said to have accompanied drawings of Egyptian gods as an imprecation and was also a magic sign of Seth; in addition, it is known to have been used by Christians (see below). Sulzberger (1925: 388–91) gives the main interpretations advanced. His own interpretation of the Y is quite fanciful (*'le braiment douloureux de l'âne crucifié'*), and cannot be seriously entertained. A completely satisfactory explanation has, as far as I know, not yet been adduced, however, and the evidence is not conclusive enough to include the graffito here as an example of the use of the Y as a Christian symbol.

20 I thank Ms Susan Davies for illustrations of the object and for additional information ahead of publication.

VI LINKS WITH PAGAN RELIGIONS AND PRACTICES

1 The evidence

1 Lewis notes that, as the type is so simple, some may have been missed when there has been an absence of votive objects.

2 And even artefacts: Dyggve (1951: fig. I.15) illustrates an example of this from Salona, where a pagan altar had been inverted, hollowed out and used as an *aspersorium.*

3 *Delubra non habemus, aras non habemus.* Nor is *ara* used in the Jerome Bible: e.g. Matthew 5.23 reads, *si ergo offeres munus tuum ad altare et ibi recordatus fueris quia frater tuus habet aliquid adversum te . . .*

4 Cf. Thomas (1981: 116; 149), who suggests that the word *altare* was loosely used in the early Church, and that in the Water Newton inscription it refers to 'church' rather than 'altar'. Both *ara* and *altare* are found in classical literature, but the latter is the less common and appears to have been favoured in poetic works.

5 *Statim itaque simulacra proiicientes, fabricam templi in ecclesiae speciem commutarunt.* Also Rufinus, *Historia ecclesiastica* 2.4; Augustine, *Sermo* 163.2; Jerome *In Esaiam* 7 (p. 279 Vallarsi), etc.

6 See Boon (1983) for a study of Romano-British domestic shrines.

7 Professor Trevor Bryce (pers. comm.): a comment made in the context of another ancient civilisation, but holding true here as well.

8 Cf. Paulinus of Nola, who, writing in the fourth or fifth century, also takes the view that Christ's burial was an expensive one (*Epistulae* 13.20).

9 Not *De resurrectione carnis* 127, as given by Green.

10 It might be argued that the late Roman poet, Prudentius, gives an account of a regular Christian burial in his *Cathemerinon* 10; it has been pointed out, however, that Prudentius wrote for a literary audience and his work presumably reflected 'the faith [and, one supposes, the burial practices] of lettered Roman Christians of the fourth and fifth centuries' (Rutherford 1980:20), rather than the burial practices of a rural and mainly unlettered society in distant Britain. Further evidence that Roman Christian burial custom was a fairly simple affair may be taken from pre-Carolingian European burial: 'Theodore's Penitential', written some time after 690, follows the 'Roman custom', that is, burial on the day of death. Burial on the next day was 'an exceptional alternative' for monks and clergy (Bullough 1983: 191; *Ordines Romani* (Andrieu 1948) 49.4).

11 See especially Cumont (1922) and Richmond (1950) for discussions of the pagan view of the afterlife.

12 Alternatively, it could merely be a method of ensuring that the dead did not come back to haunt the living. (My thanks to Professor Keith Branigan for this observation.) Ucko (1969–70: 265–7) gives several other reasons for the *burial* of grave goods, some of which have nothing to do with a belief in an afterlife.

13 On the other hand, as has been suggested in the chapter on the identification of cemeteries, they may have been merely following a fashion in burial.

14 That is, the orderly early Roman cemetery (Wheeler 1943: 348–9), not to be confused with the 'war cemetery' of *c*. AD 44 (Wheeler 1943: 351–6).

15 Those grave goods which occur only in feature 6, and not in other presumed Christian cemeteries, will not be discussed here. Objects such as spindle whorls and jet pins reflect pagan beliefs, but feature 6 has been seen as a group of burials of newly converted Christians, with an initial pagan grave (Macdonald 1979: 430). See especially Alcock (1980) and Macdonald (1979: 406–14) on grave furniture in the Roman period.

16 This figure of 1.2 per cent is well below that of the Lankhills cemetery, where, of 237 intact graves, nineteen, or 8 per cent, had coins in the mouth (Clarke 1979: 147–9).

17 Brief mention is made here of one further object indicating Celtic influence, an iron tumbler lock lift key found in a grave at Butt Road II (C. Crossan, pers. comm.). It is the only known key found in presumed Christian cemeteries of the fourth century. See Black (1986b: 222) for a note on keys as Celtic grave goods.

18 The only known toilet set in a putative Christian cemetery was found in Butt Road II (C. Crossan, pers. comm.).
19 e.g. at Bath Gate, Cirencester and Trentholme Drive, York.
20 e.g. Radley I.
21 e.g. Lynch Farm and Radley II.
22 e.g. Frilford and Lankhills.
23 e.g. Hirst (1980: fig. 14.1b).
24 The structure at Lincoln, in the North Cemetery outside Newport Arch, is described as a narrow trench bordered by *loculi*. Richmond says it is unknown whether these were cremations or inhumations, but he thinks they were probably inhumations, and represented burials by a burial club, according to an inscription found nearby.
25 The enclosure with two burials at Queensford Farm, Oxfordshire, will not be discussed here, as it seems to have been a sixth-century feature.
26 See Sulzberger (1925: 366–7) and Cabrol and Leclerq (1920–53: vol. 3, col. 515 s.v. *'croix et crucifix'*) for differing views.
27 e.g. *RIB* 295, 376, 682.
28 e.g. Jessup (1954: pl. XIII); Toller (1977: 19, 27, 72–4).
29 The association by the early Church of baptism and death has already been noted in Chapter V.

2 Assessment

1 That is, the cemeteries at Brean Down, Cannington and Lamyatt Beacon, and the temple/church site at Uley. It is more likely, however, that religious continuity at these sites was the result of the monastic movement which developed independently of Rome in the western parts of Britain.
2 This is, of course, a simplistic interpretation, and ignores the influence on Rome of the Greek and other civilisations. For this study, however, a differentiation is made merely between Roman and Celtic influence and practices.

VII CONCLUSIONS

1 Summarised by Thomas (1981: 53–60), but see also Myres (1960), Thompson (1984) and Markus (1986).
2 Other cemeteries in the area have been excavated but not reported. (Information kindly supplied by Mr David Miles.)
3 And, to a lesser extent, in the areas where there was a military presence. It would be well not to over-estimate the role of the Roman army in the spread of Christianity, however. On available data, there was very strong evidence for Christianity only at Richborough, although the density map shows a Christian presence at York, along parts of Hadrian's Wall and around Caerleon. There is no evidence, as yet, from Chester, where one might expect it, if the army had, in fact, played a major role in the spread of Christianity. That most of the British army, under the guidance of Germanus and Lupus, sought baptism before the 'Alleluia victory' of 429 (Bede, *Historia ecclesiastica* 1.20), suggests that there had been no strong tradition of Christianity within the Roman army only a couple of decades before.

4 So Thomas (1981: 140).

5 e.g. Radford (1967: 105–6).

6 So Frend (1979: 137; 1982: 8).

7 e.g. Sulpicius Severus, *Chronicon* 2.41.

8 This, of course, refers to house churches after the Peace of the Church in 313. The size of putative house churches in Britain suggests small congregations only.

9 Thomas (1981: figs 30, 32). He does not say which European churches he uses for his sample.

10 A situation already proposed by Frend (1979: 131–2; 1982: 10), who based his findings on the literary evidence.

11 To this list should be added the buildings at Uley, which constitute a special case. Here, the site does not appear to have been christianised until after the pagan revival, the first church being built around 380 and the second early in the fifth century. As has been mentioned earlier, the evidence, as yet unpublished, suggests that the site was occupied by a monastic order in its later life.

12 Plus or minus 80 (information kindly supplied by Mr Michael Jones).

13 At Nettleton, there is a complete absence of pagan characteristics. Two burials at Icklingham had deliberate grave goods (one a coin in the mouth, the other a pile of jewellery at the foot of the grave), and another wore a bronze bracelet, but this may not necessarily have been significant; the position of the three graves suggests that none of these burials was among the earliest or the latest in any burial sequence in the cemetery. At Ashton, where the only possible pagan feature is that of stones in graves, there is no evidence for an increase in the deposition of these stones in graves towards the extremities of the cemetery, where one might expect the last burials to be made.

14 At Poundbury, the latest burials seem not only to have been of a poorer type, but were also, on occasion, shallower than the earlier ones; yet, although some were dug above earlier graves, they did not disturb these burials. Those presumed to be the latest at Ancaster were at the western and least-organised part of the cemetery, and included a handful of north–south, flexed and prone burials.

15 It is possible that Cannington belongs to the same class of site as Uley, its longevity attributable to a monastic succession after the Roman occupation.

16 e.g. at Carrawburgh, where, although a Mithraeum had been destroyed early in the fourth century, perhaps by zealous Christians in the garrison, on coin evidence the shrine of Coventina continued in use until the fifth century (Lewis 1966: 88). Altars were also found dedicated *nymphis et genio loci* (Smith 1962: 62). Even in an area with a strong Roman presence, the local Celtic deities were not totally eliminated.

17 The discarding of objects of considerable value seems very curious unless seen as the work of iconoclasts.

18 The dismantling of what may have been a rather insubstantial baptistery at Icklingham (West 1976: 74–8) may also possibly suggest this.

19 Another site which may have been a victim of the resurgence of paganism is Chedworth. A stone, inscribed with a *chi-rho*, from what had probably been a christianised water shrine was reused as a step to a baths suite. Goodburn (1979: 24) suggests various explanations for the final use of the stone. In view of the evidence for pagan activity in the south-west in the late fourth century, a reversion to paganism is a likely explanation.

20 That is, when set against the developments of the Church in Europe, the British Church would have seemed primitive to Augustine in 597 (e.g. Bede, *Historia ecclesiastica* 2.2). (I thank Bro. Eoin de Bhaldraithe for this observation). See also Markus (1986: 199–200), who suggests, in relation to the Pelagian controversy, that 'local [i.e. British] orthodoxy became heresy only in relation to the faith of the "overseas" Churches'.

21 Sulpicius Severus, *Vita Martini* 13–15, in which he relates the conversion of many parts of the countryside to Christianity. See also James (1988: 124), for a description of fifth-century Gaul.

BIBLIOGRAPHY

Archaeological and secondary sources

Abbreviations for the titles of journals are in accordance with the system adopted by the Council for British Archaeology. In addition, BAR = British Archaeological Reports, CBA = Council for British Archaeology and RR = Research Report.

Aitken, M. (1987) *Found at Richard Cound: The Kingsholm Dig*, Gloucester: Richard Cound.

Alcock, J.P. (1980) 'Classical religious practice and burial practice in Roman Britain', *Archaeol. J.* 137: 50–85.

Allen, J.R. (1887) *Christian Symbolism in Great Britain and Ireland*, London: Whiting.

Akeley, T.C. (1967) *Christian Initiation in Spain c.300–1100*, London: Darton, Longman & Todd.

Anderson, T. (1987) 'Cirencester: an osteo-archaeological analysis of the Bath Gate cemetery', unpublished project report in partial completion of requirements for MA, Department of Archaeology and Prehistory, Sheffield University.

Andrieu, M. (1948) *Les Ordines Romani du haut moyen âge II: Les Textes*, Louvain: Spicilegium Sacrum Lovaniense.

Anon. (1927) 'Notes: medieval hone from Ireland', *Antiq. J.* 7: 322–3.

Anon. (1940) 'Roman Britain in 1939: sites explored', *J. Roman Stud.* 30: 155–82.

Anon. (1957) 'Roman Britain in 1956: sites explored', *J. Roman Stud.* 47: 198–226.

Anon. (1961–3) 'Excavations and fieldwork in Wiltshire 1962: Winterbourne Down', *Wiltshire Archaeol. and Natur. Hist. Magazine* 58: 470.

Anon. (1974) 'Lincolnshire', *East Midlands Archaeol. Bull.* 10: 10–40.

Anon. (1978) 'The Cambridge shrine', *Curr. Archaeol.* 61: 58–60.

Anthony, I.E. (1968) 'Excavations in Verulam Hills Field, St Albans, 1963–4', *Hertfordshire Archaeol.* 1: 9–50.

ApSimon, A.M. (1965) 'The Roman temple on Brean Down, Somerset', *Proc. Univ. Bristol Spelaeolog. Soc.* 10.3: 195–258.

ApSimon, A.M., Donovan, D.T. and Taylor, H. (1961) 'The stratigraphy and archaeology of the Late Glacial and Post Glacial deposits at Brean Down, Somerset', *Proc. Univ. Bristol Spelaeolog. Soc.* 9.2: 67–136.

Arthur, P. (1977) 'Eggs and pomegranates: an example of symbolism in Roman Britain', 367–74 in J. Munby and M. Henig (eds), *Roman Life and Art in Britain* (Pt ii) BAR B ser. 41, Oxford.

Ashby, T., Hudd, A.E. and King, F. (1911) 'Excavations at Caerwent, Monmouthshire on the site of the Romano-British city of Venta Silurum, in the years 1909 and 1910', *Archaeologia* 62: 405–45.

Atkinson, R.J.C. (1952–3) 'Excavations in Barrow Hills Fields, Radley, Berks, 1944–45: the Romano-British inhumation cemetery', *Oxoniensia* 17–18: 1–35.

Baddeley, St C. (1930) 'The Roman-British temple, Chedworth', *Trans. Bristol Gloucestershire Archaeol. Soc.* 52: 255–64.

Barley, M.W. and Hanson, R.P.C. (eds) (1968) *Christianity in Britain, 300–700*, Leicester: University Press.

Barnard, L.W. (1967) *Justin Martyr,* Cambridge: University Press.

Bartlett, R. (1987) 'A Late Roman buckle from Harlow temple, Essex', *Essex Archaeol. Hist.* 18: 115–20.

Bedwin, O. (1981) 'Excavations at Lancing Down, West Sussex', *Sussex Archaeol. Coll.* 119: 37–55.

Bennett, C.M. (1962) 'Cox Green Roman villa', *Berkshire Archaeol. J.* 60: 62–92.

Birley, R.E. and Birley, A. (1962) 'Housesteads *vicus*, 1961', *Archaeol. Aeliana* 4th ser. 40: 117–33.

Black, E.W. (1983) 'Ritual dog burials from Roman sites', *Kent Archaeol. Rev.* 71: 20–22.

—— (1986a) 'Christian and pagan hopes of salvation in Romano-British mosaics', 147–58 in M. Henig and A. King (eds), *Pagan Gods and Shrines of the Roman Empire*, OUCA Monograph 8, Oxford: University Press.

—— (1986b) 'Romano-British burial customs and religious beliefs in South-East England', *Archaeol. J.* 143: 201–39.

Bober, P.P. (1951) 'Cernunnos: origin and transformation of a Celtic deity', *American J. Archaeol.* 55: 13–51.

Boileau, J. (1847) Untitled note on Venta Icenorum in 'Archaeological intelligence: Roman period', *Archaeol. J.* 4: 72–3.

Boon, G.C. (1962) 'A Christian monogram at Caerwent', *Bull. Board Celtic Stud.* 19: 338–44.

—— (1974) *Silchester: The Roman Town of Calleva*, London: David & Charles.

—— (1976) 'The shrine of the head, Caerwent', 163–76 in G.C. Boon and J.M. Lewis (eds), *Welsh Antiquity: Essays . . . presented to H. N. Savory*, Cardiff: National Museum of Wales.

—— (1983) 'Some Romano-British domestic shrines and their inhabitants', 33–55 in B. Hartley and J. Wacher (eds), *Rome and Her Northern Provinces*, Gloucester: Alan Sutton.

Bradford, J.S.P. and Goodchild, R.G. (1939) 'Excavations at Frilford, Berks, 1937–8', *Oxoniensia* 4: 1–70.

Brailsford, J.W. (1947) *The Mildenhall Treasure*, London: British Museum.

Brandenburg, H. (1968) 'Bellerophon christianus?' *Römische Quartalschrift* 63: 49–86.

—— (1969) 'Christussymbole in frühchristlichen Bodenmosaiken', *Römische Quartalschrift* 64: 75–138.

Branigan, K. (1977a) *Gatcombe: The Excavation and Study of a Romano-British Villa Estate 1967–1976*, BAR B ser. 44, Oxford.

—— (1977b) *The Roman Villa in South-West England,* Bradford-on-Avon: Moonraker.

—— (1980) *Roman Britain*, London: Reader's Digest.

Braun, J. (1932) *Das christliche Altargerät*, Munich: Heuber.

Brewster, T.C.M. (1976) 'Garton Slack (near Drifford, Humberside N)', *Curr. Archaeol.* 55: 104–16.

Brooks, H. (1989) 'The Stanstead temple', *Curr. Archaeol.* 117: 322–5.

Brooks, N.P. (1977) 'The ecclesiastical topography of early medieval Canterbury', 487–98 in M.W. Barley (ed.), *European Towns – Their Archaeology and Early History*, CBA, London: Academic Press.

Brown, P.D.C. (1971) 'The church at Richborough', *Britannia* 2: 225–31.

Brunaux, J.L. (1988) *The Celtic Gauls: Gods, Rites and Sanctuaries* (D. Nash trans.), London: Seaby.

Bryant, R. (1980) 'Excavations at St Mary de Lode, Gloucester 1978–79', *Glevensis* 14: 4–12.

Bullough, D. (1983) 'Burial, community and belief in the early medieval west', 177–201 in P. Wormald, D. Bullough and R. Collins (eds) *Ideal and Reality in Frankish and Anglo-Saxon Society*, Oxford: Blackwell.

Bushe-Fox, J.P. (1926) *First Report on the Excavation of the Roman Fort at Richborough, Kent*, Soc. Antiq. RR 6: Oxford.

—— (1928) *Second Report of the Excavation of the Roman Fort at Richborough, Kent*, Soc. Antiq. RR 7: Oxford.

—— (1949) *Fourth Report on the Excavation of the Roman Fort at Richborough, Kent*, Soc. Antiq. RR 16: Oxford.

Buxton, L.H.D. (1921) 'Excavations at Frilford', *Antiq. J.* 1: 87–97.

Cabrol, F. and Leclerq, H. (1920–53) *Dictionnaire d'Archéologie Chrétienne et de Liturgie* (15 vols), Paris: Letouzey et Ané.

Cahn, H. and Kaufmann-Heinemann, A. (eds) (1984) *Der spätrömische Silberschatz von Kaiseraugst*, Derendingen: Habegger.

Cattaneo, E. (1940) 'L'Intinctio nella Liturgia Ambrosiana' *Ephemerides Liturgicae*, 54: 182–205.

Chadwick, H. (1967) *The Early Church*, Harmondsworth: Penguin.

Chadwick, N. (1970) *The Celts*, Harmondsworth: Penguin.

Chambers, R.A. (1978) 'Two radio-carbon dates from the Romano-British cemetery and settlement at Curbridge, Oxon.', *Oxoniensia* 43: 252–3.

—— (1984) 'Radley, Oxon: Barrow Hills (SU 515983) the Roman cemetery', *South Midlands Archaeol.* 14 (Newsletter of CBA Regional Group 9): 119–20.

—— (1987) 'The late- and sub-Roman cemetery at Queensford Farm, Dorchester-on-Thames, Oxon.', *Oxoniensia* 52: 35–69.

Charlesworth, D. (1959) 'Roman glass in Northern Britain', *Archaeol. Aeliana* 4th ser. 37: 33–58.

—— (1978) 'Roman Carlisle', *Archaeol. J.* 135: 115–37.

Chenet, G. (1941) *La Céramique gallo-romaine d'Argonne du IVᵉ siècle et la Terre Sigilée decorée à la Molette*, Mâcon: Protat.

Child, H. and Colles, D. (1971) *Christian Symbols*, New York: Scribner.

Clarke, G. (1979) *Pre-Roman and Roman Winchester Part II: The Roman Cemetery at Lankhills* (Winchester Studies 3), Oxford: Clarendon.

—— (1982) 'The Roman villa at Woodchester', *Britannia* 13: 197–228.

Clarke, L.G.C. (1931) 'Roman pewter bowl from the Isle of Ely', *Proc. Cambridge Antiq. Soc.* 31: 66–75.

Clifford, E.M. (1938) 'Roman altars in Gloucestershire', *Trans. Bristol Gloucestershire Archaeol. Soc.* 60: 297–307.

Cocks, A.H. (1921) 'A Romano-British homestead in the Hambledon Valley, Bucks', *Archaeologia* 71: 141–98.

Collingwood, R.G. (1930) *Archaeology of Roman Britain*, London: Methuen.

Collis, J. (1977a) 'Owslebury (Hants) and the problem of burials on rural settlements', 26–74 in R. Reece (ed.), *Burial in the Roman World*, CBA RR 22: London.

—— (1977b) 'Pre-Roman burial rites in North Western Europe', 1–12 in R. Reece (ed.), *Burial in the Roman World*, CBA RR 22: London.

Colyer, C. and Gilmour, B. (1978) 'St Paul-in-the-Bail Lincoln', *Curr. Archaeol.* 63: 102–5.

Conder, C.R. and Kitchener, H.H. (1881–3) *The Survey of Western Palestine* (3 vols), London: Committee of the Palestine Exploration Fund.

Cookson, N.A. (1984) *Romano-British Mosaics: A Reassessment and Critique of some Notable Stylistic Affinities*, BAR B ser. 135: Oxford.

Cotton, M.A. (1956–7) 'Weymouth Hill, 1953', *Berkshire Archaeol. J.* 55: 48–68.

Cross, F.L. and Livingstone, E.A. (eds) (1984) *The Oxford Dictionary of the Christian Church*, 2nd rev. edn, Oxford: University Press.

Crummy, N. (1983) *The Roman Small Finds from Excavations in Colchester 1971–9*, Colchester Archaeol. Report 2, Colchester: Colchester Archaeological Trust.

Crummy, P. (1980) 'The temples of Roman Colchester', in W. Rodwell (ed.), *Temples, Churches and Religion in Roman Britain* (2 vols), BAR B ser. 77: Oxford.

—— (1984) *In Search of Colchester's Past*, 2nd edn, Colchester: Colchester Archaeol. Trust.

—— (1989). *Secrets of the Grave*, Colchester: Colchester Archaeol. Trust and Essex County Council.

Cumont, F. (1922) *After Life in Roman Paganism*, New Haven: Yale University Press.

Cunliffe, B.W. (ed.) (1968) *Fifth Report on the Excavations of the Roman Fort at Richborough Kent*, Soc. Antiq. RR 23: London.

—— (1978) *Iron Age Communities in Britain*, 2nd edn, London: Routledge & Kegan Paul.

—— (1983) *Danebury: Anatomy of an Iron Age Hillfort*, London: Batsford.

Curle, A.O. (1921) 'The recent discovery of silver at Traprain Law', *Antiquaries Journal* 1: 42–7.

—— (1923) *The Treasure of Traprain*, Glasgow: Maclehouse Jackson.

Curwen, E.C. (1943) 'Roman lead cistern from Pulborough, Sussex', *Antiq. J.* 23: 155–7.

Dalton, O.M. (1901) *Catalogue of the Early Christian Antiquities and Objects from the Christian East in the Department of British and Mediaeval Antiquities of the British Museum*, London: British Museum.

—— (1922) 'Roman spoons from Dorchester', *Antiq. J.* 2: 89–92.

Daniélou, J. (1964) *Primitive Christian Symbols* (D. Attwater trans.), London: Burns & Oates.

Davies, G. (1977) 'Burial in Italy up to Augustus', 13–19 in R. Reece (ed.), *Burial in the Roman World*, CBA RR 22: London.

Davies, J.G. (1962) *The Architectural Setting of Baptism*, London: Barrie & Rockliffe.

Davies, S.M., Stacey, L.C. and Woodward, P.J. (1986) 'Excavations at Alington Avenue, Fordington, Dorchester, 1984/85: interim report', *Proc. Dorset Natur. Hist. Archaeol. Soc.* 107: 101–10.

de Bhaldraithe, E. (1990) 'Daily Eucharist: the need for an Early Church paradigm', *The American Benedictine Revue* 41: 378–440.

de Jong, J.P. (1951) 'Le rite de la commixtion dans la messe romaine', *Revue Bénédictine* 61: 15–37.

De Rossi, G.B. (1857–61) *Inscriptiones Christianae Urbis Romae* 1, Rome, with Supplement I, ed. I. Gatti, Rome (1915).

—— (1864–77) *La Roma sotterranea Cristiana*, (3 vols), Rome (reprinted 1966, Frankfurt: Minerva).

Diehl, D. (1926) 'Un nouveau trésor d'argenterie syrienne', *Syria* 7: 105–20.

Dix, B. (1984) 'Ashton Roman Town: archaeological rescue excavation', *Durobrivae* 9: 26–7.

Dix, G. (1954) *The Shape of the Liturgy*, 2nd edn, London: Dacre.

Donovan, H.E. (1933) 'Excavations at Bourton on the Water', *Trans. Bristol Gloucestershire Archaeol. Soc.* 55: 377–81.

—— (1934) 'Excavation of a Romano-British building at Bourton on the Water', *Trans. Bristol Gloucestershire Archaeol. Soc.* 56: 98–128.

Downey, R. *et al.* (1980) 'The Hayling Island temple and religious connections across the Channel', 289–301 in W. Rodwell (ed.), *Temples, Churches and Religion in Roman Britain* (2 vols), BAR B ser. 77: Oxford.

Drew, C.D. (1931) 'The excavations at Jordan Hill. 1931', *Proc. Dorset Natur. Hist. Archaeol. Soc.* 53: 265–76.

Drew, C.D. (1932) 'The excavations at Jordan Hill and Preston, 1932', *Proc. Dorset Natur. Hist. Archaeol. Soc.* 54: 15–34.

Drew, C.D. and Selby, K.C. (1937) 'First interim report on the excavations at Colliton Park, Dorchester 1937–1938', *Proc. Dorset Natur. Hist. Archaeol. Soc.* 59: 1–14.

Drury, P.J. (1972) 'Preliminary report: the Romano-British settlement at Chelmsford, Essex: *Caesaromagus*', *Trans. Essex Archaeol. Soc.* 4: 3–29.

—— (1980) 'Non-classical religious buildings in Iron Age and Roman Britain: A Review', 45–78 in W. Rodwell (ed.), *Temples, Churches and Religion in Roman Britain* (2 vols), BAR B ser. 77: Oxford.

—— (1984) 'The temple of Claudius at Colchester reconsidered', *Britannia* 15: 7–50.

Durham, B. and Rowley, T. (1972) 'A cemetery site at Queensford Mill, Dorchester', *Oxoniensia* 37: 32–7.

Duval, P.M. (1961) *Paris antique*, Paris: Hermann.

Dyggve, E. (1951) *History of Salonitan Christianity*, Oslo: Aschehoug.

Eddy, M.R. and Turner, C. (1982) *Kelvedon: The Origin and Development of a Roman Small Town*, Chelmsford: Essex County Council Occas. Paper 3.

Edwards, D. (1977) 'The air photographs of the Norfolk Archaeological Unit: second report', *East Anglian Archaeol.* 5: 225–37.

Ellison, A. (1980) 'Natives, Romans and Christians on West Hill, Uley: an interim report on the excavation of the ritual complex of the first millennium A.D.', 305–28 in W. Rodwell (ed.), *Temples, Churches and Religion in Roman Britain* (2 vols), BAR B ser. 77: Oxford.

Engemann, J. (1972) 'Anmerkungen zu spätantiken Geräten des Alltagslebens mit christlichen Bildern, Symbolen und Inschriften', *Jahrbuch für Antike und Christentum* 15: 154–73.

Engleheart, G.H. (1903) 'The Roman villa at Fifehead Neville', *Proc. Dorset Natur. Hist. Archaeol. Soc.* 24: 172–7.

Erikson, R.T. (1982) 'Syncretic symbolism and the Christian Roman mosaic at Hinton St Mary: a closer reading', *Proc. Dorset Natur. Hist. Archaeol. Soc.* 102: 43–8.

Esmond Cleary, S. (1987) *Extra-mural areas of Romano-British towns*, BAR B ser. 169: Oxford.

Evans, C. (1984) 'A shrine provenance for the Willingham Fen hoard', *Antiquity* 58: 212–14.

Evans, G. and Pierpoint, S. (1986) 'Divers coffins and the bones of men', *London Archaeologist* 5: 202–6.

Farrar, R.A.H. (1957) 'Archaeological fieldwork in Dorset 1956: the Frampton villa, Maiden Newton', *Proc. Dorset Natur. Hist. Archaeol. Soc.* 78: 81–3.

Faull, M.L. (1977) 'British survival in Anglo-Saxon Northumbria', 1–55 in Laing L. (ed.), *Studies in Celtic Survival*, BAR B ser. 37: Oxford.

Ferguson, G. (1961) *Signs and Symbols in Christian Art*, New York: Oxford University Press.

Fishwick, D. (1988) 'Imperial sceptre heads in Roman Britain', *Britannia* 19: 399–400.

Fletcher, E. and Meates, G.W. (1969) 'The ruined church of Stone-by-Faversham', *Antiq. J.* 49: 273–94.

—— (1977) 'The ruined church of Stone-by-Faversham: second report', *Antiq. J.* 57: 67–72.

Fox, C. and Lethbridge, T.C. (1926) 'The La Tène and Romano-British cemetery, Guilden Morden, Cambs.', *Proc. Cambridge Antiq. Soc.* 27: 49–63.

Fox, G.E. (1887) 'The Roman villa at Chedworth, Gloucestershire', *Archaeol. J.* 44: 322–36.

Fox, G.E. and Hope, W.H.St J. (1893) 'Excavations on the site of the Roman city at Silchester, Hants in 1892', *Archaeologia* 53: 539–73.

France, N.E. and Gobel, B.M. (1985) *The Romano-British Temple at Harlow*, ed. F.R. Clark and I.K. Jones, West Essex Archaeol. Group, Gloucester: Alan Sutton.

Frend, W.H.C. (1955) 'Religion in Roman Britain in the fourth century A.D.', *J. Brit. Archaeol. Ass.* 3rd ser. 18: 1–18.

—— (1961) 'Der Donatismus und die afrikanische Kirche', *Wissenschaftliche Zeitschrift der Martin-Luther-Universität Halle-Wittenberg* 10/1: 53–62.

—— (1968) 'The christianization of Roman Britain', 37–49 in M.W. Barley and R.P.C. Hanson (eds), *Christianity in Britain, 300–700*, Leicester: University Press.

—— (1979) '*Ecclesia Britannica*: prelude or dead end?', *J. Eccles. Hist.* 30: 129–44.

—— (1982) 'Romano-British Christianity and the West: comparison and contrast', 5–16 in S.M. Pearce (ed.), *The Early Church in Western Britain and Ireland*, BAR B ser. 102: Oxford.

—— (1984) *The Rise of Christianity*, London: Darton, Longman & Todd.

—— (1984–5) 'Syrian parallels to the Water Newton treasure?', *Jahrbuch für Antike und Christentum* 27–8: 146–50.

Frere, S.S. (1940) 'A survey of archaeology near Lancing', *Sussex Archaeol. Coll.* 81: 141–72.

—— (1975) 'The Silchester church: the excavations by Sir Ian Richmond in 1961', *Archaeologia* 105: 277–302.

—— (1983) 'Roman Britain in 1982: sites explored', *Britannia* 14: 279–356.

—— (1984a) 'Roman Britain in 1983: sites explored', *Britannia* 15: 266–332.

—— (1984b) *Verulamium Excavations III*, OUCA Monograph 1, Oxford: University Press.

—— (1985) 'Roman Britain in 1984: sites explored', *Britannia* 16: 251–316.

—— (1986) 'Roman Britain in 1985: sites explored', *Britannia* 17: 363–427.

—— (1989) 'Roman Britain in 1989: sites explored', *Britannia* 20: 258–326.

Fulton, D. (1975) 'The skeletal material', 129–30 in R. Jones, 'The Romano-British farmstead and its cemetery at Lynch Farm, near Peterborough', *Northamptonshire Archaeol.* 10: 94–137.

Garrucci, P.R. (1872) *Storia dell' Arte Cristiana nei Primi Otto Secoli* (7 vols), Prato: Giachetti.

Gilbert, H.M. (1978) 'The Felmington Hall hoard, Norfolk', *Bull. Board Celtic Stud.* 28: 159–87.

Gillam, J.P. and Daniels, C.M. (1961) 'The Roman mausoleum on Shorden Brae, Beaufront, Corbridge, Northumberland', *Archaeol. Aeliana* 4 ser. 39: 37–61.

Giovagnoli, D.E. (1935) 'Una collezione di vasi eucaristici scoperti a Canoscio', *Rivista di Archeologia Cristiana* 12: 313–28.

Goodburn, R. (1979) *The Roman Villa at Chedworth*, London: National Trust.

Goodchild, R.G. (1946) 'The origins of the Romano-British forum', *Antiquity* 20: 70–7.

—— (1953) 'The curse and the ring', *Antiquity* 27: 100–2.

Goodenough, E.R. (1953–68) *Jewish Symbols in the Greco-Roman World* (13 vols), New York: Bollingen Foundation.

Gough, M. (1961) *The Early Christians*, London: Thames & Hudson.

—— (1973) *The Origins of Christian Art*, London: Thames & Hudson.

Green, C.J.S. (1967) 'Interim report on discoveries in the Roman cemetery at Poundbury, Dorchester', *Proc. Dorset Natur. Hist. Archaeol. Soc.* 88: 108–10.

—— (1968) 'Interim report on excavations at the copse site in the Roman cemetery, Poundbury, Dorchester', *Proc. Dorset Natur. Hist. Archaeol. Soc.* 89: 133–5.

—— (1969) 'Interim report on excavations in the Roman cemetery, Poundbury, Dorchester 1968', *Proc. Dorset Natur. Hist. Archaeol. Soc.* 90: 171–3.

—— (1970) 'Interim report on excavations in the Roman cemetery, Poundbury, Dorchester 1969', *Proc. Dorset Natur. Hist. Archaeol. Soc.* 91: 183–6.

—— (1971) 'Interim report on excavations in the Roman cemetery, Poundbury, Dorchester 1970', *Proc. Dorset Natur. Hist. Archaeol. Soc.* 92: 138–40.

—— (1972) 'Interim report on excavations at Poundbury, Dorchester 1971', *Proc. Dorset Natur. Hist. Archaeol. Soc.* 93: 154–6.

—— (1973) 'Excavations for the Dorchester Excavation Committee, interim report 1972: Poundbury Camp', *Proc. Dorset Natur. Hist. Archaeol. Soc.* 94: 80–1.

—— (1974) 'Interim report on excavations at Poundbury, Dorchester 1973', *Proc. Dorset Natur. Hist. Archaeol. Soc.* 95: 97–100.

—— (1975) 'Interim report on excavations at Poundbury, Dorchester, 1974', *Proc. Dorset Natur. Hist. Archaeol. Soc.* 96: 56.

—— (1976) 'Interim report on excavations at Poundbury, Dorchester 1975', *Proc. Dorset Natur. Hist. Archaeol. Soc.* 97: 53.

—— (1977a) 'Dorchester', in L. Keen (ed.), 'Dorset archaeology in 1976', *Proc. Dorset Natur. Archaeol. Soc.* 98: 54–62.

—— (1977b) 'The significance of plaster burials for the recognition of Christian cemeteries', 46–53 in R. Reece (ed.), *Burial in the Roman World*, CBA RR 22: London.

—— (1981) 'Dorchester' in L. Keen (ed.), 'Dorset archaeology 1979', *Proc. Dorset Natur. Hist. Archaeol. Soc.* 101: 133–43.

—— (1982) 'The cemetery of a Romano-British community at Poundbury, Dorchester, Dorset', 61–76 in S.M. Pearce (ed.), *The Early Church in Western Britain and Ireland*, BAR B ser. 102: Oxford.

Green, C.J.S. *et al.* (1982) 'A Roman coffin-burial from the Crown Building site, Dorchester: with particular reference to the head of well-preserved hair', *Proc. Dorset Natur. Hist. Archaeol. Soc.* 103: 67–100.

Green, M. (1976) *A Corpus of Religious Material from the Civilian Areas of Roman Britain*, BAR B ser. 24: Oxford.

—— (1983) *The Gods of Roman Britain*, Aylesbury: Shire.

—— (1986) *The Gods of the Celts*, Gloucester: Alan Sutton.

Grimes, W.F. (1955) 'London', in Anon., 'Roman Britain in 1954', *J. Roman Stud.* 45: 137–8.

Grinsell, L.V. (1957) 'The ferryman and his fee: a study in ethnology, archaeology and tradition', *Folklore* 68: 257–69.

—— (1961) 'The breaking of objects as a funerary rite', *Folklore* 72: 475–91.

—— (1986) 'The christianisation of prehistoric and other pagan sites', *Landscape History* 8: 27–37.

Grover, J.W. (1867) 'Pre-Augustine Christianity in Britain', *J. Brit. Archaeol. Assoc.* 23: 221–30.

—— (1868) 'On a Roman villa at Chedworth', *J. Brit. Archaeol. Assoc.* 24: 129–35.

Gsell, S. (1901) *Les Monuments antiques de l'Algérie* (2 vols), Paris: Ancienne Librairie Thorin.

Guy, C.J. (1977) 'The lead tank from Ashton' *Durobrivae* 5: 10–11.

—— (1978) 'A Roman lead tank from Burwell, Cambridgeshire', *Proc. Cambridge Antiq. Soc.* 68: 2–4.

—— (1981) 'Roman circular lead tanks in Britain', *Britannia* 12: 271–6.

—— (1989) 'The Oxborough lead tank', *Britannia* 20: 234–7.

Hadman, J. (1984) 'Ashton 1979–82', *Durobrivae* 9: 28–30.

Hadman, J. and Upex, S. (1977) 'Ashton, 1976', *Durobrivae* 5: 6–9.

Hall, A.F. (1946) 'A Roman walled cemetery at Colchester', *Archaeol. J.* 101: 69–90.

Hammerson, M. (1978) 'Excavations under Southwark cathedral', *London Archaeologist* 3: 206–12.

Harman, M., Lambrick, G., Miles, D. and Rowley, T. (1978) 'Roman burials around Dorchester on Thames', *Oxoniensia* 43: 1–16.

Harman, M., Molleson, T.I. and Price, J.L. (1981) 'Burials, bodies and beheadings in Romano-British and Anglo-Saxon cemeteries', *Bull. Brit. Mus. Nat. Hist.* 35: 145–88.

Harvey, R.A. (1981) *A Commentary on Persius*, Brill: Leiden.

Hassall, M.W.C. and Tomlin, R.S.O. (1979) 'Roman Britain in 1978: inscriptions', *Britannia* 10: 339–56.

—— (1980) 'Roman Britain in 1979: inscriptions', *Britannia* 11: 403–17.

—— (1981) 'Roman Britain in 1980: inscriptions', *Britannia* 12: 369–96.

—— (1983) 'Roman Britain in 1982: inscriptions', *Britannia* 14: 343.

—— (1989) 'Roman Britain in 1988: inscriptions', *Britannia* 20: 327–45.

Haverfield, F. (1914) 'Roman silver in Northumberland', *J. Roman Stud.* 4: 1–12.

Hawkes, C.F.C. (1946) 'Roman Ancaster, Horncastle and Caistor', *Archaeol. J.* 103: 17–25.

Hawkes, S.C. (1973) 'A late Roman buckle from Tripontium', *Trans. Birmingham Warwickshire Archaeol. Soc.* 85: 145–59.

Hawkes, S.C. and Dunning, G.C. (1961) 'Soldiers and settlers in Britain, fourth to fifth century', *Medieval Archaeol.* 5: 1–70.

Hefele, C.J. (1894) *A History of the Christian Councils, from the Original Documents, to the Close of the Council of Nicea A.D. 325* (W.R. Clark trans.), Edinburgh: Clark.

Henderson, A. (1938) *Pagan and Christian Symbols*, London: Skeffington.

Henig, M. (1977) 'Death and the maiden: funerary symbolism in daily life', 347–66 in J. Munby and M. Henig (eds), *Roman Life and Art in Britain* (Pt ii) BAR B ser. 41, Oxford.

—— (1978) *A Corpus of Roman Engraved Gemstones from British Sites*, 2nd edn, BAR B ser. 8: Oxford.

—— (1980) 'Art and cult in the temples of Roman Britain', 91–113 in W. Rodwell (ed.), *Temples, Churches and Religion in Roman Britain* (2 vols), BAR B ser. 77: Oxford.

—— (1982) 'Orphic church defended', *Curr. Archaeol.* 83: 375.

—— (1983) 'A probable chi-rho stamp on a pair of compasses', *Proc. Dorset Natur. Hist. Archaeol. Soc.* 105: 159.

—— (1984a) 'James Engleheart's drawings of a mosaic at Frampton 1794', *Proc. Dorset Natur. Hist. Archaeol. Soc.* 106: 143–6.

—— (1984b) *Religion in Roman Britain*, London: Batsford.

—— (1986) '"*Ita intellexit numine inductus tuo*": some personal interpretations of deity in Roman Religion', 159–70 in M. Henig and A. King (eds), *Pagan Gods and Shrines of the Roman Empire*, OUCA Monograph 8, Oxford: University Press.

—— (1987) 'An early Christian signet ring from the Roman villa at Moor Park', *Hertfordshire Archaeol.* 9 (1983–6): 184–5.

Henig, M. and King, A. (eds) (1986) *Pagan Gods and Shrines of the Roman Empire*, OUCA Monograph 8, Oxford: University Press.

Henry, F. (1965) *Irish Art in the Early Christian Period (to 800 A.D.)*, London: Methuen.

Hewitt, A.T.M. (1971) *Roman Villa West Park, Rockbourne* (privately published).

Hingley, R. (1982) 'Recent discoveries of the Roman period at the Noah's Ark Inn, Frilford, South Oxfordshire', *Britannia* 13: 305–9.

Hirst, S. (1980) 'Some aspects of the analysis and publication of an inhumation cemetery', 239–52 in P. Rahtz, T. Dickinson and L. Watts, *Anglo-Saxon Cemeteries 1979: The Fourth Anglo-Saxon Symposium at Oxford*, BAR B ser. 82: Oxford.

Hopkins, K. (1983) *Death and Renewal*, Cambridge: University Press.

Horne, B. (1981) 'Romano-Celtic temples in the third century', in A. King and M. Henig, (eds) *The Roman West in the Third Century*, BAR Int. ser. 109: 21–6.

Hull, M.R. (1958) *Roman Colchester*, Soc. Antiq. RR 20: Oxford.

Hulme, F.E. (1899) *The History, Principles and Practice of Symbolism in Christian Art*, 3rd edn, London: Swan Sonnenschein.

Huskinson, J. (1974) 'Some pagan mythological figures and their significance in early Christian art', *Papers Brit. School Rome* 42: 68–97.

Hutchinson, V.J. (1986) *Bacchus in Roman Britain: The Evidence for his Cult* (2 vols), BAR B ser. 151: Oxford.

Insley, M. (1982) 'Littlecote', *Curr. Archaeol.* 82: 350.

Ireland, S. (1986) *Roman Britain: A Sourcebook*, London: Croom Helm.

James, E. (1988) *The Franks*, Oxford: Blackwell.

Janthoudidis, S.A. (1903) 'Χριστιανικαὶ ἐπιγραφαὶ ἐκ κρήτς', *Ἀθηνᾶ* 15: 4, 95, 97, 163.

Jenkins, F. (1976) 'Preliminary report on the excavations at the church of St Pancras at Canterbury', *Canterbury Archaeol.* 1975–6: 4–5.

Jessup, R.F. (1954) 'Excavation of a Roman barrow at Holborough, Snodland', *Archaeol. Cantiana* 69: 1–61.

—— (1959) 'Barrows and walled cemeteries in Roman Britain', *J. Brit. Archaeol. Assoc.* 3rd ser. 22: 1–32.

Johns, C.M. (1986a) 'Faunus at Thetford: an early Latian deity in late Roman Britain', 93–104 in M. Henig and A. King (eds), *Pagan Gods and Shrines of the Roman Empire*, OUCA Monograph 8, Oxford: University Press.

—— (1986b) 'The Roman silver cups from Hockwold, Norfolk', *Archaeologia* 108: 1–13.

Johns, C.M. and Potter, T.W. (1983) *The Thetford Treasure: Roman Jewellery and Silver*, London: British Museum.

—— (1985) 'The Canterbury late Roman treasure', *Antiq. J.* 65: 313–51.

Johnson, F.E. (ed.) (1969) *Religious Symbolism*, New York: Kennikat.

Jones, C., Wainwright, G. and Yarnold, E. (1978) *The Study of Liturgy*, London: SPCK.

Jones, E.W. and Horne B. (1981) 'The skeletons', 37–44 in C.L. Matthews, 'A Romano-British inhumation cemetery at Dunstable', *Bedfordshire Archaeol. J.* 15: 4–137.

Jones, M.J. (ed.) (1984) *Lincoln: Twenty-one Centuries of Living History*, Lincoln: Lincoln Archaeology Trust.

Jones, M.J., Gilmore, B. and Camidge, K. (1982) 'Lincoln', *Curr. Archaeol.* 83: 366–71.

Jones, R. (1975) 'The Romano-British farmstead and its cemetery at Lynch Farm, near Peterborough', *Northamptonshire Archaeol.* 10: 94–137.

Jones, R.F.J. (1981) 'Cremation and inhumation – change in the third century', 15–19 in A. King and M. Henig (eds), *The Roman West in the Third Century*, BAR Int. ser. 109: Oxford.

—— (1984) 'Death and distinction', 219–25 in T.F.C. Blagg and A.C. King (eds), *Military and Civilian in Roman Britain*, BAR B ser. 136: Oxford.

Kajanto, I. (1965) *The Latin Cognomina*, Helsinki: Finnish Society of Sciences (reprinted 1982, Rome: Bretschneider).

Kean, P.F. (1968) 'An inhumation burial in the Roman cemetery at Poundbury, Dorset', *Proc. Dorset Natur. Hist. Archaeol. Soc.* 89: 144.

Kendall, G. (1982) 'A study of grave orientation in several Roman and post-Roman cemeteries from southern Britain', *Archaeol. J.* 139: 101–23.

King, A. (1983) 'The Roman church at Silchester reconsidered', *Oxford J. Archaeol.* 2: 225–37.

Kraay, C.M. (1942) 'An early Christian object from Icklingham, Suffolk', *Antiq. J.* 22: 219–20.

Krautheimer, R. (1965) *Early Christian and Byzantine Architecture*, Harmondsworth: Penguin.

Kruta, V. and Forman, W. (1985) *The Celts of the West*, London: Orbis.

Layard, N.F. (1925) 'Bronze crowns and a bronze headdress from a Roman site at Cavenham Heath, Suffolk', *Antiq. J.* 5: 258–65.

Leech, R.H. (1974) 'Lamyatt Beacon, Lamyatt', *Archaeological Excavations, 1973:* Department of the Environment 57–8.

—— (1980) 'Religion and burials in South Somerset and North Devon', 329–66 in W. Rodwell (ed.), *Temples, Churches and Religion in Roman Britain* (2 vols), BAR B ser. 77: Oxford.

—— (1981) 'The excavation of a Romano-British farmstead and cemetery on Bradley Hill, Somerton, Somerset', *Britannia* 12: 177–252.

—— (1973–82) *Somerset Lamyatt Beacon*, London: HMSO.

—— (1986) 'The excavation of a Romano-Celtic temple and a later cemetery on Lamyatt Beacon, Somerset', *Britannia* 17: 259–328.

Lethbridge, T.C. (1936) 'Further excavations in the early Iron Age and Romano-British cemetery at Guilden Morden', *Proc. Cambridge Antiq. Soc.* 36: 109–19.

Levison, W. (1941) 'St Alban and St Albans', *Antiquity* 15: 337–59.

Lewis, M.J.T. (1966) *Temples in Roman Britain*, Cambridge: University Press.

Ling, R. (1982) 'Littlecote', *Curr. Archaeol.* 82: 350.

Liversidge, J. (1959) 'A new hoard of Romano-British pewter from Icklingham', *Proc. Cambridge Antiq. Soc.* 52: 6–10.

—— (1977) 'Roman burials in the Cambridge area', *Proc. Cambridge Antiq. Soc.* 67: 11–38.

Loizel, M. (1977) 'Le cimetière gallo-romain du bas-Empire de Marteville', *Cahiers Archéologiques de Picardie* 4: 151–203.

Macdonald, J.L. (1977) 'Pagan religions and burial practices in Roman Britain', 35–8 in R. Reece (ed.), *Burial in the Roman World*, CBA RR 22: London.

—— (1979) 'Religion', 404–33 in G. Clarke, *Pre-Roman and Roman Winchester Part II: The Roman Cemetery at Lankhills*, Winchester Studies 3, Oxford: Clarendon.

McRoberts, D. (1965) 'The ecclesiastical character of the St Ninian's Isle treasure', 224–46 in A. Small (ed.), *The Fourth Viking Congress*, Edinburgh: Oliver & Boyd.

McWhirr, A.D. (1973) 'Cirencester, 1969–1973: ninth interim report', *Antiq. J.* 53: 191–218.

McWhirr A.D. *et al* (1982) *Cirencester Excavations II: Romano-British Cemeteries at Cirencester*, Cirencester: Cirencester Excavation Committee.

Mancinelli, F. (1981) *Catacombs and Basilicas*, Florence: Scala.

Mango, M.M. (1986) *Silver from Early Byzantium: The Kaper Koraon and related Treasures*, Baltimore: Walters Art Gallery.

Markus, R.A. (1986) 'Pelagianism: Britain and the Continent', *J. Eccles. Hist.* 37: 191–204.

Martimort, A.G. (1961) *L'Eglise en Prière*, Paris: Desclée.

Matthews, C.L. (1981) 'A Romano-British inhumation cemetery at Dunstable', *Bedfordshire Archaeol. J.* 15: 4–137.

Mattingly, H. and Pearce, J.W.E. (1937) 'The Coleraine hoard', *Antiquity* 11: 39–45.

Mawer, C.F. (1989) 'A lost Roman ring from Suffolk', *Britannia* 20: 237–41.

Meates, G.W. (1955) *Lullingstone Roman Villa*, London: Heinemann.

—— (1979) *The Roman Villa at Lullingstone, Vol. I: The Site*, Kent Archaeol. Soc. Monograph 1.

—— (1987) *The Lullingstone Roman Villa Vol. II: The Wall Paintings and Finds* Kent Archaeol. Soc. Monograph 3.

Middleton, J.H. (1882) 'Notes on some Christian rings and other antiquities found on the site of a Roman villa, at Fifehead Neville, Dorset', *Proc. Soc. Antiq.* 9: 66–9.

Milne, S. (1988) 'Roman temple find changes view of London', *The Guardian*: 3 July 1988.

Milojčić, V. (1968) 'Zu den spätkaiserzeitlichen und merowingischen Silberlöffeln', *Bericht der Römisch-Germanischen Kommission* 49: 111–52.

Morris, J.R. (1968) 'The date of St Alban', *Hertfordshire Archaeol.* 1: 1–8.

Morris, R. (1983) *The Church in British Archaeology*, CBA RR 47: London.

Morris, R. and Roxan, J. (1980) 'Churches on Roman buildings', 175–92 in W. Rodwell (ed.), *Temples, Churches and Religion in Roman Britain* (2 vols), BAR B ser. 77: Oxford.

Munby, J. and Henig, M. (eds) (1977) *Roman Life and Art in Britain* (Pt ii) BAR B ser. 41, Oxford.

Myres, J.N.L. (1960) 'Pelagius and the end of Roman rule in Britain', *J. Roman Stud.* 50: 21–36.

Næss, J-R. (1970) 'The significance of orientation elements in Iron Age burial customs at Voss: a tentative interpretation', *Norwegian Archaeol. Rev.* 3: 73–83.

Neal, D.S. (1981) *Roman Mosaics in Britain*, Britannia Monograph 1: London.

Noakes, K.W. (1978) 'From New Testament times until St Cyprian', 80–94 in C. Jones, G. Wainwright and E. Yarnold, *The Study of Liturgy*, London: SPCK.

Nock, A.D. (1932) 'Cremation and burial in the Roman empire', *Harvard Theol. Rev.* 25: 321–67.

North, J.A. (1976) 'Conservatism and change in Roman religion', *Papers Brit. School Rome* 44: 1–12.

Northcote, J.S. and Brownlow, W.R. (1869) *Roma Sotterranea*, London: Longmans, Green, Reader, and Dyer.

O'Dell, A.C. (1959) 'The St Ninian's Isle silver hoard', *Antiquity* 33: 241–68.

Oliver, V.L. (1923) 'The Pre-Roman and Roman occupation of the Weymouth district', *Proc. Dorset Natur. Hist. Archaeol. Soc.* 44: 31–55.

O'Neill, B.H.St J. (1935) 'Coins from Jordan Hill Roman temple', *Proc. Dorset Natur. Hist. Archaeol. Soc.* 57: 140.

O'Neill, H.E. and Toynbee, J.M.C. (1958) 'Sculptures from a Romano-British well in Gloucestershire', *J. Roman Stud.* 48: 49–55.

Page, W. (ed.) (1908) *The Victoria History of the Counties of England: Buckinghamshire*, Vol. II, London: Constable.

—— (1911) *The Victoria History of the Counties of England: Suffolk*, Vol. I, London: Constable.

—— (1914) *The Victoria History of the Counties of England: Hertfordshire*, Vol. IV, London: Constable.

Painter, K.S. (1965) 'A Roman silver treasure from Canterbury', *J. Brit. Archaeol. Ass.* 3rd ser. 28: 1–15.

—— (1968) 'The Roman site at Hinton St Mary, Dorset', *Brit. Mus. Q.* 32: 15–31.

—— (1971) 'Villas and Christianity in Roman Britain', *Brit. Mus. Q.* 35: 156–75.

—— (1972) 'A late-Roman silver ingot from Kent', *Antiq. J.* 52: 84–92.

—— (1976) 'The design of the Roman mosaic at Hinton St Mary', *Antiq. J.* 56: 49–54.

—— (1977a) *The Mildenhall Treasure*, London: British Museum.

—— (1977b) *The Water Newton Early Christian Silver*, London: British Museum.

Parfitt, K. and Green, M. (1987) 'A chalk figurine from Upper Deal, Kent', *Britannia* 18: 295–298.

Pearce, S.M. (ed.) (1982) *The Early Church in Western Britain and Ireland*, BAR B ser. 102: Oxford.

Penn, W.S. (1967) 'Possible evidence from Springhead for the Great Plague of A.D. 166', *Archaeol. Cantiana* 82: 263–71.

Petch, D.F. (1961) 'A Roman lead tank, Walesby', *Lincolnshire Architect. Archaeol. Soc. Reports and Papers* 9: 13–15.

Phillips, C.W. (ed.) (1970) *The Fenland in Roman Times*, London: Royal Geographical Society.

Piggott, S. (1968) *The Druids*, London: Thames & Hudson.

Potter, T.W. (1982) 'A fourth century silver spoon', *Antiq. J.* 62: 375–7.

Powell, T.G.E. (1959) *The Celts*, rev. edn, London: Thames & Hudson.

Pownall, J. (1792) 'Account of some sepulchral antiquities discovered at Lincoln', *Archaeologia* 10: 345–9.

Radford, C.A.R. (1967) 'The early Church in Strathclyde and Galloway', *Medieval Archaeol.* 11: 105–26.

—— (1968) 'The architectural background on the Continent', 19–36 in M.W. Barley and R.P.C. Hanson (eds), *Christianity in Britain, 300–700*, Leicester: University Press.

—— (1971) 'Christian origins in Britain', *Medieval Archaeol.* 15: 1–12.

Raftery, B. (1981) 'Iron age burials in Ireland', 173–204 in D. Corrain (ed.), *Essays and Studies presented to M. J. Kelly*, Cork: Tower.

Rahtz, P.A. (1969) 'Cannington hillfort 1963', *Somerset Archaeol. Natur. Hist.* 113: 56–71.

—— (1977) 'Late Roman cemeteries and beyond', 53–64 in R. Reece (ed.), *Burial in the Roman World*, CBA RR 22: London.

—— (1978) 'Grave orientation', *Archaeol. J.* 135: 1–14.

Ramm, H.G. (1971) 'The end of Roman York', 179–99 in R.M. Butler (ed.), *Soldier and Civilian in Roman Yorkshire*, Leicester: University Press.

Ramsay, W.M. and Bell, G. (1909) *The Thousand and one Churches*, London: Hodder & Stoughton.

Rawes, B. (1977) 'A Romano-British site on the Portway', *Glevensis* 11: 31–2.

—— (1978) 'The Portway Roman site at Upton St Leonards', *Glevensis* 12: 11–12.

RCHM (1962) *Eburacum*, London: HMSO.

—— (1970) *Dorset*, Vol. II.3, London: HMSO.

—— (1975) *Dorset*, London: HMSO.

RCHM (England) (1983) 'West Park Roman villa, Rockbourne, Hampshire', *Archaeol. J.* 140: 129–50.

Read, C.H. (1898) 'List of pewter dishes and vessels found at Appleshaw and now in the British Museum', *Archaeologia* 56: 7–12.

Reece, R. (ed.) (1977) *Burial in the Roman World*, CBA RR 22: London.

Rennie, E.B. (1984) 'Excavations at Ardnadam, Argyll, 1965–82', *Glasgow Archaeol. J.* 11: 13–39.

Richardson, H. (1980) 'Derrynavlan and other early church treasures', *J. Roy. Soc. Antiq. Ireland* 110: 92–115.

Richmond, I.A. (1943) 'Roman legionnaires at Corbridge, their supply base, temples and religious cults', *Archaeol. Aeliana* 4th ser. 21: 127–224.

—— (1945) 'A Roman vat of lead from Ireby, Cumberland', *Trans. Cumberland Westmorland Antiq. and Archaeol. Soc.* n.s. 45: 163–71.

—— (1946) 'The Roman city of Lincoln', *Archaeol. J.* 103: 26–56.

—— (1950) *Archaeology and the After-life in Pagan and Christian Imagery*, London: Oxford University Press.

—— (1959a) 'Roman Britain in 1958: sites explored', *J. Roman Stud.* 49: 102–39.

—— (1959b) 'The Roman villa at Chedworth 1958–59', *Trans. Bristol Gloucestershire Archaeol. Soc.* 78: 5–23.

—— (1963) 'Roman Essex', 1–23 in R.B Pugh (ed.), *The Victoria History of the Counties of England: Essex*, Vol. III, London: Oxford University Press.

Rock, (Canon) (1869) 'Celtic spoons', *Archaeol. J.* 26: 35–51.

Rodwell, K. (1987) *The Prehistoric and Roman Settlement at Kelvedon, Essex*, CBA RR 33 (Chelmsford Archaeol. Trust Report 6): London.

Rodwell, W. (1980a) 'Temple archaeology: problems of the present and portents for the future', 211–41 in W. Rodwell (ed.), *Temples, Churches and Religion in Roman Britain* (2 vols), BAR B ser. 77: Oxford.

—— (ed.) (1980b) *Temples, Churches and Religion in Roman Britain* (2 vols), BAR B ser. 77: Oxford.

—— (1980c) 'Temples in Roman Britain: a revised gazetteer', 557–85 in W. Rodwell (ed.), *Temples, Churches and Religion in Roman Britain* (2 vols), BAR B ser. 77: Oxford.

Rodwell, W.J. and Rodwell, K.A. (1977) *Historic Churches: A Wasting Asset*, CBA RR 19: London.

—— (1985) *Rivenhall: Investigations of a Villa, Church, and Village, 1950–1977*, CBA RR 55 (Chelmsford Archaeol. Trust Report 4): London.

Rogers, C.F. (1903) *Baptism and Christian Archaeology*, Oxford: Clarendon.

Rook, A.G. (1973) 'Excavations at the Grange Romano-British cemetery, Welwyn, 1967', *Hertfordshire Archaeol.* 3: 1–30.

Ross, A. (1959) 'The human head in insular pagan Celtic religion', *Proc. Soc. Antiq. Scotland 1957–8* 91: 10–43.

—— (1967) *Pagan Celtic Britain: Studies in Iconography and Tradition*, London: Routledge & Kegan Paul.

Rostovtseff, M. (1923) 'Commodus-Hercules in Britain', *J. Roman Stud.* 13: 91–109.

Rowell, G. (1977) *The Liturgy of Christian Burial*, London: Alcuin Club/SPCK.

Rutherford, R. (1980) *The Death of a Christian: The Rite of Funerals*, New York: Pueblo.

Schiller, G. (1972) *Iconography of Christian Art* (J. Seligman trans.), 2 vols, London: Lund Humphries.

Shelton, K.J. (1981) *The Esquiline Treasure*, London: British Museum.

Sherlock, D. (1973) 'Zu einer Fundliste antiker Silberlöffel', *Bericht der Römisch-Germanischen Kommission* 54: 203–11.

—— (1978–80) 'An inscribed spoon from Caistor St Edmund', *Norfolk Archaeol.* 37: 346–9.

—— (1984) 'An inscribed spoon from Canterbury', *Archaeol. Cantiana* 100: 81–6.

Small, A., Thomas, C. and Wilson, D.M. (1973) *St Ninian's Isle and its Treasure*, Aberdeen University Studies Series 152, Oxford: University Press.

Smith, D.J. (1962) 'The shrine of the nymphs and the *genius loci* at Carrawburgh', *Archaeol. Aeliana* 4th ser. 40: 59–81.

—— (1978) 'Regional aspects of the winged corridor villa in Britain', 117–47 in M. Todd (ed.), *Studies in the Romano-British Villa*, Leicester: University Press.

—— (1983) 'Orpheus mosaics in Britain', 315–28 in *Mosaïque: Recueil d'hommages à Henri Stern*, Paris.

Smith, R.F. (1987) *Roadside Settlements in Lowland Roman Britain*, BAR B ser. 157: Oxford.

Stafford, P. (1985) *The East Midlands in the Early Middle Ages*, Leicester: University Press.

Startin, D.W.A. (1982) 'Excavations at the Old Vicarage, Fordington, Dorchester', *Proc. Dorset Natur. Hist. Archaeol. Soc.* 103: 43–66.

Stead, I.M. (1967) 'A La Tène III burial at Welwyn Garden City', *Archaeologia* 101: 1–62.

Stebbing, W.P.B. (1937) 'Pre-Roman, Roman and post-Roman pottery from burials at Worth, East Kent', *Antiq. J.* 17: 310–13.

Stephens, G.R. (1985) 'Caerleon and the martyrdom of Ss Aaron and Julius', *Bull. Bd. Celtic Stud.* 32: 326–35.

—— (1987) 'A note on the martyrdom of St Alban', *Hertfordshire Archaeol.* 9 (1983–86): 20–1.

Sulzberger, M. (1925) 'La symbole de la croix et les monogrammes de Jésu chez les premiers Chrétiens', *Byzantion* 2: 337–448.

Taylor, H.M. and Taylor, J. (1965) *Anglo-Saxon Architecture*, Vol. I, Cambridge: University Press.

Thomas, C. (1971) *The Early Christian Archaeology in North Britain*, Oxford: University of Glasgow.

—— (1981) *Christianity in Roman Britain to A.D. 500*, London: Batsford.

—— (1986) 'Recognizing Christian origins: an archaeological and historical dilemma', 121–5 in L.A.S. Butler and R.K. Morris (eds), *The Anglo-Saxon Church: Papers on History, Architecture and Archaeology in Honour of Dr H. M. Taylor*, CBA RR 66: London.

Thompson, E.A. (1984) *Saint Germanus of Auxerre and the End of Roman Britain*, Studies in Celtic History 6, Bury St Edmunds: Boydell.

Toller, H. (1977) *Roman Lead Coffins and Ossuaria in Britain*, BAR B ser. 38: Oxford.

Toynbee, J.M.C. (1953) 'Christianity in Roman Britain', *J. Brit. Archaeol. Ass.* 3rd ser. 16: 1–24.

—— (1963) 'The Christian Roman mosaic, Hinton St Mary, Dorset', *Proc. Dorset Natur. Hist. Archaeol. Soc.* 85: 116–21.

—— (1964a) 'A new Roman mosaic pavement found in Dorset', *J. Roman Stud.* 54: 7–14.

—— (1964b) *Art in Britain under the Romans*, Oxford: Clarendon.

—— (1968) 'Pagan motifs and practices in Christian art and ritual in Roman Britain', 177–92 in M.W. Barley and R.P.C. Hanson (eds), *Christianity in Britain, 300–700*, Leicester: University Press.

—— (1971) *Death and Burial in the Roman World*, London: Thames & Hudson.

—— (1978) 'A Londinium votive leaf or feather and its fellows', 128–47 in J. Bird, H. Chapman and J. Clark (eds) *Collectanea Londiniensia: Studies presented to R. Merrifield*, London and Middlesex Arch. Soc. Special Paper 2, London.

—— (1981) 'Apollo, beasts and seasons: some thoughts on the Littlecote mosaic', *Britannia* 12: 1–5.

Turner, B.R.G. (1982) *Ivy Chimneys, Witham: An Interim Report*, Essex County Council Occas. Paper 2, Chelmsford.

Ucko, P.J. (1969–70) 'Ethnography and archaeological interpretation of funerary remains', *World Archaeol.* 1: 262–77.

Vita-Finzi, C. and Higgs, E.S. (1970) 'Prehistoric economy in the Mount Carmel area of Palestine: site catchment analysis', *Proc. Prehistoric Soc.* 36: 1–37.

Volbach, W.F. (1965) 'Il Tesoro di Canoscio', 'Ricerche sull'Umbria Tardo-Antica e Preromanica', *Atti del II Convegno di Studi Umbri Gubbio 1964*: 303–16.

Wait, G.A. (1986) *Ritual and Religion in Iron Age Britain* (2 vols), BAR B ser. 149: Oxford.

Wall, J. (1965) 'Christian evidences in the Roman period: the Northern Counties Part I', *Archaeol. Aeliana* 4th ser. 43: 201–25.

—— (1966) 'Christian evidences in the Roman period: the Northern Counties Part II', *Archaeol. Aeliana* 4th ser. 44: 147–64.

—— (1968) 'Christian evidences in Roman South-West England', *Trans. Devonshire Assn. for the Advancement of Science Literature and Art* 100: 161–78.

Walters, B. (1981) 'Littlecote', *Curr. Archaeol.* 80: 264–8.

—— (1984) 'The "Orpheus" mosaic in Littlecote Park, England', 433–42 in R.F. Campanati (ed.), *Atti del III Colloquio Internazionale sul Mosaico Antico*, Ravenna.

Ward-Perkins, J.B. (1954) 'Constantine and the origins of the Christian basilica', *Papers Brit. School Rome* 22: 69–90.

Warne, C. (1872) *Ancient Dorset* (privately published).

Warwick, R. (1968) 'The skeletal remains', 113–76 in L.P. Wenham, *The Romano-British Cemetery at Trentholme Drive*, York, London: HMSO.

Watts, D.J. (1988a) 'Circular lead tanks and their significance for Romano-British Christianity', *Antiq. J.* 68: 210–22.

—— (1988b) 'The Thetford Treasure: a reappraisal', *Antiq. J.* 68: 55–68.

—— (forthcoming) 'Infant burials and Romano-British Christianity', *Archaeological J.* 146.

Webber, F.R. (1971) *Church Symbolism*, 2nd rev. edn, Detroit: Gale Research.

Webster, G. (1975) 'Small towns without defences', 55–66 in W. Rodwell and T. Rowley (eds) *Small Towns of Roman Britain*, Vol. II, BAR B ser. 15: Oxford.

—— (1984) 'The function of the Chedworth Roman "villa"', *Trans. Bristol Gloucestershire Archaeol. Soc.* 101: 5–20.

—— (1986) *The British Celts and Their Gods under Rome*, London: Batsford.

Webster, L.E. and Cherry, J. (1973) 'Medieval Britain in 1972', *Medieval Archaeol.* 17: 138–88.

Wedlake, W.J. (1982) *The Excavation of the Shrine of Apollo at Nettleton, Wiltshire 1956–71*, Soc. Antiq. RR 40: London.

Wells, C. (1968) 'General observations on the skeletal analysis', 40–2 in I.E. Anthony, 'Excavations in Verulam Hills Field, St Albans, 1963–4', *Hertfordshire Archaeol.* 1: 9–50.

—— (1976) 'The human burials', 103–19 in S. West, 'The Romano-British site at Icklingham', *East Anglian Archaeol.* 3: 63–126.

—— (1982) 'The human burials', 135–202 in McWhirr A.D. *et al.*, *Cirencester Excavations II: Romano-British Cemeteries at Cirencester*, Cirencester: Cirencester Excavation Committee.

Wenham, L.P. (1968) *The Romano-British Cemetery at Trentholme Drive, York*, London: HMSO.

West, S. (1976) 'The Romano-British site at Icklingham', *East Anglian Archaeol.* 3: 63–126.

Wheeler, R.E.M. (1943) *Maiden Castle*, Soc. Antiq. RR 12: London.

Wheeler, R.E.M. and Wheeler, T.V. (1932) *Report on the Excavation of the Prehistoric, Roman and Post-Roman site at Lydney Park, Gloucestershire*, Soc. Antiq. RR 9: London.

—— (1936) *Verulamium: A Belgic and Two Roman Cities*, Soc. Antiq. RR 11: London.

Whimster, R. (1981) *Burial Practices in Iron Age Britain*, BAR B ser. 90: Oxford.

Whiting, W. *et al.* (1931) *Report on the Excavation of the Roman Cemetery at Ospringe, Kent*, Soc. Antiq. RR 8: London.

Wickenden, N.P. (1988) *Excavations at Great Dunmow, Essex: A Romano-British Small Town in the Trinovantian Civitas*, East Anglian Archaeol. Rep. 41 (Chelmsford Archaeol. Trust Rep. 7), Chelmsford: Essex County Council.

Wild, J.P. (1970) *Textile Manufacture in the Northern Roman Provinces*, Cambridge: University Press.

Williams, H. (1912) *Christianity in Early Britain*, Oxford: Clarendon.

Williams, R. (1984) 'Bancroft Mausoleum', *South Midlands Archaeol.* (Newsletter of CBA Regional Group 9) 14: 21–6.

Wilson, C.E. (1981) 'Burial within settlements in Southern Britain during the pre-Roman Iron Age', *Univ. London Instit. Archaeol. Bull.* 18: 127–69.

Wilson, D. (1986) 'Excavation at Wortley near Wotton under Edge: first interim report 1985', *Glevensis* 20: 41–4.

Wilson, D.R. (1965) 'Roman Britain in 1964: sites explored', *J. Roman Stud.* 55: 199–220.

—— (1968) 'An early Christian cemetery at Ancaster', 197–9 in M.W. Barley and R.P.C. Hanson (eds), *Christianity in Britain, 300–700*, Leicester: University Press.

—— (1969) 'Roman Britain in 1968: sites explored', *J. Roman Stud.* 59: 198–234.

—— (1970) 'Roman Britain in 1969: sites explored', *Britannia* 1: 269–305.

Wilson, P.R. (1988) 'The Richborough font – some additional structural detail', *Britannia* 19: 411–12.

Wright, R.P. (1955) 'Roman Britain in 1954: inscriptions', *J. Roman Stud.* 45: 145–9.

—— (1965) 'Roman Britain in 1964: inscriptions', *J. Roman Stud.* 55: 220–28.

—— (1970) 'Roman Britain in 1969: inscriptions', *Britannia* 1: 305–15.

Wright, R.P. and Hassall, M.W.C. (1973) 'Roman Britain in 1972: inscriptions', *Britannia* 4: 324–27.

Yarnold, E.J. (1970) 'The ceremonies of initiation in the *De Sacramentis* and *De Mysteriis* of St Ambrose', *Studia Patristica* 10: 453–63.

—— (1971) *The Awe-Inspiring Rites of Initiation*, Slough: St Paul Publications.

—— (1978) 'The fourth and fifth centuries', 95–110 in C. Jones, G. Wainwright and E. Yarnold, *The Study of Liturgy*, London: SPCK.

NAME INDEX

Notes: Ancient and mediaeval writers are in italics
bp. = bishop, m. = martyr, s. = saint

273

PLACE INDEX

GENERAL INDEX